SOLDIERS OF REASON

SOLDIERS OF REASON

The RAND Corporation
and the Rise
of the American Empire

Alex Abella

Harcourt, Inc.

Orlando   Austin   New York   San Diego   London

www.HarcourtBooks.com

Library of Congress Cataloging-in-Publication Data
Abella, Alex.
Soldiers of reason: the RAND Corporation and the rise of
the American empire/Alex Abella.—1st ed.
p.   cm.
Includes bibliographical references and index.
1. RAND Corporation—History.   2. RAND
Corporation—Influence.   3. Research institutes—United
States—History—20th century.   4. Military research—
United States—History—20th century.   5. United States—
Intellectual life—20th century.   6. United States—Foreign
relations—1945–1989.   7. United States—Foreign
relations—1989–   8. United States—Military policy.
I. Title
AS36.R35A24   2008
355'.070973—dc22   2007030691
ISBN 978-0-15-101081-3

Text set in Sabon
Designed by Lydia D'moch

Printed in the United States of America
First edition
A C E G I K J H F D B

To my wife and children, who never wavered.

Ad astra per aspera.

Killing, too, is a form of our ancient wandering affliction.

—Rainer Maria Rilke

The Matrix is everywhere. It is all around us. Even now, in this very room. You can see it when you look out your window or when you turn on your television. You can feel it when you go to work . . . when you go to church . . . when you pay your taxes.

—*The Matrix* (1999)

Reason's dream creates monsters.

—Francisco José de Goya y Lucientes

Contents

SOLDIERS OF REASON

Foreword

*If we had lost the war, we'd all have been
prosecuted as war criminals.*

—AIR FORCE GENERAL CURTIS LEMAY,
in *The Fog of War*

I FIRST BECAME aware of RAND's existence in the cauldron of one
of the most controversial conflicts in modern American history, the
Vietnam War. The occasion was a rally at Columbia University in
1970. Two years earlier, New York City police had brutally ended
a controversial student occupation at our Morningside Heights campus, resulting in hundreds wounded and arrested. My turn to get my
share of abuse came on a sultry April night, when again New York's
finest were summoned to end an antiwar protest that concluded, like
so many of the era, with shattered windows, burning trash cans,
clouds of tear gas, and the thumping of heads by police clubs to the
cry of "Up against the wall, m . . . f . . . !"

Some of my codemonstrators had procured Molotov cocktails—
or at least, what they thought were such—and ran to toss them
at the building housing computers doing work for the RAND Corporation. When I asked what RAND was and why it deserved such

violence, I was told it was a think tank in California, a place where war criminals conducted research on how to defeat the Vietcong and perpetuate the ruling classes, the "establishment." In the event, my impassioned compadres did not accomplish their goal—the sudden arrival of dozens of blue uniforms sent us all scattering. Those who escaped repaired for a postmortem at the university watering hole, the West End. There, consoled by soggy fries, steins of beer, and boilermakers, white-bread revolutionaries told me tall tales in which RAND played the simultaneous role of Dr. Strangelove and Svengali—both deranged genius and puppet master.

Flash forward thirty-some years to a signing in Los Angeles for my last book, a study of Hitler's secret terrorist plot against the United States. As I autographed away at the Westwood bookstore, I greeted a friend from RAND who had come to lend his support. The odd conjunction of terrorism, RAND, and books was sudden inspiration. Had anyone ever done a book on RAND? Was such a thing even possible, given the top-secret research still being conducted at the think tank? It might be difficult, but undoubtedly worth trying. Just what was RAND up to nowadays?

When I approached RAND leaders to get their cooperation for the project, I never imagined they would ultimately give their consent. RAND was too secretive, too wrapped up in mystery. A staffer told me that in the past RAND actually had paid a public relations person to keep its name *out* of the newspapers.

All the same, my idea for a book on the organization journeyed from level to level, beginning with friends inside RAND, to the public relations office, and onward and upward until ultimately I made my pitch to top management at a 7:30 A.M. meeting, as though we were in the Pentagon. In typical RAND mode, management took a vote, asking not just a yes or no answer but also an ordinal on a scale—one being extremely negative and ten extremely positive. Out of five ballots cast, I received an average grade of seven, which I was told was the second highest they had given to any project in years.

One of the managers confided that he thought agreeing to this book was either the brightest or the dumbest move RAND had ever made.

RAND opened its files to me, put me in touch with its researchers and analysts, and placed no restriction on my writing save that I use no classified material. I agreed with some trepidation, fearing that the use of declassified information would make the story bland and inconsequential. I need not have worried. Most of the materials still marked top secret deal with the development of nuclear weapons and, important as that is, it only illustrates a portion of the extraordinarily wide-ranging influence RAND has had on the world. Once I began my research on the sixty-year-plus RAND history, I was staggered by the abundance of material encompassing so many fields, activities, people, and events. That was how I found out that my friends at the West End so many years ago, as often happens in bull sessions, had gotten their facts wrong. It was not RAND conducting counterinsurgency studies at Columbia, but another think tank, the Institute for Defense Analyses. Moreover, Columbia had canceled its contract with the IDA in the wake of the 1968 student takeover.

Nonetheless, my fellow students were not too far off in their characterization. RAND had conducted extensive research on how to defeat the Vietcong and more in Vietnam. Its very raison d'être at its founding had been to advise the Air Force on how to wage and win wars. And at that very moment in 1970, RAND was transmuting the lessons it had learned in the fields of war into precepts of urban planning, turning New York City into a research laboratory for its controlling vision of a perfect society.

RAND was, and is, the essential establishment organization. Throughout its history, RAND has been at the heart of that interweaving of Pentagon concupiscence and financial rapacity that President Eisenhower aimed to call the military-industrial-legislative complex. RAND has literally reshaped the modern world—and very few know it.

———

RAND SITS BY the beach in Santa Monica, squeezed in between
city hall and the pier, in what for decades was a run-down part of
the California coastline until the real estate boom turned the dowdy
retirement community into Beverly Hills by the sea.

RAND's old buildings—a two-story boxcar intersecting a five-
story slab, now demolished—were designed to be like a campus
without students, just faculty thinking about the vicissitudes of their
specialty.* Even the long hallways that had to be negotiated to access common areas were meant to get people out of their rooms and
interacting with one another. The new RAND building was paid for
in large part by the sale of the lot the previous one was sited on. This
new structure is as much a reflection of our era, all curves and glass
and postmodern Koolhaas cool, as the earlier one was of its own an-
gular, midcentury modernist manner. One thing remains the same:
it is still hard to go in a straight line from one point to another;
everything is interconnected, with the specific purpose of promot-
ing the flow of people and information.

For RAND has always been about ideas, about what-ifs, about
pie in the sky. At one point RAND could have been like TRW, a defense contractor with dozens of factories, thousands of workers, and
multimillion-dollar budgets. Instead, its leaders deliberately chose
the life of the mind, the power of the idea whose time has come, at
the expense of fame and fortune.

That was why a general, a San Francisco lawyer, and an aircraft
manufacturer conspired to establish it as a center of military-
sponsored scientific research and development, a factory of ideas, a
think tank. Even its name was muscular—and cryptic: RAND.† Not
an ivory tower but a group of consiglieri who would advise the gov-

---

* Tradition has it that mathematician John Williams, one of the first five people to be hired
at RAND, was influential in this design.
† RAND stands for research and development. Or, as wags have been saying since its inception, research and no development.

ernment—specifically, the United States Air Force—on how best to wage and win wars.

Over time, RAND disguised its mission by filing incorporation papers with California's secretary of state that its purpose was "To further and promote scientific, educational, and charitable purposes, all for the public welfare and security of the United States of America."[1] Its true aim—which never needed to be discussed as it was so plain to see—was to have its analysts become the advocates, planners, and courtiers of an ever-expanding America that, like the Creator, sought to refashion the world in its own image. And who could argue otherwise? For in the unexamined syllogism of the time, America was good and everyone wants to be good so everyone should be like America. We know what is best, said the politicians in Washington. Trust us.

In the 1950s, RAND helped the Eisenhower administration square off against the specter of thermonuclear war with the Soviet Union. In the 1960s, RAND filled the top political posts of the American involvement in Southeast Asia and the War on Poverty. The 1980s Reagan devolution of smaller government and interventionist foreign policy can be traced directly to RAND thinkers, while the Persian Gulf War, Operation Iraqi Freedom, and the reorganization of the Pentagon in the so-called Revolution in Military Affairs were all the culmination of plans long gestated by RAND alumni.

RAND's role goes beyond the national security field. In the late 1950s, trying to come up with a way to carry on communications in the event of a nuclear attack, a RAND engineer developed the concept of packet switching, which became the foundation of the Internet. In the health field, a ten-year RAND study resulted in the spread of co-payments for medical insurance plans. RAND also initiated the discipline of terrorism studies, which had long been the province of conspiracy theorists and political extremists. Nowadays RAND analysts continue this tradition of problem solving, publishing hundreds of books and pamphlets pointing out the best, which is to say, the most rational, solutions to the many problems of the world—hunger, war, drug trafficking, even traffic jams.

Although RANDites presaged the Internet and arguably saved America from nuclear annihilation, of equal importance is the little-known fact that RAND has changed the way everyone in the West thinks about government—what people owe it and what it owes them.

While attempting to divine dangers that up to then had been impossible to imagine, RAND analysts stumbled onto a brilliant discourse that provided both a way to maximize efficiency in government and a philosophical foundation for the West's ideological struggle with the Communist bloc. RAND accomplished this through rational choice theory, a concept that holds that self-interest, unleavened by collective concerns such as religion or patriotism, is the hallmark of the modern world.

Rational choice may have been created to defeat communism, but in so doing, it staged a total transformation of people's daily lives—from the amount of taxes they pay, to the way their children are schooled, to the health services they receive, to the way their wars are fought. It also opened the door to the violent reaction of tribal Islamic societies, where the collective good is paramount and for whom the cult of the individual as represented by rational choice is cultural death.

In a very real, very tangible way, in this great maelstrom of consumerism called Western civilization, all of us are the bastard children of RAND. Put in everyday terms, RAND's rational choice theory is the *Matrix* code of the West. The RAND concept of numbers and rationality constitutes a reality that must be explained before it can be seen—much less understood.

Think of this book then as the red pill that will make visible the secret world that rules us all.

PART 1

1

A Great Beginning

The RAND Corporation's the boon of the world
They think all day long for a fee
They sit and play games about going up in flames
For Counters they use you and me.

— "The RAND Hymn," by MALVINA REYNOLDS

ON OCTOBER 1, 1945, less than two months after the dropping of two nuclear bombs on Japan, the commanding general of the U.S. Army Air Forces boarded a flight from Washington, D.C., to San Francisco on a trip he was certain would be as momentous as the Manhattan Project.

A man of medium stature, with pudgy features, clear eyes, and a constant smile, General Henry Harley "Hap" Arnold was a true believer in the power of the Air Force. He was one of only nine people ever to earn the rank of five-star general and the only one with that rank in the Air Force. He had received his military pilot license in 1912, and since then had pushed for an Air Force independent of the Army; he never wavered in his conviction of the usefulness of maximum destructive power in combat. On hearing doubts on the legitimacy of the Allied fire bombing in Dresden,

Germany, Arnold wrote, "We must not get soft. War must be destructive and to a certain extent inhuman and ruthless."[1]

General Arnold had welcomed the development and deployment of nuclear bombs—especially since it had fallen to the Army Air Force to deliver, and thus control, that mightiest of weapons. (By 1947 President Truman would cleave the Air Force from its Army concatenation, setting up both services as rivals for the Pentagon's largesse.) But Arnold was concerned that the amazing concentration of scientific minds that had made possible the Manhattan Project would prove hard to duplicate under peacetime conditions.

Washington had recruited talent from far and wide for its crusade against the Axis. The production capabilities and sheer output of the country's industries (General Motors, Ford, U.S. Steel, General Electric) had been harnessed by the best and the brightest minds from the country's top scientific research centers (MIT, Princeton, Columbia), giving the world radar, jet fighters, the atom bomb. In the span of four years, the country had grown from a second-rate power to the greatest military behemoth in history. It was the dawn of the American New Order. Like ancient Athens and her league, it would be an empire of the willing—America's allies willed her to rule the world and rule the world she would.

Yet now that the battle was won, the unlikely alliance that had guided the United States to victory was splitting apart. Businesses wanted to make money and scientists wanted to do research. Few wanted to put up with the military's restrictions and low pay. General Arnold feared that if everybody went back to industry or academia, America's enemies could one day hold sway. The likeliest adversary: our erstwhile wartime ally, the Soviet Union.

Already in March 1946, former British prime minister Winston Churchill had warned about an Iron Curtain descending on Europe.[2] Soviet leader Joseph Stalin had shattered his wartime alliance with the United States, and his troops, firmly in control of Central and Eastern Europe, were pressuring Italy and France. Soviet boots seemed ready to crush all political opposition; it was only a matter of time before a major American-Soviet conflict developed. That was why Arnold was flying to California, to find a way to hire the best brains in the country, put them together in a space they could call their own, and have them come up with weapons nobody had ever imagined.

Even in the midst of the war, a year earlier, Arnold had requested his chief scientific adviser, a colorful Hungarian named Theodore von Kármán (who was also director of the Guggenheim Laboratories), to devise a plan to entice scientists to continue working for the Air Force during peacetime. Kármán had come up with a report called "Toward New Horizons," which called for the establishment of a new kind of scientific community, "a nucleus for scientific groups such as those which successfully assisted in the command and staff work in the field during the war," a university without students and with the Air Force as its only client.[3] In other words, a prototype for the organization that would become RAND. Arnold had been delighted with the plan, but the exigencies of the war had made him put it aside until the right moment. That moment came when lean, steely-jawed, blue-eyed former test pilot Franklin R. Collbohm, visiting from California, came into Arnold's office one day in September of 1945.

A fanatically fit former marine, Collbohm swam in his pool every morning, rain or shine, before going to work.[4] He had fled his childhood environs in upstate New York for the wide skies and opportunities of the West as soon as he could, eventually becoming the right-hand man of Donald Douglas, head of Douglas Aircraft, America's largest airplane manufacturer, and the special assistant to Arthur E. Raymond, the company's vice president and head of engineering.

Arnold and Collbohm had met in 1942, when Collbohm procured nascent radar technology being developed at the Massachusetts Institute of Technology for the Army Air Force.[5] Both men shared a passion for aircraft and a deep love for the armed forces, to the point that they might have been inverse images of each other—Arnold advocating for scientists among the military and Collbohm standing up for the Air Force among the intelligentsia.

Like Arnold, Collbohm was concerned with the imminent dispersal of the best brains the United States could hire, and had approached a number of officials in Washington, D.C., about finding a way to retain top scientists after the war, with little success. When he finally came to Arnold's office, though, Collbohm did not even have to finish describing his idea for setting up an advisory group of independent scientists consulting for the military before the general slapped his desk and exclaimed, "I know just what you're going to tell me. It's the most important thing we can do." He told Collbohm to call Douglas right away to enlist his cooperation; they were to meet at California's Hamilton Air Force Base in two days. Collbohm was to have a list of all the things required to make the project come to fruition—the men, the machines, the money.[6]

Collbohm grabbed the first plane he could out of Washington, a B-25 bomber, and landed at Douglas's Santa Monica plant. He gathered all the Douglas officials he needed for the meeting and then looked for a plane to get them to the San Francisco Bay Area. The only aircraft available was President Roosevelt's private plane, a Douglas C-54 dubbed "The Sacred Cow," so Collbohm and his people grabbed that and flew to Hamilton in it, arriving at the base just an hour ahead of Arnold, with barely enough time to round up a luncheon for the meeting.[7]

When the general's B-21 rumbled into Hamilton Air Force Base, waiting for him were Collbohm, Raymond, and Douglas, whose daughter had married Arnold's son. Arnold had brought with him Edward Bowles, a consultant from MIT who had collaborated with Collbohm in setting up the first instance of coordinated civilian and military efforts in wartime planning, the B-29 Special Bombardment Project in 1944.[8]

Lunch was served and the men got to work. One of the chief concerns of the meeting was how the new organization would help develop the technology of long-distance missiles, which Arnold was convinced was the wave of the future. Arnold and his group were adamant that only the Air Force and no other branch of the armed forces should control the new weapon. By the time he finished his coffee, Arnold had pledged $10 million from unspent wartime research money to set up the research group and keep it running independently for a few years. Arthur Raymond suggested the name Project RAND, for research and development. Collbohm nominated himself to head the group while he looked for a permanent director.[9] (His temporary stay would eventually stretch to more than twenty years.) And so was RAND conceived.

At first, Project RAND had no specific definition of purpose other than the very general outline hashed out in Hamilton Field—a civilian outfit to come up with new weapons. But how? Besides long-range missiles, what other kind of weapons? How many? Arnold, Collbohm, Bowles, and Douglas exchanged memos, letters, and suggestions on the future of the organization for months, but final details were not worked out until General Curtis LeMay came into the picture in late December.

Gruff, aggressive, demanding, and some would say demented, LeMay was the coldest of the cold warriors. With his bulldog swagger and "never surrender" attitude, he served as a prototype for several generals in the movie *Doctor Strangelove,* advocating massive attacks on the enemy—whichever enemy America happened to be facing at the time, although usually the Soviet Union—while chomping on a stogie.[10]

Named Air Force Deputy Chief of Air Staff for Research and Development, LeMay included among his responsibilities the supervision of the new research group. Whether purposely or by the sheer serendipity that can accompany government work, LeMay turned out to be the ideal candidate to shepherd the fledgling organization.

With typical impatience, he tore through the red tape hindering the birth of RAND—at one point gathering all the Air Force bureaucrats needed for budget approval in one room and refusing to let them leave until they signed off on Project RAND's exact mission. Finally, on March 1, 1946, RAND officially was delivered. Its charter was clear: "Project RAND is a continuing program of scientific study and research on the broad subject of air warfare with the object of recommending to the Air Force preferred methods, techniques and instrumentalities for this purpose."[11]

Unlike other government contractors, RAND would be exempt from reporting to a contracting command. Instead, the unfiltered results would be delivered straight to LeMay. LeMay made sure that Project RAND could accept or reject Air Force suggestions for research and that RAND alone would determine the overall balance of its research. In exchange, the Air Force would receive information on intelligence, plans, and programs to optimize the value of its research; nevertheless, the project in no way was meant to exempt the Air Force from its own decision-making responsibilities.[12] In other words, RAND would always be subservient to the Air Force when it came to deciding what would get made and how.

Arnold, Collbohm, and LeMay proved prescient on the government's need for continued assistance from independent civilian scientists in peacetime. Within a few years, a new mind-set would take hold in government: science, rather than diplomacy, could provide the answers needed to cope with threats to national security—especially vis-à-vis the growing Soviet military menace.

The United States had demobilized its armed forces after World War II; new weapons, such as the atomic bomb, were seen as cheaper and more efficient than keeping large numbers of soldiers stationed abroad. Rather than nationalize key military industries, as Great Britain and France had done, the U.S. government opted to contract out its scientific research development to private concerns. The pri-

vate sector, not bound by the procurement and personnel requirements of the Pentagon, could create new weapons faster and cheaper.
RAND would be a bridge between the two worlds of military planning and civilian development.[13]

President Truman's main scientific adviser, Vannevar Bush, had
published an acclaimed report, "Science, the Endless Frontier," in
which he advocated continual and ever-greater government expenditures on what he called "basic research," that is, the generation of
new knowledge without constraints.[14] Therefore, LeMay's insistence
that RAND's independence be guaranteed, and that it should not be
assigned to crash projects but instead carry out research of a long-
range nature, was supported at the highest levels of the armed forces
as well.[15] General Eisenhower, then Chief of Staff of the Army,
pointed out in a memorandum dated April 30, 1946, that

> *The Army must have civilian assistance in military planning
> as well as for the production of weapons . . . Scientists and
> industrialists must be given the greatest possible freedom to
> carry out their research . . .* Scientists and industrialists are
> more likely to make new and unexpected contributions to
> the development of the Army if detailed conditions are held
> to a minimum . . . There appears to be little reason for du-
> plicating within the Army an outside organization which by
> its experience is better qualified than we are to carry out
> some of our tasks. The advantages to our nation in economy
> and to the Army in efficiency are compelling reasons for this
> procedure.[16]

If Arnold and his group were the founding fathers of RAND,
there is no doubt that LeMay was its godfather. Unlike some of his
privileged confreres, LeMay was of humble origins, earning his first
commission through the Reserve Officers' Training Corps instead

of West Point. Enamored of airplanes since first seeing them at age five, when, in his words, he decided that "flying was next to the divine," LeMay became a legendary pilot in the Army Air Corps. In 1937 he found the battleship *Utah* in the vast waters off the California coast and dropped water bombs on it during a military exercise, even though he had been given the wrong coordinates for the ship's location. The following year he led squads of B-17s to South America to display their range and effectiveness in national defense.[17]

When the war began, LeMay was a group commander for the Eighth Air Force; within eighteen months, he had risen from lieutenant colonel to major general and air division commander on the strength of his organizational skills and take-no-prisoners attitude. His skill as a gifted tactician brought him to the attention of Arnold, who was bringing a powerful new bomber, the B-29, into service. He picked LeMay to take it to the theater where bombers were most urgently needed, China. There LeMay coordinated efforts to fight the Japanese invaders with Mao Tse-tung, the Communist leader who had been conducting a civil war against the Nationalist regime of Generalissimo Chiang Kai-shek. Arnold subsequently sent LeMay to the Marianas, where, as head of the 21st Bomber Command, LeMay would oversee the controversial raids over Japanese cities in 1945.

It was in the Marianas that LeMay first worked with Collbohm, Raymond, and Bowles. The three civilians had been assigned by Douglas to run a study aimed at improving the effectiveness of the B-29 during the sorties over Japan. Using a new technique called operational research, Collbohm and his group discovered that B-29s could fly longer, better, and safer from their bases by discarding most of their armor. The conclusion was counterintuitive to most pilots, who were opposed to flying without extra protection from Japanese attacks; however, when implemented, the change proved amazingly valuable to the war effort. LeMay wrote that never before had any of his bombers been as accurate as the B-29s stripped as per the recommendation of Collbohm's team.[18]

The operational research concept had been developed in Great Britain during World War II to measure and improve the efficacy of new weapons systems—such as bomber aircraft, long-range rockets, torpedoes, and radar. OR, as it was first known, gathered, analyzed, and compared all kinds of data to answer the pressing questions of military commanders: What kind of payload allows a given bomber to destroy its intended target with the greatest impact? How should antiaircraft guns be placed to fend off enemy attacks? How large should naval convoys be? In short, it applied standard scientific methodology to the art of war. State your objective, analyze available data, propose the improvements, experiment in the field, examine the results, and, voilà, the solution.

Strangely enough, such a practical approach to military matters had rarely been taken before, and never of this magnitude by so many diverse minds. P. M. S. Blackett,[19] a Nobel Prize winner in physics and one of the creators of OR, believed in the value of what he called "mixed teams," groups that charged scientists from different fields with dissecting a problem and proffering the most efficient solution.* At one point their efforts proved so successful in the improvement of aircraft antisubmarine depth charges that the German enemy believed Allied forces had come up with new weaponry. In the United States, OR became known as operational analysis, and, as Fred Kaplan writes, "By the end of the war, every U.S. Army Air Force Unit had its own operational analysis division."[20] Scientists were not only asked to gather data and create new weapons but also became involved in the very planning of the war

---

* When Blackett explained his approach to American military leaders, he said he had tried all kinds of professions for his teams, except for lawyers. Misunderstanding Blackett's sardonic humor, the U.S. Air Force hired as its first OR chief an attorney who later became a Supreme Court justice, John Marshall Harlan.

effort. RAND would become the supreme embodiment of that approach to war.

The success of the B-29 project, though, would later prove horrifying to many people around the world, for the payloads were incendiary bombs designed to inflict the greatest amount of damage to the civilian population of Japan. Hundreds of thousands of people burned to death; homes, shops, and buildings of no apparent military value were consumed by the fiery rain that fell from the low-flying B-29s night after night. The tactic had been used previously by the Allies in Europe, most infamously during the bombing of Dresden, which had killed 25,000 civilians[21]—but never before by Americans, who had deliberately avoided civilian populations. The need to conquer Japan overruled any qualms the United States might have had. Japanese civilians were classified as admissible military targets.

The benefits and disadvantages of the raids, like those of the dropping of the atomic bomb, have been debated for decades; historians have weighed the unconditional surrender of Japan and its concomitant saving of American soldiers' lives against the wholesale slaughter of a civilian population. One thing is certain: the carpet bombing of Japan left the founding fathers of RAND—and the future secretary of defense Robert McNamara, who also collaborated on the B-29 project—with the reputation of looking only to the practical aspect of a problem without concern for morality. Their numbers-driven perspective had the effect, intentional or not, of divorcing ethical questions from the job at hand. Eventually RAND doctrine would come to view scientists and researchers as facilitators, not independent judges. As LeMay himself said, "All war is immoral. If you let that bother you, you're not a good soldier."[22]

ON MARCH 1, 1946, when its birth charter was signed, RAND had a handful of consultants on its payroll but only four full-time employees: Collbohm; James E. Lipp, who headed the Missiles Department; J. Richard Goldstein, a longtime colleague of Collbohm's, as associate director; and L. E. Root, who had been one of Douglas Aircraft's leading engineers. Raymond, while still working for Douglas, served as general supervisor. Because of security concerns, they were housed in a section of the main Douglas plant in Santa Monica closed off from the rest of the building by a thick glass door. The fledgling RANDites had already received their first assignment from LeMay: an inquiry into the possibility of launching an orbiting satellite by spaceship.

The project arose out of the Air Force's interest in developing intercontinental ballistic missiles. LeMay requested that RAND scientists prepare the study quickly because the Navy Bureau of Aeronautics was already working with Wernher von Braun and other captured Nazi scientists on a similar rocket project. LeMay wanted to outmaneuver his rivals and preserve the Air Force's exclusive right to the military uses of space. Within a month, RAND's four employees, with the help of consultants, wrote a farseeing report, breathtaking in its intellectual daring and self-assured to the point of arrogance. "Preliminary Design of an Experimental World-Circling Spaceship"[23] was the world's first comprehensive satellite feasibility assessment.[24]

LeMay wanted vision and details, and he got both to spare. The RAND report was prophetic in advocating the use of multiple-stage rockets, specifying maximum desired acceleration rates, and recommending studies on alcohol–liquid oxygen and liquid hydrogen–liquid oxygen as propellants. It also spelled out many of the eventual uses of man-made satellites, such as weather forecasting, communications, spying, and, especially, propaganda.

As the report stated,

Whose imagination is not fired by the possibility of voyaging out beyond the limits of our earth, traveling to the Moon, to Venus and Mars? Such thoughts when put on paper now seem like idle fancy. But, a man-made satellite, circling our globe beyond the limits of the atmosphere, is the first step. The other necessary steps would surely follow in rapid succession.[25]

The oftentimes lyrical study served its purpose well and the Navy project was shelved. As Air Force chief of staff General Hoyt Vandenberg consequently put it, the Air Force had "logical responsibility" for satellites. To prevent further disputes with other branches, the Department of Defense brokered an agreement whereby the Air Force took charge of "strategic"—that is, intercontinental—missiles, while the Army was granted authority to develop "tactical" or battlefield-use missiles.[26]

Internecine competition among branches of the armed forces for new and improved weapons systems was nothing out of the ordinary at the time. For decades, chiefs of staff had fought tenaciously to expand their bailiwicks at the expense of the other services. The main role of the secretary of defense was seen as that of a mediator between the competing branches, which always battled for an ever-greater slice of the Pentagon budget. "The secretaries of Defense and of the other three services usually tend toward a narrow view of their administrative function, and incline to avoid if they can intervention in what they call 'strictly military decisions,' though they are not always permitted to," wrote military analyst Bernard Brodie. "Since they are normally selected for talents in fields other than the military and rarely tarry long in their high public posts, their modesty is probably for the best."[27] The practice of brotherly back-stabbing would not end until President Kennedy's appointment of Robert McNamara to head the Pentagon in 1961, with a mandate to tame the military.

With RAND firmly in the role of intellectual gunslinger for the Air Force, Collbohm was pressed to beef up RAND's permanent staff. His fifth hire, John Davis Williams, would mold the intellectual environment and structural growth of the think tank for years to come through his choice of new employees, expansion into diverse fields of study, and even the very shape of the building that housed RAND.

An obese, genial, and charmingly eccentric mathematician, Williams was director of the newly created Mathematics Division—and Collbohm's de facto right-hand man.[28] He personified what would become hallmarks of RANDites—a love of pleasures of the flesh, a dedication to abstract theory, and a sense of absolute self-righteousness married to an amoral approach to politics and policy. While he coolly advocated a preemptive nuclear attack on the Soviet Union that would annihilate millions, he also published a book on game theory called *The Compleat Strategyst,* which he mordantly described as "a soporific on all unpleasant passions."[29] Williams believed that every human activity could be understood and explained by numerical rationality. From the start, one of his pet projects at RAND was developing a theory of war along the lines of Einstein's grand unified theory of physics. Like that project, Williams's dream of a general theory of war would prove chimerical.

Williams contracted with one of the most renowned mathematicians of the era, John von Neumann, to help him develop the general theory of war. In a typical Williams twist, he informed von Neumann that his contribution was to be his thoughts while he shaved every day—and only those thoughts he had while shaving, no more, no less. For that von Neumann was paid $200 a month—the average monthly salary at the time.[30]

A wrestling aficionado and amateur pool shark, Williams had a penchant for things that went very fast in the dark. He bought a Jaguar sports coupe and exchanged its original engine for a Cadillac behemoth, which allowed him to take the vehicle out for spins at midnight down the Pacific Coast Highway at over 150 miles per hour. As a precaution, he also installed state-of-the-art radar equipment in the car to forfend the friendly ministrations of the California highway patrol.

Born to a wealthy family that indulged his eccentricities, Williams owned a house in tony Pacific Palisades, which had been built for a millionaire before the Great Depression. The house had been too big to sell in its original condition at the man's death so a wily developer had cut it up into five rectangular slices, demolishing the second and fourth slices. Williams bought the middle house; the actress Deborah Kerr bought the first. Williams threw frequent, well-attended soirees, so well lubricated that at times his brilliant guests would be rolling around on the ground, drunk.[31] (This was common conduct among mathematicians, who believed in the "therapeutic effects" of alcohol consumption; at Princeton University, the famous physicist J. Robert Oppenheimer was so free with the booze that his house was nicknamed Bourbon Manor.[32])

SOON THE GROWING number of projects assigned or suggested to RAND by the Air Force, as well as those the ever-growing number of full-time employees came up with, dictated that there would be a corps of university-based consultants in different disciplines. By 1947 the list of RAND consultants included such luminaries as Nobel Prize–winning physicist Luis W. Alvarez from the University of California at Berkeley; Samuel S. Wilks, from Princeton University, an expert on mathematical statistics; and George B. Kistiakowsky, a leader in physical chemistry out of Harvard University.[33] Many of these were recruited to help RAND design what was intended to be the most powerful weapon in the world—the "super," the top-secret H, or hydrogen, bomb meant to be thousands of times more powerful than the twenty-kiloton blasts that leveled Hiroshima and Nagasaki.

Collbohm and Williams also hired a number of industrial subcontractors to handle such things as research on the capabilities of propeller turbines and delivery of high-intensity radiation to distant points. For the first two years of its existence, RAND allocated the lion's share of its Air Force research funds for applied science projects to subcontractors like Bell Telephone, Boeing Aircraft, and Collins Radio Company.[34] Gradually, though, RAND moved away from applied studies and began to concentrate on scientific theory and structure.

Refining the concept of operational analysis, RANDites, led by Williams, set out to create an analytical system that would identify policy choices, evaluate them scientifically, and allow policy makers to base their choices on ostensibly rational, objective criteria.[35] It came to be called systems analysis, and became one of the most notable and controversial contributions of RAND to the national policy-making structure. It also allowed RAND to pioneer the field of nuclear analysis—that is, the ways and means by which nuclear weapons would be deployed and the enormous consequences thereof. Yet, in spite of the collective brilliance of RAND, there would be one area of science that would forever elude it, one whose absence would time and again expose the organization to peril: the knowledge of the human psyche.

2

The Human Factor

IN 1946, screenwriter Leo Rosten received a mysterious call from one of his college classmates, an economics professor at Stanford named Allen Wallis. Though years later Rosten would write two bestselling comic novels, *The Education of H*Y*M*A*N K*A*P*L*A*N* and *Captain Newman, M.D.*,[1] at the time he was making a comfortable living as a Hollywood rewrite man—albeit one with somewhat unusual qualifications.

Born in Poland, Rosten was a psychologist, a trained economist, and a political scientist, having studied at the University of Chicago and the London School of Economics. During the war, he had worked as deputy director of the Office of War Information, and for a while had been an assistant to Lowell Mellett, one of President Roosevelt's aides. Rosten also had participated in producing the Why We Fight series of propaganda films for the Army, which had enlisted the talent of such directors as John Ford and Frank Capra.

Even though he was no longer in the public sector, when his friend Wallis asked him to meet with a man named John Williams, who was involved with top-secret work, Rosten said yes.

A few hours later Williams called and asked if he could bring Frank Collbohm to the meeting. When the duo showed up, Rosten was stunned by the unlikely pair. Williams was north of 300 pounds, orotund, and messy, while Collbohm was lean, leathery, and laconic. The moment Rosten showed them into his living room and closed the doors, so neither his wife nor two young children would interrupt, Williams spoke.

"We should tell you that you have been cleared. We had a security check run on you. There are certain things that will develop in the course of this conversation which we are permitted to tell you, but which you must regard as strictly off-the-record."

Collbohm then briefly sketched the origins and purpose of Project RAND, but without mentioning its top-secret goal of research into intercontinental missiles. After a while Rosten asked, "Now, why are you talking to me?"

Williams replied that for months they had felt that their staff was incomplete, as they were facing certain problems that they didn't have the knowledge to deal with.

"Like what?" asked Rosten.

Collbohm cut in: "Well, we think we know a lot about planes, and other devices, but there's one thing we don't know much about, and that is a certain machine that weighs—oh, between 160 to 185 pounds, is between five-feet-eight and six feet, and is called a 'pilot.'"[2]

The people at RAND were stumped by human behavior. Their work on a general theory of war, the Air Force–commissioned studies of pilot reaction during enemy attack, the whole panoply of RAND's defense projects hinged on human psychology. And their numbers-oriented philosophy could not figure that out.

Williams and Collbohm picked Rosten's brain, wanting to know how to improve the morale of a group engaged in stress activity, how to gauge a possible enemy's intentions, how human behavior was changed by group dynamics. The three talked into the night on that occasion and then met again several times with other members of the small group of RAND employees, exploring means of introducing social sciences into the hard research RAND was already conducting. Years later Rosten would recall that at their meetings Collbohm seemed inscrutable; he could never figure out the degree to which Collbohm was skeptical of psychology. Williams, on the other hand, was receptive, sympathetic, and enthusiastic. He was also egocentric, sarcastic, and supercilious, insisting on being at the center of all conversations.

When after a few months it became clear that RAND would definitely be starting a social science department, Williams and Collbohm asked Rosten to head it. Rosten declined, citing his writing schedule, but instead offered to set up a conference in New York where they could recruit some of the best minds in the field. Rosten warned Collbohm and Williams that they would be hampered by the fact that RAND was sited at Douglas, since some of the social scientists would not want to work at an aircraft company. They might also feel embarrassed by RAND's reputation, as Rosten had found out that "in some circles in Southern California, RAND was a sinister acronym for some diabolic group of war-mongers."[3]

The conference was to be held at the New York Economic Club September 14 to 19, 1947. Williams, who had an irrational fear of planes, took a train to New York while Rosten bowed out at the last minute because of a screening of his new movie. The meeting was chaired by Warren Weaver, who, in his opening remarks, stated what could be considered the RAND creed:

> I assume that everyone here is devoted to what can broadly be called the rational life. He believes fundamentally that there is something to this business of having some knowledge, and some experience, and some insight, and some

analysis of problems, as compared with living in a state of ignorance, superstition, and drifting-into-whatever-may-come . . . I think that we are interested not in war but in peace . . . I assume that every person in this room is desperately dedicated to the ideals of democracy, and to so running our own business, so cleaning our own house, and so improving our own relations with the rest of the world that the value of those ideals in which we believe becomes thereby evident.[4]

Although the conference ostensibly was to identify, measure, and control the factors important to the waging and winning of wars, the meeting also served as an introduction to RAND for the thirty scholars who had accepted the expenses-paid invitation. Rosten had solicited research projects, and participants had submitted about one hundred papers. Among the topics were American foreign policy, the economic war potential of the United States and the Soviet Union, methods of attitude measurement, and the reliability of prediction. Those present included anthropologist Ruth Benedict from Columbia University; historian Bernard Brodie from Yale; philosopher Abraham Kaplan from the University of California at Los Angeles; sociologists Herbert Goldhamer from the University of Chicago and Hans Speier from the New School for Social Research; as well as economists Charles Hitch from Oxford University and Jacob Viner from Princeton.

Over the years, most of the people who attended that 1947 conference would become consultants to RAND. But that steamy September in New York, Williams made offers of full employment to only two prominent figures, Speier and Hitch, asking them to become the first directors of the social science and economics divisions, respectively.[5]

Speier was a German refugee who had escaped Nazi Germany in 1933 and joined the New School for Social Research in New York, where he was part of the University in Exile, composed of newly displaced German and Austrian scholars.[6] A shy, self-effacing man whose field was international politics, Speier was a specialist in propaganda and civic social structures, both issues of critical importance in the conduct of war. He readily accepted Williams's offer.

The other recruit's background was even more germane to RAND's future work—a fact that had prompted Collbohm to authorize payment of his ticket from Rio de Janeiro, where he was conducting research.[7] Hitch was an Arizona-born Harvard graduate, a Rhodes scholar, and an Oxford don. Joining the U.S. Army in 1943, he was eventually assigned to the Office of Strategic Services, the antecedent of today's Central Intelligence Agency.[8] While in the OSS, Hitch had conducted OR for a section called Research and Experiments Department Number 8, using reverse analysis to estimate the efficacy of British bombing raids over Germany (they concluded that less than one-half of the bombs reached their intended targets and those that did affected only slightly the Nazi war machine).[9]

Hitch knew firsthand how economic and statistical computations could aid policy decisions in government, and he was sorely tempted by Williams's offer to join RAND in California, though at the time he was comfortably ensconced in Oxford with his family. Hitch would later call the decision to join RAND the hardest of his life—but ultimately he signed on and moved to Santa Monica.

Speier began formal operations of the RAND Social Science Department in 1948, a few short months after the New York conference. From the start, he had difficulty convincing scholars in international politics to break away from East Coast–based academic centers. Out of necessity, the department established two social science offices: one in Washington, D.C., that concentrated on political analysis, and the other at RAND headquarters in Santa Monica, focusing on human behavior.[10] This geographical separation inadvertently foiled Williams's original plan to integrate into the

RAND fold the entire faculty of social scientists, so that their historical, humanistic perspective on issues would counterbalance the numbers-oriented analytic tendencies of the "hard" scientists: the mathematicians, physicists, and economists who already were thriving in Santa Monica. Over time, the remoteness of political scientists from the center of RAND power at Santa Monica—they would not move west until the mid-1950s—would cause the near absolute predominance of a quantitative, mathematical focus on RAND work, particularly in nuclear strategy.

Rosten remained a RAND consultant, but his involvement with daily operations diminished, ceasing altogether when he moved to New York in 1954. Before his departure, though, Rosten was instrumental in two other major developments at the think tank. He persuaded Speier to hire the noted historian Bernard Brodie away from Yale, where he was unhappy over the neglect of his work. Rosten also suggested that H. Rowan Gaither, the attorney who was drafting the RAND articles of incorporation, contact the Ford Foundation about funding RAND.

RAND's incorporation in 1948 was a mutually desired manumission from the Douglas Aircraft Company. For the idiosyncratic bunch that had migrated to RAND, life at Douglas had not been without difficulties. As Williams recounted,

> The matter of hours of work were . . . a substantial trial. Academic people have irregular habits and have never taken kindly to the eight-to-five routine. We had one man who rarely showed up before two o'clock, and another who almost never went home—this, mind you, in an organization where they physically locked the doors at about five, and kept them locked until about eight in the morning. Well, they changed this for us so people could work nights and weekends.

We had a lot of trouble about blackboards. About the very concept of a blackboard in every office! I can remember Cecil Weihe, our procurement chief, saying, "What's the matter with these people? Can't they write on paper?" Now this may sound as though I'm getting down to awfully fine details—but the chalk was worse than the blackboards. The company had no policy on blackboards, so we could get one in every office. But they did have a policy on chalk, stating that each blackboard could have two (or was it three?) pieces of chalk; and of course, our people wanted four colors. We had quite a flap on chalk.[11]

Although nominally autonomous, Project RAND had come to be seen as an appendage of Douglas. After a while, RAND found it difficult to obtain detailed information from Air Force contractors to prepare analyses of defense problems since contractors were wary of supplying confidential proprietary information that might be leaked to a competitor. Moreover, many analysts were reluctant to be associated with RAND, believing that RAND could not really be objective as long as it was under Douglas sponsorship.[12]

For its part, Douglas Aircraft saw RAND as a growth choking the life of the parent body. Since the Air Force was going out of its way to avoid even the impression of favoritism, Douglas executives felt the company's association with the think tank was hurting Douglas's chances of landing lucrative contracts. Even the Air Force was unhappy, frustrated that the millions of dollars it was spending on Project RAND were not bearing the desired results because of these conflicts.[13] To solve these problems, early in 1948 Collbohm asked Gaither to find an acceptable way to sever RAND's links to Douglas. Collbohm had made the acquaintance of the well-connected San Francisco attorney during World War II, when Gaither worked as assistant director to the Radiation Laboratory at MIT and was a consultant to the National Defense Research Committee.

At Collbohm's request, Gaither drafted a memorandum on the different forms RAND could take after its separation from Douglas, among them becoming an affiliate of a prominent university like Princeton or the University of Chicago, or transforming itself into a for-profit business. In the end, Collbohm decided that RAND's best chance for an independent future was as a nonprofit corporation.[14] The articles of incorporation specified that RAND would have no stock or stockholders; its earnings would benefit only the corporation and not any individual; and while it might derive profit from contract fees, all moneys beyond what was needed for running the organization would be plowed back into it. Technically the trustees, chosen from among the cream of the country's universities, laboratories, foundations, and communications and finance companies, would own the corporation.[15] Management, analysts, and researchers—that is to say, the people who actually constituted the RAND business—would be working for the trustees. Strangely enough for an ostensibly independent business organization, all of RAND's contracts were with the Air Force—although in theory RAND would be at liberty to pursue other contracts after incorporation, as long as they did not interfere with its basic commitment to the Air Force. This reflected Collbohm's intense allegiance to his former employer. As he said, "Civilians come and go. The Air Force stays forever."[16]

After discussions with Collbohm, Raymond, and Larry Henderson of RAND, Air Force Chief of Staff Carl Spaatz signed off on the rebirth of the organization, saying consent would be given "when we are satisfied that the new corporation is in existence and is capable of discharging the contract obligations as effectively as the Douglas Company."[17]

Gaither informed Collbohm that to start independent operations RAND would need $1 million—the equivalent of about $10 million in 2007 dollars. Using Gaither's connections, they prevailed on San Francisco–based Wells Fargo Bank to offer a $600,000 line of credit, promising that RAND would come up with the other $400,000. Both Henry Ford II and Benson Ford promised $400,000. Its new stated mission, worked out by Collbohm and Williams, signified a vision of RAND as something more than just a weapons incubator: "To further and promote scientific, educational and charitable purposes, all for the public welfare and security of the United States of America."[18]

RAND's new mission statement meshed perfectly with the objectives of the Ford Foundation. The largest philanthropic organization of the time, the foundation was in the process of reorganizing itself to lend financial support for world peace and the advancement of scientific knowledge.[19] Gaither not only obtained a much needed commitment of close to half a million dollars from the Ford Foundation for RAND but he also became the foundation's president.[20] Thus from the outset, an enduring link was established between the two seminal civilian institutions of the Cold War.[21]

In a statement he crafted after assuming the presidency of the foundation, Gaither stated as his goal a society where technocrats ruled using objective analysis. Philanthropy, in his view, should not only help the needy but also advise those responsible for the formulation of policy, replacing partisan controversy with objective fact. "This very non-partisanship and objectivity gives the [Ford] foundation a great positive force, and enables it to play a unique and effective role in the difficult and sometimes controversial task of helping to realize democracy's goals."[22] The Ford Foundation's close alignment with U.S. government policies continued throughout the 1950s, with Gaither supporting foundation efforts to underwrite American political and psychological warfare. According to some scholars, Ford Foundation presidents after Gaither even went so far as to drop by the National Security Council and ask if there were projects the NSC wanted funded.[23] (Years after his death, Gaither would become a bête noire of conspiracy theorists; he was blasted as a closet Socialist who, as president of the Ford Foundation, was advancing the cause of a one-party, one-world government that would eventually merge the United States with the Soviet Union. Considering all the work that Gaither conducted and offered to conduct for the Central Intelligence Agency while at the Ford Foundation, this accusation seems groundless.[24])

IF ANY PERIOD can be called the shiniest of the golden years for RAND, there is little doubt that the handful of years following the think tank's incorporation was it. The Air Force, in essence, wrote the organization a blank check, saying: Here's the money, now go and think up ways to spend it to improve the nation's defenses against the Soviet Union as you see fit.

RAND grew at a dizzying pace, attracting a host of new consultants by its sponsorship of conferences and summer study groups, as well as by its relationship with industrial subcontractors. One of those subcontracting relationships resulted in the invention of new uses for titanium, a lightweight metal of great military importance for the development of supersonic vehicles—not to mention modern jewelry.[25]

To attract more academic researchers, RAND instituted a change in its nomenclature, as it sought to become truly a campus without students. Divisions, originally named sections—which smacked of the military—became departments, which then grew exponentially to include a host of disciplines. Soon RAND was hiring not only mathematicians and engineers but astronomers, psychologists, logicians, historians, sociologists, aerodynamicists, statisticians, chemists, economists, and even computer scientists.[26] No test for ideological correctness was given to join, but then none was needed. The nation's best and brightest joining RAND knew what they were signing on for, and readily accepted the vision of a rational world—America and its Western allies—engaged in a life-and-death struggle with the forces of darkness: the USSR.

With the expansion of RAND, an esprit de corps was born, a common assumption of men with a common enemy.* Beyond those shared beliefs about the Cold War, a number of factors worked to create an extremely tight-knit group at the think tank: its privileged position as the favorite of the Air Force (itself the golden boy of the armed forces by virtue of being the guardian of the ultimate weapon, the nuclear bomb); RAND's remoteness from the political power plays of Washington, D.C.; and the relative youth of the researchers.[27] RANDites working on top-secret projects were only free to discuss the details of their work with vetted colleagues. Like undercover agents, they hid the precise nature of their work even from their families. Most were brilliant young men with postgraduate degrees from the nation's top academic institutions; many had also served as junior officers during World War II. They knew they were bright, and they made sure everyone else knew it. This knowledge of their intellectual superiority bred a contempt for officialdom and an overweening arrogance that can still be detected among some of the surviving analysts today, more than fifty years later.

Williams, Collbohm, and the RAND board firmly believed that collegial competition was the best way to encourage original, creative thinking. RANDites were therefore always trying to outdo each other in all fields. Essays and working papers were circulated among colleagues for comments, which were always copious and controversial. New projects were examined by so-called murder boards, regularly scheduled departmental meetings where RANDites took brutal pleasure in shooting down shaky ideas. There was an annual tennis tournament; analysts also raced in local boating competitions with a small catamaran they built called *The Dreamer,* which they

---

*   Until the 1960s RAND employed few women as anything more than office assistants or secretaries. As late as 2004, RAND faced problems in its apparent disparity of treatment of women, with female employees filing a massive sexual discrimination lawsuit against the corporation.

occasionally took out on overnight cruises.[28] During work breaks, they puttered around with golf clubs in the building's inner court-yard lawn. At RAND parties, they tried to outdo one another in their appreciation of fine food, wine, and music, especially after the arrival of the mathematician and nuclear strategist Albert Wohlstet-ter, who was a world-class gourmand. Wives also participated in the spirit of competition through a cooking club, where spouses vied to prepare the most exotic recipes.[29]

RANDites even revived the old Prussian game of Kriegspiel, a kind of three-dimensional blind chess favored by nineteenth-century European military planners. They played it so much during the lunch hour that some researchers avoided the lunchroom altogether because of the mess the distracted researchers would leave behind.[30] Life at RAND was a boy's conception of what a man's life should be, down to the fragrant pipe tobacco, fast cars, and clubby exclusivity.

FOR A PLACE where thinking the unthinkable was supposed to be the common coin, strangely enough there was virtually no internal RAND debate on the nature of the Soviet Union or on the validity of existing American policies to contain it. RANDites took their cues from the military's top echelons—their monolithic faith in American righteousness would not be shattered until a new, ques-tioning generation, and a more complex conflict, the Vietnam War, came around.

Most internal documents written by RAND analysts through the 1940s and 1950s demonstrate a consistent belief that nuclear weapons were not only necessary but desirable to curb Soviet ag-gression, and that America was, unfortunately, much too passive in the face of the Soviet threat. Some RANDites, like Williams, believed in preemptive nuclear war on Russia as a prelude to an American-controlled world government—a body apart from the United Nations, which even then was viewed as an ineffectual den of contemptible prevaricators.

As an Air Force dependent, RAND eagerly propagated the military's belief that Moscow was out to devour the world. A book by RAND analyst Nathan Leites, *The Operational Code of the Politburo,* became house doctrine, and more than fifty years later, RAND analysts were still quoting it admiringly. Leites wrote his book in 1949 based on his reading of the works of Marx and Lenin; in it he posited an insatiable Soviet empire driven by doctrinal principles to attempt the territorial conquest of the globe.[31] Only the use of aggressive force could stop the Communist tide. Leites's work stood in marked contrast to the extant strategy of political containment developed by the former U.S. ambassador to the Soviet Union, George F. Kennan.

After World War II, when Moscow began to swallow up Eastern Europe, Ambassador Kennan sent what came to be known as "The Long Telegram." In his 10,000-word cable to President Truman in 1946, Kennan advocated containment of the Marxist giant through vigilance and example, not necessarily by the use of military force—the mere threat of it would be sufficient, in his view, to hold off the Soviets. The following year, under the sobriquet "X," Kennan published a lengthened form of his essay with the title "The Sources of Soviet Conduct" in the magazine *Foreign Affairs.*[32] For several years Kennan's guidelines were the operative code of American relations toward the Soviet Union. However, by 1950, after the successful detonation of the Soviet Union's first atomic weapon, administration policy changed from the passive, ideological containment advocated by Kennan to the open military competition urged by Leites. A notable RAND associate, Paul Nitze, brought about that change almost single-handedly.

A former Wall Street banker, the independently wealthy Nitze had entered government service as an aide to President Franklin Delano Roosevelt. During World War II, he had been vice chairman of the Strategic Bombing Survey, which put him in touch with the founding members of RAND, Arnold, LeMay, and Collbohm. Having replaced Kennan as head of the president's policy planning staff,[33] Nitze wrote a memorandum for the National Security Council on how to conduct foreign policy in the nuclear age.[34] The paper, called NSC-68, warned apocalyptically, in the spirit of Leites, about the "Kremlin's design for world domination" and the constant threat that presented to the United States:

> The Soviet Union, unlike previous aspirants to hegemony, is animated by a new fanatic faith, antithetical to our own, and seeks to impose its absolute authority over the rest of the world. The [Soviet] design, therefore, calls for the complete subversion or forcible destruction of the machinery of government and structure of society in the countries of the non-Soviet world and their replacement by an apparatus and structure subservient to and controlled from the Kremlin. To that end Soviet efforts are now directed toward the domination of the Eurasian land mass. The United States, as the principal center of power in the non-Soviet world and the bulwark of opposition to Soviet expansion, is the principal enemy whose integrity and vitality must be subverted or destroyed by one means or another if the Kremlin is to achieve its fundamental design.[35]

The paper also warned that with the Soviet buildup of atomic capability, the Kremlin might very well stage a surprise attack, with 1954 as the year of maximum danger, unless the United States substantially and immediately increased its armed forces and civil defenses. NSC-68 was forwarded to President Truman around the time that Soviet-backed North Korea launched an invasion of South Korea, an American ally. Nitze's warning about Communist designs worked so well that President Truman adopted NSC-68 as the official policy of the land and increased the national defense budget by almost $40 billion.

That year, 1950, the United States possessed approximately 298 atomic weapons.[36] Although we now know that the Soviet Union held only a handful of nuclear weapons, American policy makers, having little hard evidence, assumed the worst: that Moscow had built up a large arsenal and that its air force was capable of delivering the bombs to the United States. Moreover, in the eyes of the American public at large, it wasn't just Moscow that threatened the United States; there was plenty to fear from all quarters.

Just the previous year China had fallen to Communist rebels led by Mao Tse-tung, who had chased the forces of the former U.S.-backed Chinese strongman Generalissimo Chiang Kai-shek across the strait to Taiwan. A wave of recrimination had broken over the United States; cries of "Who lost China?" blared in newspaper editorials and in Congress.[37] In addition, the first Soviet atomic explosion—and the well-founded suspicion that Soviet spies had given Moscow the key to the bomb—unleashed fears of a Communist fifth column in this country. The House Un-American Activities Committee began holding hearings on the supposed infiltration of Communist Party members and sympathizers in the film industry, while a previously unknown senator from Wisconsin, Joseph Mc-Carthy, commenced clamoring about a vast Communist conspiracy in the federal government. A nationwide witch hunt for Communists ensued, with people in many professions being forced to sign loyalty oaths to the government if they wanted to preserve their jobs. Anyone suspected of being just a Communist sympathizer—a "pinko" or a "fellow traveler"—found himself unable to hold anything other than the most menial job. Ironically, one of the victims of the witch hunt was the man responsible for the atomic bomb, the head of the Manhattan Project, noted physicist J. Robert Oppenheimer. Suspected of Communist leanings, if not actual spying, he was stripped of his security clearance and blacklisted from top-secret government work.[38]

RAND's hawkish views of Soviet intentions, distilled in Leites's works and Nitze's jeremiads, fit the paranoia of the age, the national terror over an impending nuclear conflict, the abhorrence of anything that wasn't true-blue American. Nevertheless, RAND analysts believed that with hard work, dedication, and sacrifice—and the prescriptions issuing from Santa Monica—there might still be a future worth living. One of these RAND prescriptions would pull the world from the brink of possible nuclear annihilation, while another would rewrite the basic concepts of social welfare, politics, and government in America and the West.

3

The Wages of Sin

THE MUSHROOM CLOUD that rose out of the desert sands at Alamogordo, New Mexico, on July 16, 1945, blazed with a cosmic power that Brigadier General Thomas Farrell, the deputy to the director of the Manhattan Project, called "unprecedented, magnificent, beautiful, stupendous and terrifying."[1] The handful of scientists and military present at the creation of the nuclear era would forever be divided in their reaction to the bomb. Some, like physicists Edward Teller and Ernest Lawrence, saw nothing but the divine glory of their life's work flashing before their eyes. Others, like Enrico Fermi, made jokes and took bets as to whether the bomb's chain reaction would destroy the atmosphere of the entire country, the entire world, or just the state of New Mexico.[2]

By contrast, the head of the Manhattan Project, J. Robert Oppenheimer, although outwardly proud of his creation, was overcome by immense foreboding and regret. On witnessing the blast he recalled the words of the *Bhagavad Gita*, the Hindu sacred text in which the god Vishnu appears in his multiarmed guise and intones, "Now I have become death, the destroyer of worlds." Oppenheimer's remorse over creating the world's most dangerous weapon hounded him for the rest of his life, for he felt that physicists, who once had lived in an Edenic garden of knowledge, had now "known sin."[3]

Oppenheimer would go to his death trying to make amends for his brilliant contribution to the ranks of war, urging unilateral American disarmament and a halt to nuclear proliferation.[4] Many of his fellow scientists would also do their share to put the nuclear genie back in the bottle. But for those who studied war, the blasts at Alamogordo, Hiroshima, and Nagasaki demanded neither mea culpas nor apologies for the fall of man; the radioactive start of the nuclear era heralded a new world they could get in order. Perhaps the most prominent of these was the man credited with the concept of nuclear deterrence, RAND military historian Bernard Brodie, who upon seeing the newspaper headlines of the explosion at Hiroshima exclaimed, "Everything that I have written is obsolete." Months later, having plunged into a dark period of reflection, he would write, "Thus far the chief purpose of our military establishment has been to win wars. From now on its chief purpose must be to avert them. It can have almost no other useful purpose."[5]

Until he joined RAND in 1951, Brodie knocked about from college faculty to college faculty, unable, whether consciously or not, to fit into any one particular slot. In this, he echoed Albert Wohlstetter and so many others who came to RAND, people seeking an ivory tower that would shelter them from the buffeting winds of cultural orthodoxy.

The child of a poor Jewish family from Chicago's South Side, Brodie was short, nearsighted, and fascinated with power. Enamored of armies and horses, he lied about his age and at sixteen enlisted in the National Guard, back when the guard still trained its members on horses. Graduating from the University of Chicago in

1939, he taught at Princeton, where he met the future RAND Sovietologist Nathan Leites. From there Brodie moved to yet another Ivy League college, Dartmouth, where he was let go by the dean for being "too big a man in your field to fit into any future plans of the Department."[6] During the war Brodie served in the Office of Naval Intelligence, writing propaganda tracts broadcast to German U-boats to convince their crews to surrender. He had been named to the Political Science Department of Yale just five days before the bombing of Hiroshima.

Up to the moment that Hiroshima changed the modern world, Brodie's reputation had been based on two works that capitalized extensively, if unexpectedly, on the conflagration in Europe. His graduate school dissertation, titled *Sea Power in the Machine Age,* was published by the Princeton University Press shortly after Pearl Harbor. The Navy immediately ordered 1,600 copies, making it a bestseller for the academic presses of the time. The reception to the work was so encouraging that Brodie's publisher asked for another. Brodie complied with *A Layman's Guide to Naval Strategy;* the book was promptly snapped up by the U.S. Navy Reserve Officers' Training Corps, which bought 15,000 copies. Not bad for a man who had never even been to the ocean.[7]

Brodie, of course, was not the only scientist to observe that the atomic bomb changed the rules of all the games—bellicose and political—that nations played. Calls for a new order were heard throughout the Western world. Just as the awful carnage of World War I brought forth the desire for a collective world government that would finally usher in a new era of peace, many observers in the post–World War II era asked for the creation of a world body that would be entrusted with the use of this new and sublimely dangerous atomic arsenal. Noted British philosopher Bertrand Russell lobbied for such a world organization, as did Norman Cousins, the publisher of the *Saturday Review,* the most influential literary magazine in America at the time, who wrote, "There is no need to talk of the difficulties in the way of world government. There is need only to ask whether we can afford to do without it."[8] Even Oppenheimer favored limiting use of the bomb to a transnational organization very much like the United Nations.[9]

Then there were those who argued for preemptive war, to deny the Soviets—or any other enemy—the ability to ever be the aggressor by striking first without provocation. Several congressmen voiced the idea of destroying the Soviet Union shortly after the end of the war; even Secretary of State Dean Acheson privately toyed with the notion of permanently disarming the Soviets while it was still easy to do.[10] Perhaps the most prominent figure in the military establishment to come out in favor of preventive war was Secretary of the Navy Francis Matthews, who openly declared, "To have peace we should be willing, and declare our intention, to pay any price, even the price of instituting a war to compel cooperation for peace . . . We would become the first Aggressors for Peace."[11] For this opinion, President Truman immediately cashiered Matthews. Truman publicly rebuked all those who would strike first without provocation as un-American—even though years later in his memoirs he would admit to the existence of plans to stage a preventive nuclear attack if the Soviet Union threatened to invade Western Europe.[12]

To Brodie, preventive war, although desirable in theory, was tantamount to disaster. He argued at the time that attacking first without provocation would run so strikingly counter to the American tradition of fair play and to the national history of nonaggression that any military gain on the battlefield would be lost in the political arena. That was his conclusion even before the Soviet Union detonated its own atomic weapon in 1949. From that point on, Brodie felt there would never be any guarantee that American forces would be able to destroy all of the Soviet bombers and all of their nuclear weapons. It would take only one bomber to get through for the carnage on the American side to be unbearable.

The road to a permanent, albeit unstable, peace would have to go through the sloughs of nuclear preparedness before reaching the city of disarmament.

Asked by Yale's Institute of International Studies to contribute to *The Absolute Weapon,* a book exploring the case for control of atomic weapons, Brodie submitted its two most influential articles, "War in the Atomic Age" and "Implications for Military Policy." Brodie had previously immersed himself in scientific literature on the bomb to better understand the physical structure of it and to learn whether enough of the critical uranium ore supplies existed for its manufacture. He concluded that the atomic bomb had changed the very nature of war and that his field of specialty, naval studies, would play only a minor role in any future conflict.[13]

In his articles, Brodie argued that superiority in the number of bombs, or in the aircraft to deliver them, would not guarantee victory in a nuclear exchange. Since the materials for making the bomb were scarce, its best and highest use would be for attacking population centers. Furthermore, since all it took was one bomb to wreak unthinkable havoc, what was really needed was a way to deter war in the first place. This deterrence could be achieved only by having the capacity to retaliate after a first strike. Each side "must fear retaliation [since] the fact that it destroys the opponent's cities some hours or even days before its own are destroyed may avail it little."[14]

Brodie's thinking evolved further with the growing political turmoil in Western Europe and what was seen as the continuous Soviet encroachment on the free world. The CIA had had its hands full fighting off a Communist insurgency in Greece, while in Italy the Communist Party had come within a whisker of electoral triumph. In 1948 the democratic government of Czechoslovakia had fallen to a Communist coup d'état, while later that year, Soviet troops in still-divided Germany blockaded Berlin.[15] Meanwhile the United States had quickly demobilized the bulk of its troops as the nation veered away from a wartime economy.[16] It seemed to Brodie that along with political containment of the Soviet Union, America had no choice but to use its atomic arsenal as the major military means of controlling the expansionist Soviets.

New public information about the continuing scarcity of raw materials for the bomb caused Brodie to rethink his position that superiority in the number of atomic bombs was not an automatic advantage. It would indeed be effective superiority for America to have a three- or five-to-one margin over the Soviets, especially if the bombs were delivered to specific targets, not just to cities at random. But what targets? When? How?

Because it seemed to him that no one in the military was focusing on these questions, in 1949 Brodie decided to write a book about the subject. *Strategy of Air Power* was his original title—it would take him ten years to complete and would be called ultimately *Strategy in the Missile Age*. Brodie studied carefully official surveys and statistics on the effect of Allied bombing during World War II. He compared the actual impact of the bombing with the results that had been prophesied in the 1920s and 1930s by analysts such as the Italian brigadier general Giulio Douhet and the American general Billy Mitchell,* who had envisioned a future where airplanes were the ultimate weapon, rendering large armies or navies unnecessary.[17]

Brodie learned that the Allied bombing campaign had not had the expected impact, and that the Nazi industrial machine in fact had stood up very well to the onslaught; toward the end of the war, however, bombing had crippled two very important industries—liquid fuel and chemicals. Since the Soviet economy was less resilient than Germany's had been, and the effect of atomic weapons would be so much more extensive, he felt the United States should study its targets systematically and efficiently so as not to waste its advantage.

---

* Billy Mitchell, a controversial proponent of air warfare, was RAND founder Frank Collbohm's hero and inspiration.

Following the publication of some of these thoughts in a magazine article, Brodie was approached by General Lauris Norstad, the Air Force Vice Chief of Staff, who in turn convinced his boss, Chief of Staff Hoyt Vandenberg, to hire Brodie as a consultant. Brodie's charge was to examine and comment on how to improve the Strategic Air Command's target list, the 1945–46 Strategic Bombing Survey.[18]

The Army Air Force had formed SAC after World War II to plan and direct the use of the latest and most advanced weapons. Following the Air Force's split from the Army, the Joint Chiefs of Staff had charged SAC with battlefield delivery of the atomic bomb. Although by the end of 1948 there were only fifty nuclear bombs ready, the Atomic Energy Commission—at the time in charge of the development and production of the bombs—promised a stockpile of 400 A-bombs by 1951.[19]

RAND's godfather, General Curtis LeMay, had been named head of SAC after his successful completion of the American airlift during a Soviet blockade of Berlin in 1948. He found a command that was largely disabled—for example, all the B-29 bombers in Europe were nonoperational—and disoriented. He argued convincingly with the Joint Chiefs of Staff to give first priority to his needs; within two months, he had readied more than sixty planes for atomic missions.[20] He also made sure that the Atomic Energy Commission delivered on its promise of a swelling nuclear arsenal.

Brodie was ecstatic. At last he had gained the access to secrets of nuclear policy he had long been dreaming of: he would be going from the outer rings to the dark heart of the matter. He took a leave of absence from Yale and began questioning Pentagon planners about their rationale for the targets on the list. Brash and self-assertive, Brodie was not bothered by the negative reactions he provoked, as he knew he was the nation's most renowned civilian military strategist. He failed to realize that he was a walking oxymoron in the eyes of Pentagon brass, who felt only the military had the proper training and moral fiber to decide the nation's conduct in war. Moreover, Brodie unknowingly strayed into a hornet's nest when it came to the selection of targets.

SAC command, headed by LeMay, advocated massive attacks against the Soviet Union, dropping the entire stockpile of atomic bombs on seventy cities in the so-called Sunday punch. But Air Force staff analysts—with the approval of the Joint Chiefs—had come up with a different plan, one that distinguished between three kinds of targets: Delta, for "*disruption* of the vital elements of the Soviet war-making capacity"; Bravo, for "*blunting* of Soviet Capacities to deliver an atomic bomb"; and Romeo, for "*retardation* of Soviet advances into Western Europe."[21]

To LeMay, such distinctions were anathema. He had learned in combat that the principles of war advocated throwing everything but the kitchen sink at your enemy at the beginning of the conflict, in what was called "concentration of attack."[22] Anything else was specious hogwash.

Brodie had been hired, then, to add intellectual heft to the anti-LeMay arguments. When he examined the competing plans, Brodie was appalled by both. While the air staff analysts at least differentiated the targets and their effectiveness in stopping a Soviet aggression, they did not exactly know where all the targets were located. Moreover, they could not quite explain the specific results of each kind of bombing. Brodie, for instance, failed to understand why the planners thought that eliminating electrical power plants would instantly collapse the Soviet economy or "kill the nation." As for LeMay's plan, Brodie had already gone on the record that indiscriminate bombing of cities was ineffective. He personally told LeMay he did not understand his concept of the Sunday punch, especially when the Soviet Union had so few bombs to begin with. Brodie advocated using a "reserve force" of nuclear missiles as a deterrent to the Soviet Union. He held that if Moscow knew the

United States had enough firepower left after a surprise attack to inflict mortal damage to its enemy, the Soviets would be much more reluctant to use their nuclear arsenal first.

LeMay's opposition ultimately proved insurmountable. Brodie submitted a memorandum to Vandenberg, urging selectiveness of attack, reminding him that a nuclear war with the Soviet Union might very well turn out to be a two-way affair. If the United States withheld some of its forces, attacking only certain targets so as to convince the Soviets of the futility of further aggression, "that might be a small price to pay for the sake of avoiding total war."[23]

Historians still are not certain what Vandenberg's reaction was to Brodie's recommendation, although he did ask Brodie to chair a special advisory panel on strategic bombing effectiveness. But when Norstad, who had been Brodie's benefactor in the Air Force, was transferred to Europe, other Vandenberg aides who were opposed to Brodie and his ideas succeeded in having Brodie's contract, in his own words, "rather abruptly terminated."

Looking for a job, and reluctant to return to Yale, in 1951 he signed on with Hans Speier at RAND, for whom he had done some consulting a few years earlier. Brodie, having finally found the intellectual home he craved, would wind up staying for fifteen years—even though his relationship with RAND would be stormy and full of profound disappointments, as well as triumphs and acclaim.*

AMERICA'S POSTWAR STRUGGLE with the Soviet bloc was not just military. It was also ideological—and the stakes seemed to be the future of Western civilization.

---

* Brodie's history at RAND was not extraordinary in that last regard. A close reading of the relationship between RAND's most prominent analysts and the institution shows the same pattern—enthrallment and acclaim, followed by (and sometimes concurrent with) criticism, then institutional attack and rupture. It would also happen to Brodie's intellectual archrival, mathematician Albert Wohlstetter, as well as physicist and futurologist Herman Kahn.

Up until the end of World War II, there was a widespread belief among American and European intellectuals that capitalism was on the losing side of history. As Joseph Schumpeter, the famed Austrian economist, put it, "Can capitalism survive? No. I do not think it can."[24] Soviet-style communism, with its faith in a Hegelian movement of history that culminated in a Marxist workers' paradise, was seen as the inevitable wave of the future. Even though history or the spirit of the times manifested itself through individuals, adhesion to the collective will was to be the ruling principle of society. The value of individuals was determined by their degree of submission to the collective will, as interpreted by the all-knowing and all-powerful Communist Party leadership. This was antithetical to American notions of free will, individual rights, and limited government.

To combat the Communist credo, postwar American intellectuals sought a version of history that eliminated once and for all the Marxist dogma: "From each according to his ability, to each according to his needs." The new doctrine would substitute the oppressive, omniscient Marxist state with a system that championed the right of individuals to make their own choices and their own mistakes. That doctrine, elaborated at RAND in 1950, was called rational choice; its main proponent, a twenty-nine-year-old economist named Kenneth Arrow.

The bulk of Arrow's work at RAND is still classified top secret. This much we know: arriving at RAND as a summer intern in 1948, after studying statistics at Columbia University and working for the reform-oriented Cowles Commission,* Arrow received a confidential-level security clearance with the task of establishing a collective "utility function" for the Soviet Union. That function meant to establish

---

* The Cowles Commission was an economics research institute in Chicago whose work redefined the field of econometrics in the 1940s and 1950s. Besides Arrow, several RAND economists were associated with Cowles, including Tjalling Charles Koopmans, Gerard Debreu, and Herbert Simon.

a fixed set of preferences in the conduct of Russian leaders in international affairs, that is, what would give them the greatest satisfaction as a group—for example, whether they would rather invade
Poland or Manchuria, and under which conditions. RAND needed
the function so its analysts could simulate the actions of the Soviet
oligarchs—especially the highly unpredictable Joseph Stalin—during
a nuclear conflict. Due to the lack of information about the her-
metic Stalinist system at the time, Western policy makers were constantly forced to substitute speculation for hard evidence. (This was
the time of the Sovietologists, political necromancers who divined the
political influence of Politburo members according to their closeness
to Stalin in group pictures at Red Square.)

Arrow's original task of finding a utility function for the Soviets forced him to examine the assumptions behind the notion of a
collective utility—in other words, to study how a group arranges its
preferences so that everyone in the group has equivalent satisfaction
from a set of choices. At its core, such a function presupposed that
group choices could be set up in axiomatic order—that is, that a certain desired result would rank as A, another as B, another as C,
etc.—and that eventually a group consensus would emerge. Arrow's
surprising conclusion was that in any decision-making body with at
least two players faced with at least three different outcomes, unless
there is a "dictator" or someone whose will is imposed on the others, no one could come to an agreement.[25]

Here Arrow and the other RAND analysts made a momentous,
and some would say misguided, choice: they assumed that life is de-
terministic. The underlying assumption of their studies was that by
examining the mathematical probabilities of particular courses of
action, and tabulating each in assumed order of preference, one
could predict how a person would choose. It is life as a numbers
game, its corollary being the common fallacy of geeks and science
freaks: that which doesn't compute can be safely disregarded. While

rankings and probabilities may apply to actuarial tables and insurance payouts, the dynamics of individual and group psychology are too varied and complex to fit in the kind of formula Arrow proposed. Years later RANDites would ruefully acknowledge the futility of attempting to reduce human behavior to numbers, but in 1950, it was the vernal season of math at RAND, and its analysts were all too enamored of computation as the key to human behavior. Nonetheless, their assumption resulted in a discovery that profoundly altered Western culture. By seeking to numeralize life, to reduce it to a series of equations, formulas, and theorems, Arrow developed a theory of human behavior that was, improbably, as earthshaking as Marxist dialectics.

At its most basic, Arrow's work demonstrated in formal terms— that is, in mathematical expression—that collective rational group decisions are logically impossible. Arrow's paradox, or Arrow's impossibility theorem, as it came to be called, presented an unshakable mathematical argument that destroyed the academic validity of most kinds of social compact.* Arrow utilized his findings to concoct a value system based on economics that destroyed the Marxist notion of a collective will. To achieve this result, Arrow freely borrowed elements of positivist philosophy, such as its concern for axiomization, universally objective scientific truth, and the belief that social processes can be reduced to interactions between individuals.[26]

Arrow assumed that individuals were rational, that they had consistent preferences that they sought to maximize for their own

---

* Of course, society still has laws and people do agree to work together, so at times a non-professional reader of Arrow's work feels tipped headfirst into Alice's rabbit hole, where the Red Queen's words mean just what she wants them to mean. One is also reminded of the conundrum of the ancient Greek philosopher Zeno, who posited that no rabbit can ever outrun a turtle in a race, for each time the rabbit takes one step, the turtle takes another smaller one, until at the end, no matter how many leaps the rabbit might take, the turtle will still be ahead, even if only by an infinitesimal distance.

selfish benefit. Arrow also assumed that reason, as he defined it, was not culturally relative but identical in all human beings, who act according to the same rules of logic.

Furthermore, Arrow assumed the objectivity of science—that its laws are universal and that there aren't two different sets of choices for capitalist and Communist societies, as some economists had theorized before World War II. (Marx claimed that scientific knowledge was relative, depending on cultural conditions.) Moreover, Arrow posited the individual as the ultimate arbiter of decision, using the phrase "consumers' sovereignty" to signal individual preference as the basic building block of any economic system.

Arrow's impossibility theorem, then, lay a theoretical foundation for universal scientific objectivity, individualism, and "rational choice" while undermining Marxism, totalitarianism, and idealistic democracy. Simply put, he posited that immutable, incontrovertible science tells us the collective is nothing, the individual is all.

Over the next few decades, Arrow's rational choice theory would become a mainstay of economics and political science; by the 1960s, when masses of RANDites would move into the federal government, it would redefine the foundations of public policy by assuming that self-interest defines all aspects of human activity. Altruism, patriotism, and religion, when taken into consideration at all, would be factored in as variates of selfishness. When applied to corporations, the theory exempted them from any social responsibility other than that owed to their shareholders—as though companies existed in a social vacuum. When applied to government and public officials, it denied qualities such as selflessness and acting for the public good, viewing public officials as egoistical agents seeking to maximize their own power and budgets, thus equating diligence with self-aggrandizement and good government with veiled tyranny. From there it would be only a rhetorical half step to President Ronald Reagan's dictum that government is the problem and not the solution.[27]

———

ARROW'S REVOLUTIONARY work on rational choice paralleled RAND research in the brand-new field of game theory. This academic discipline meant to take the mathematical structure of parlor games such as poker—one of John Williams's favorite pastimes—and apply it to economics, politics, foreign policy, and other spheres of activity.

In 1950, Williams's fascination with game theory prompted him finally to hire full-time the father of the discipline, John von Neumann, instead of only paying him for his thoughts while he shaved. A deceptively mild-mannered Hungarian mathematician who dressed in conservative three-piece suits, von Neumann spoke seven languages. He boasted a prodigious memory that allowed him to recall entire books after one reading and to repeat more than fifty lines of computer programming language without a single error. Also, like Williams, he was an advocate of all-out preemptive nuclear war on the Soviet Union.

As if to offset his intellectual prowess, von Neumann was a fan of children's games and toys, a hard-drinking party animal, and an inveterate jokester who loved to collect limericks. He quoted one of his favorite rhymes in a letter to his wife, Klara:

> There was a young lady from Lynn
> Who thought that to love was a sin.
> But when she was tight
> It seemed quite alright,
> So everyone filled her with gin![28]

In spite of the fact that many mathematicians consider von Neumann's work on algebras, quasi-ergodic hypotheses, and lattice theory his greatest accomplishment, it was game theory that brought him the greatest honor in the Cold War era. He and Princeton economist Oskar Morgenstern cowrote the book that lay the foundation for the field, *Theory of Games and Economic Behavior*.[29]

Morgenstern and von Neumann assumed that players in every game are rational and that any given situation has a solution, a rational outcome. Neumann coined the term "zero-sum game," referring to a set of circumstances in which a player stands to gain only if his opponent loses. He also originated the concept of the minimax theorem, which posits that every finite, two-person, zero-sum game has a rational solution, as long as the interests of the two people are completely opposite.

By the mid-1950s, RAND became the world center for game theory, employing future Nobel Prize winner John Nash and renowned economists Melvin Dresher, Merrill Flood, Anatol Rapoport, Lloyd Shapley, and Martin Shubik. In fact, it is difficult to think of any of the major figures in game theory who did not work for RAND at some point during that period. Research developed at RAND at the time and its findings were later applied to such diverse fields as economics—from which game theory had originally sprung—biology, computer science, and business.[30]

One of the favorite games developed by RAND analysts in the 1950s was called the prisoner's dilemma, variations of which had existed for thousands of years. It went something like this:

Suppose that two men have been arrested by the police and charged with a particular crime, say, the theft of a very valuable diamond, which has not been recovered. The police keep the suspects apart, so the prisoners cannot communicate with each other. Each one is told that if he tells where the diamond is hidden, he will be able to plea-bargain to a lesser charge, and will do just six months in jail. The prisoner who doesn't confess will get all the blame and receive a ten-year sentence. If both men confess, they will both get two years in prison. The prisoners, however, know that if they keep quiet, that is, if neither one confesses and the police do not find the diamond, they will both be released. Neither can learn what the other's decision is until he makes his own—and the decision is irrevocable.

What do you do? was the question RAND researchers asked of people participating in the experiment. Do you cooperate with your fellow prisoner—that is, keep quiet and hope that your partner in crime does likewise and you both get off scot-free? Or do you confess—or as RAND mathematicians called it, defect—saying it's every man for himself, so I better strike the best deal I can on my own?

Arguments can be made for and against both defecting and co-operating. The one for defecting says the choice is simultaneous and that your choice cannot affect the other. Therefore, you are better off on your own, getting what you can since no matter what you will get some time off the sentence. It is a Hobbesian choice for a Hobbesian world.

But think what happens if the prisoner cooperates with his fellow prisoner. Not only does he win his freedom, he gets to keep the diamond. Of course, the problem is, how do you know the other guy won't think of himself first and cut his own deal, leaving you with ten years behind bars? It takes a lot of trust. Yet the rewards for trust are enormous for both players.

The prisoner's dilemma is not as arcane or trivial as it might appear, for it addresses the conflict between individual and collective rationality. What is in a player's best interest, and how do you know you have chosen correctly? When applied to societies, the prisoner's dilemma has profound implications that could well determine whether a nation chooses a path to armament, conflict, and war, or disarmament, cooperation, and peace. Witness the case of Oppenheimer, father of the nuclear bomb and head of the general advisory committee to the Atomic Energy Commission. He recommended to Secretary of State Acheson that the United States not develop the hydrogen bomb, so as to provide "limitations on the totality of war and thus eliminating the fear and raising the hope of mankind." In other words, the United States would tell Stalin we will not build it, so you don't have to either. To this idealistic argument, Acheson, ever the wary diplomat, replied, "How can you persuade a paranoid adversary to 'disarm by example'?"[31] The Truman administration echoed Acheson's skepticism and ultimately, in 1950, approved the development of the H-bomb.

RAND analysts found that the responses to the prisoner's dilemma given by different test subjects instantly revealed the political and philosophical predisposition of the prisoner. Cooperators, those who trust their fellow prisoner—like Oppenheimer—are usually liberals. They are willing to put themselves at risk in order to obtain a better life. They hope to create a better, safer society by raising taxes—everyone contributes what they can afford to the common good—while seeking the assistance of foreign nations by treaties and alliances to achieve peace abroad.

Defectors, on the other hand, are usually conservatives who feel others cannot be trusted to go against their apparent self-interest. They favor going it alone to get the best results—and in the political arena, believe in keeping taxes low, avoiding treaties, and looking out for their own interest themselves because they see the common good as the aggregate of individual, self-interested decisions. Like Adam Smith, defectors believe in an invisible hand guiding the affairs of mankind—and, of course, in avoiding long prison sentences at all costs.

The prisoner's dilemma had a very direct implication for national security: disarmament. The United States and its allies, as well as the Soviet Union, faced the paradox that their nuclear arsenals provided little protection from one another if the other side really wanted to strike first. Both sides claimed they wanted to disarm, yet each was wary of the other hiding its weapons—in game theory terms, the United States and the Soviets were afraid to cooperate because they feared the other side would defect. This wariness would take years to subside, and ultimately would not be eradicated until the fall of the Soviet Union at the end of the twentieth century.

By the mid-1950s, RAND researchers decided that the answer to the prisoner's dilemma is that there is no one true answer. Both defectors and cooperators are rational in their behavior, which is predicated by emotional predisposition. In other words, it is as hard to justify cooperation as it is to accept defection. Disillusioned, RANDites gave up games and game theory as a tool for national defense. Moreover, the original purpose of game theory—to try to predict the moves of the unpredictable Soviets—began to seem moot given changes in international relations. With the death of Stalin in 1953, the Soviet Union forswore the hermetism that had been its hallmark; its new leader, Nikita Khrushchev, sought contact with the West, to live in what was termed "peaceful coexistence." Because of this historical shift, deterrence became the new focus of RANDites, who utilized as their main tool what would be heralded as the quintessential RAND procedure, systems analysis. Curiously enough, systems analysis would be born out of a plan to strike preemptively at the Soviet Union.[32]

ED PAXSON, a RAND engineer, came up with the term "systems analysis" in 1947, when Williams placed him in charge of the Evaluation of Military Worth Section while RAND was still at Douglas Aircraft. Like Williams, Paxson was a fan of game theory and thought its concepts could be used profitably in war theaters.[33] Both of them also believed that there was such a thing as a grand unified theory of war, a set of rules and theorems with which one could control and master the science of armed conflict.

Paxson had been a scientific adviser to the U.S. Army Air Forces and a consultant to the U.S. Strategic Bombing Survey of 1945–46. A pockmarked, rude, chain-smoking taskmaster, he took special pleasure in shooting down fellow scientists' theories and studies. At one "murder board" briefing, he was so scathing in his comments that his fellow analyst fainted from the pressure.[34]

Paxson's notion of systems analysis derived from World War II's operational research (OR). During the war, the Achilles' heel of OR had been its constant reliance on statistics.* OR could not function without hard data, and thus was constrained to what was already known about a system. On the question of bomber formation, for example, the questions would be: How many enemy factories can we destroy with the kind of aircraft that we have? What is the most efficient way of massing them when flying to avoid excessive losses? At what speed? What altitude?

Systems analysis changed the questions and asked: How many enemy factories do we *want* to destroy? What kind of factories are we talking about and how are they defended? To accomplish our objective, what is the best route? With what kind of plane? What kind of payload?[35] In other words, while OR referred to studies of existing systems to uncover more effective ways to perform specific missions,[36] systems analysis addressed the far more complex problem of choice among alternative systems that had yet to be designed, where the degrees of freedom and uncertainty are large, and where the difficulty is deciding both what to do and how to do it.

Although it sounds somewhat like a case of the emperor's new clothes, with everyone assuming the existence of certain facts and willing themselves to see them, Paxson and the other RAND researchers were onto a very big but very simple insight: what really counts in solving the problem is defining the objective. OR *assumed* the existence of certain systems and worked to obtain the best results from what was already on hand. It was, in its essence, a very European method of adapting oneself to preexisting circumstances; one can almost hear the British undertone of, all right, lads, let's make the best of it.

---

* Curiously, many of the researchers who populated the math and economic divisions of RAND, such as Albert Wohlstetter, J. C. C. McKinsey, and Olaf Helmer, served at least some time in the U.S. Office of Statistics during the conflict.

RAND's systems analysis, on the other hand, was American to the core—it refused to be constrained by existing reality. Systems analysis asked first: What do we want out of this? What are our objectives? And if the means to accomplish them do not exist presently—the systems, weapons, aircraft, whatever—how hard would it be to create them? How costly? How long would it take?

Systems analysis was the freedom to dream and to dream big, to turn away from the idea that reality is a limited set of choices, to strive to bend the world to one's will. It was the spirit of yes we can, of belief in the endless inventiveness of man. It is the mental process of someone who sees no obstacle so great and no problem so complex that it cannot be overcome or solved.

All the same, the crux of systems analysis lies in a careful examination of the assumptions that gird the so-called right question, for the moment of greatest danger in a project is when unexamined criteria define the answers we want to extract. Sadly, most RAND analysts failed to perceive this inherent flaw in their wondrous construct. Not only that, the methodology of systems analysis required that all the aspects of a particular problem be broken down into quantities, such as a plane's cost, speed, range, fuel consumption. Those things that could not be eased into a mathematical formula— such as camaraderie, pride, morale—were left out of the analysis, even though they might be added as an appendix in case a tiebreaker was needed to decide between otherwise equal solutions.[37] By extension, if a subject could not be measured, ranged, and classified, it was of little consequence in systems analysis, for it was not rational. Numbers were all—the human factor was a mere adjunct to the empirical.

In 1949, the Air Force was abuzz with the possibility of a preemptive strike on the Soviet Union. Moscow had exploded its first atomic bomb in September, and the top brass—including LeMay— felt if war was to come, it should be sooner rather than later. Under Air Force direction, Frank Collbohm gave Paxson the job of

designing the "best" bomber for a strategic campaign against the Soviet Union. Paxson came up with a plan that illustrated both the
strong points and the shortcomings of systems analysis.

In essence, Paxson thought that when large groups of enemy
forces met, the conflict could be defined as a function of battlefield
decisions about weapons systems—bombers, fighters, etc. Such things
as aircraft control, speed, range, number, and onboard weapons could
further classify the systems. Each choice would lead to a particular
game within the overall conflict, and so, by quantifying the total
encounter, Paxson believed that he could arrive at a true science
of war.

Paxson began by concentrating on aerial bombing analysis. He
limited his choices to manned bombers powered by turboprops flying at subsonic speeds, rejecting the use of sonic-busting turbojets
as too expensive. He then concentrated on the performance and cost
analysis of the planes: their expected losses, target coverage, logistics, and auxiliary needs such as protective fighters, as well as the
phasing of the funds for research, procurement, and operations. Paxson's analysis of a weapons system also included "men, military and
civilian; maintenance and supply; real estate, both land and buildings; medical care, food service, recreation and everything else that's
essential for the operation of the system."[38] The interrelation of
these variables required massive computation, for which RAND
built its own rudimentary computer.

In addition, Paxson constructed a top-secret Aerial Combat Research Room in the basement of RAND headquarters where Navy
and Air Force flyers engaged in combat simulation. Pilots in the
room manned the controls of their aircraft, responding to enemy
aircraft seen in projected films of actual warfare situations. When,
after two years of study, Paxson compared his models of make-
believe air duels to data from actual fighting during World War II,
he found that his theory veered enormously from reality. Whereas

according to his model, pilots should score a 60 percent probability of kills, in real-life combat pilots achieved only 2 percent.

Attributing this lack of confluence to unpredictable human response (such as the fact that pilots in real life refused to expose themselves to greater danger than necessary), Paxson stubbornly plowed on with his bomber project. He and his staff calculated results for more than 400,000 bomber configurations, taking into account variables such as preferred bombing routes, expected enemy defenses, bomb coverage, and myriad other factors. The report they produced in 1950, titled *Comparison of Airplane Systems for Strategic Bombing*,[39] was chock-full of graphs, charts, equations, and tables. It boasted of how RAND systems analysis was changing military planning from an intuitive process into a more rigorous science. When RAND, with great expectations, delivered the study, the project landed with a stunning thud. Within weeks Air Force critics accused Paxson and his team of, in so many words, not seeing the forest for the bombs.

While Paxson and his team had done a brilliant job analyzing existing technologies, they failed to explore the possibility of creating new technologies out of concerns over cost. His plan to wipe out the Soviet Union envisaged flying old-fashioned propeller airplanes out of U.S. bases, using a location in Newfoundland as a staging area to mount the attacks. Air Force brass were outraged by this indifference to new weapons. The Air Force had spent millions of dollars since 1944 trying to develop a jet-powered bomber, the B-52 Stratofortress, and now to hear its house analysts suggest that all that effort be ignored so that the Air Force would fill the Russian skies with empty bombers of only minor usefulness was totally unacceptable.[40]

Paxson's study contained other basic foundational mistakes that undermined his grand theoretical edifice. It assumed Newfoundland would be the staging area for an attack on the Soviet Union, instead of hewing to the Air Force plans of flying bombers to overseas bases and attacking from those forward positions. Neither did it take into consideration the limited amount of fissile material available for bomb production over the upcoming years.

Finally, the Air Force was appalled by the report's apparent callousness of accepting an unconscionable casualty rate by equating the death of pilots to the loss of disabled machinery. (Already systems analysis was reducing desire and existence to mathematical constructs—planes to be flown, bombs to be dropped, people to be killed—in the pursuit of national policy goals.)

Unexamined criteria had doomed the project from the start. Paxson had made a cost-analysis perspective the focus of the campaign, disregarding the intrinsic value of human life. In an attempt to salvage the report, the project was handed off to another engineer, E. J. Barlow, who slimmed the original hundred-page proposal down to sixteen pages of text, erasing the intellectual arrogance that had informed the opus. A chastened Barlow admitted,

> The great dangers inherent in the systems analysis approach, however, are that factors which we aren't yet in a position to treat quantitatively tend to be omitted from serious consideration. Even some factors we can be quantitative about are omitted because of limits on the complexity of structure we have learned to handle. Finally, a systems analysis is fairly rigid, so that we have to decide six months in advance what the USAF problem is we are trying to answer—frequently the question has changed or disappeared by the time the analysis is finished.[41]

RAND's revised air defense systems analysis, when published in 1951, did little to improve the plan's standing among Air Force leaders. If this was an example of the kind of work a unified theory of war would produce, the Air Force wanted no part of it. Systems analysis as a tool, however, was far from dead. Officials in the Air Force and the aircraft industry had been impressed by the logical, quantitative techniques utilized, even if they had disagreed with the result.

Paxson had ignored the political implications of the work, for it failed to satisfy the unspoken desire of the Air Force to use RAND's work as a political weapon to convince a recalcitrant Congress to buy newer, better, and sexier armaments. The Air Force realized, however, that the rationality of systems analysis was a powerful weapon it could use in policy debates to procure bigger budgets. RAND leadership, seeing its opening, gave up on its attempt to create a general science of warfare and instead began tailoring its studies to narrower, more specific problems that lent themselves to the technique with greater ease.

One of these studies would solidify RAND's reputation in the 1950s as the foremost civilian policy adviser group to the U.S. government. It would also bring wealth and acclaim to an astute logical mathematician who was a founding father of the neoconservative movement. Using the techniques originated by Paxson, but narrowing their focus to simple but decisive questions, Albert Wohlstetter would become the leading intellectual figure at RAND. Wohlstetter's wedding of technological expertise to a finely honed sense of political theater also helped him define the national defense discipline that RANDites dominated for decades: nuclear strategy.

Whether there was war or peace, whether millions would live or die, whether the world would continue as it was or die from a suffocating nuclear winter—the fate of humanity truly hinged on the efforts of this small band of self-anointed experts. And Albert Wohlstetter was its acknowledged leader.

PART 2

4

A Talk Before Dinner

EVEN BEFORE he was a nuclear strategist or a logical mathematician, Albert Wohlstetter was an aesthete. From his youth he was drawn to the arts, eventually treating his chosen field of science as though it were a vehicle for his personal artistic expression. Wohlstetter was also a constant proponent of what today, for lack of a better word, we can only call modernity. The newest, the latest, the most cutting-edge concepts, whether in art, music, literature, or national defense, were always certain to garner his attention—so he could examine them, test them, and incorporate them into his life. Tall, fair, and self-assured to the point of arrogance, he personified the imperial ethos of the mandarins who made America the center of power and culture in the postwar Western world.

Wohlstetter was born into a prosperous Mitteleuropa Jewish family in New York, his father the owner of a company that recorded opera singers. Although his father died when he was four and the family suffered through hard times during the Depression, young Albert grew up attending the Metropolitan Opera as often as other kids went to the movies, using complimentary tickets to impress his dates. He was a painter, a musician, even joined a modern dance troupe. When young, he was an assistant to the prominent art historian Meyer Schapiro, who discovered the greatest figures of postwar American art. After Wohlstetter married Roberta Morgan, the daughter of a noted legal scholar, the two honeymooned in Mexico, viewing ancient Aztec pyramids and the works of famous Mexican muralists. During World War II, while working at the War Production Board and the National Housing Agency, Wohlstetter kept abreast of the works of modern artists and sponsored some of them for residence visas in the United States. He was a friend of both Gropius and Mies van der Rohe, and served as Le Corbusier's guide and driver during a visit by the famous architect to the East Coast.

In the early 1950s, now a national security analyst for RAND, Wohlstetter bought a spacious home in the Hollywood Hills back when the streets were dirt roads gouged out by innovative developers. Built by the architect Josef van der Car on a large wooded lot on Woodstock Road, the Wohlstetter house was a two-story, 2,400-square-foot vision of modernist light and comfort, boasting cork floors, a state-of-the-art hi-fi system, and sliding glass doors that led to cantilevered balconies. The estate was so picture-perfect that the master of modernist iconography, Julius Shulman—who happened to be a neighbor and good friend—photographed it. The Wohlstetters hired one of the most prominent garden designers of the day, Garrett Eckbo, to artfully redo the back acreage; he planted a garden and put in groves of exotic bamboo by the kidney-shaped pool.[1]

The Wohlstetters' Laurel Canyon neighborhood was a sylvan paradise in the middle of Los Angeles, just a half-hour drive down Sunset Boulevard to RAND headquarters. In the mornings, either Albert or Roberta would take their daughter, Joan, to Westland, the progressive school they had founded with friends in Santa Monica, and later to her riding lessons by Griffith Park, on the north side of the hills. Theirs was an idyllic existence, marred only in the 1950s by the political witch hunts fostered by Senator Joseph McCarthy in his drive to purge the country of all Communists and Communist sympathizers, their "fellow travelers."

The FBI had already hounded Charlie Chaplin, whom Wohlstetter had coaxed out of retirement for a benefit screening of *City Lights* for Westland School. Although one of his children attended Westland, Chaplin had been reluctant to participate in school activities; he feared being ostracized because of the rumors the FBI had spread about his Communist leanings. It had fallen to Wohlstetter, the RAND national security analyst, to gently cajole this brilliant man back into the limelight. As one of the school's directors, Wohlstetter arranged for the screening at a theater on Wilshire Boulevard in Beverly Hills. Chaplin, not wanting to draw attention to himself, had stood in line along with the other patrons to get his seat. Wohlstetter made a point of taking Chaplin and his wife by the arm and guiding them to the head of the line, to show that in art and culture political differences were insignificant.

So it was with this business with the Schwerins, the Wohlstetters' neighbors down the road. Ever since the House Un-American Committee Hearings and the Red Scare in Hollywood, the Schwerins had been mercilessly persecuted by the FBI. Screenwriters who hung out with leftists, Jules and Doris Schwerin had refused to come on bended knee before Congress to name names and plead for mercy. They had stood their ground on their constitutional rights, and because of that their writing income had dried up as the studios refused to hire them, even under pseudonyms. Doris tried working as a teacher, but there, too, their refusal to sign the loathsome loyalty oaths that had become practically standard at all levels of American life had kept them from being employable. And now the telephone calls.

It was typical FBI harassment, the agency's way of dealing with people suspected of Communist leanings. Federal agents would inform employers and neighbors that the subjects were being investigated for possible subversive activities. Employers, fearing repercussions, would fire the suspects, whose friends would abandon them and relatives would denounce them. If that wasn't enough, then the calls would come at all hours of the day and night. Gruff male voices wanting to know what they were doing, who were they associating with, what they were planning to do the following day—a petty harassment that seemed to have no end. Thus with the Schwerins. Now that their landlord had given them notice to vacate, they had come to stay with the Wohlstetters before moving back East and then to Europe, where they hoped to escape the all-seeing eye of the FBI.

Wohlstetter had just returned from Washington, and he was in no mood to brook more government nonsense. He was preparing to go out with Roberta and stepped from his bedroom into the living area on the main floor. Doris and Jules, who were staying in the den on the bottom floor, were having dinner with ten-year-old Joan and her babysitter when the phone rang.

Wohlstetter picked up the phone.

"Hello?"

A man demanded to speak to the Schwerins.

"They cannot come to the phone," said Wohlstetter. The man insisted. Wohlstetter asked the man to identify himself; the caller said he was with the FBI and wanted to ask them some questions.

"I'm sorry, but they are not available. They are my friends and as long as they are guests in my house, they do not have to answer any of your questions. They have answered enough. Now please do not call back."

Wohlstetter hung up and turned to his friends and family. They stared back slack jawed—a top nuclear analyst, a keeper of the country's nuclear secrets, refusing to cooperate with the FBI?

"That ought to do it. I don't think they'll be bothering you any-more. Come, Roberta, we'll be late."

And with that Wohlstetter took his stylish wife by the arm and set out for their dinner party with the blithe confidence of the righteous and the powerful. The FBI didn't call the Schwerins again for the rest of the time they stayed in the Wohlstetter household.

Wohlstetter's achievement was mighty impressive and pretty cheeky—particularly for someone who once had been a member of an underground Communist cell.[2]

5

The Secret Keepers

OVER THE PAST few years, an increasingly serious branch of American history, sometimes called allohistory or counterfactual history, has devoted itself to what might be called the what-if. What if the Confederacy had defeated the Union in the Civil War? What if Archduke Ferdinand had not been assassinated and World War I never happened? What if Hitler had invaded England? What if Al Gore had won Florida in 2000? It is a wonderful kind of speculation, meant to explore the essential capriciousness of fate, to examine the rationale for people's actions and the way certain forces are considered by historians to be immutable. (For instance, most believe that even if the South had won, slavery eventually would have faded away, just as if Hitler had conquered England, the United States would have stayed out of the conflict, becoming a "Fortress America" in a world controlled by Fascist allies. And if Al Gore had won the recount . . . well, some fates are too stunning to contemplate at any length.)[1]

In a similar vein, it is difficult not to wonder what would have happened to America if Albert Wohlstetter, the principal architect of the nuclear deterrence policy that determined when, where, and how thermonuclear weapons were used, had been exposed as a former Communist.

Had Wohlstetter's radical past been exposed, most likely he would have been fired and in all likelihood his crucial study on the placement of nuclear bombers, known as the basing study, would have never been written. Although today it may seem hard to believe, without the remedies advocated by the basing study, an annihilating nuclear attack by the Soviet Union would have been not only conceivable but also highly doable. Had another RAND analyst written the study, it is also doubtful the report would have had as great an impact, for few scientists anywhere could match the theatricality and efficacy of Wohlstetter's presentation. With his basing study, not only did he forfend a possible nuclear first strike by the Soviet Union, he also promoted his own career and RAND's fortunes, becoming the principal adviser to the Air Force and its Strategic Air Command.

In spite of its explosive growth after its founding in 1945, SAC had been slow to recognize the perils of its vulnerability to a Soviet surprise attack. In 1951, two years after Moscow detonated its own nuclear bomb, the Air Force finally authorized an internal study on the problem of base vulnerability. Then, almost as a redundancy, SAC asked RAND to prepare a report on where to site the bases to create the least vulnerability, without neglecting the accessibility to the enemy front line needed in case of war. That was the basing study that Wohlstetter undertook, and his results changed history.

The question then is, how did Wohlstetter manage to conceal the youthful radicalism that would have cut short his career and precluded the basing study? RAND, after all, wasn't impervious to the Communist witch hunt. The FBI required top security clearances of all researchers dealing with national secrets—especially those involving nuclear devices. Mere suspicion of having a relative who once belonged to a leftist association was grounds for suspension if not revocation of clearance. Physicists like Richard Bellman were petrified that the FBI would consider their mildly liberal politics too leftist and blacklist them. Not to mention the terror felt by Wohlstetter's friend and colleague, the top mathematician J. C. C. McKinsey. An open homosexual, McKinsey had been in a committed relationship for years when the FBI decided he was a security risk. When told that his sexual orientation could subject him to blackmail, McKinsey complained to Roberta Wohlstetter, "How can anyone threaten me with disclosure when everybody already knows?"[2] A few years after his clearance was revoked and Frank Collbohm himself had fired him, McKinsey committed suicide.[3]

One possible answer to why Wohlstetter's radical past was never outed has been suggested by his former friend and colleague Daniel Ellsberg; it is a reason both comical and surprising, given the intensity of the ideological wars that have cleft America since the Great Depression.

In the 1930s, a confluence of economic crisis and pervasive anti-Semitism had given rise to what is known as the New York School, a group of young, radical, impoverished Jewish intellectuals who sought a new way to reorganize society.[4] Centered around the City College of New York (one of the few institutions of higher learning that did not impose quotas on Jewish students), the New York School counted among its members such future distinguished intellectuals as Irving Howe, Irving Kristol, Nathan Glazer, Daniel Bell, and Albert Wohlstetter.

The children of recent immigrants—if not foreign-born themselves—like most youth, they worshipped at the altar of the new and the radical, which after the Russian Revolution and especially after the 1929 stock market crash meant leftist politics. They were drawn not just to socialism, which in some fashion had been part of American intellectual life since the nineteenth century, but to the main variants of communism as interpreted at the time: Trotskyism and Soviet Bolshevism or Stalinism.

Already in the early 1920s, when Wohlstetter's older brother, Charles, attended tuition-free City College, political radicals had taken over certain dining alcoves of the school cafeteria. Bolsheviks ruled one alcove, Trotskyites the other, while those just wanting to eat lunch sat at a third.[5] Skipping class, young intellectuals would meet to harangue one another over obscure political points, memorializing their dialectical disputes in pamphlets, broadsheets, and magazines. Some of them would use this experience as training for future careers in academia, journalism, politics, and law, such as Kristol, a Trotskyite[6] who founded the *Public Interest*[7] along with Bell and Glazer. Originally a leftist magazine, the publication over the years mirrored the political transfiguration of its creators, ultimately becoming a voice for the neoconservative movement that reshaped American politics in the 1980s.[8]

Wohlstetter followed his brother into City College in the early 1930s. In spite of the institution's well-deserved reputation as a hotbed of radical leftists and Communists, he was not particularly politically active there. He was a mathematician, a logical phenomenon who, at seventeen, wrote an article entitled "The Structure of the Proposition and the Fact" for the magazine *Philosophy of Science*, which garnered an enthusiastic response from Albert Einstein. In a letter, the renowned physicist called the piece "the most lucid extrapolation of mathematical logic he had ever read,"[9] and invited the young scholar to his home to have tea and discuss the article.

Wohlstetter's involvement with radical politics came about later, at Columbia University. Believing that the Depression would make it exceedingly difficult for him to support himself as a logician, he had applied for and received a fellowship to study law at the Morningside Heights institution. It was 1934, and Wohlstetter was moved enough by the realities of the time to take an interest in politics. Having endured his family's financial reversal, he was inclined to believe there was something radically wrong with the country's economic system. In response, he systematically studied the work of the prevalent economic figures of the time: Karl Marx, John Maynard Keynes, and Alfred Marshall. For him that involved formalizing their theories into mathematical terms so as to compare the validity of their respective views—anticipating the way RAND analysts would reduce historical arguments and beliefs into numbers and equations.[10] Concurrently, according to historian Alan Wald, Wohlstetter joined a splinter Communist group, the League for a Revolutionary Workers Party (LRWP).[11]

The LRWP was composed of neo-Trotskyites; although equally Marxist and Socialist, Trotskyites were bitter enemies of the Stalinists in the official Communist Party, accusing them of betraying the ideals of Lenin's revolution. The LRWP had been formed by B. J. Field, a former Wall Street analyst who had been expelled from the Communist Party in 1932. Under Field's command, the LRWP became involved in the 1934 New York Hotel Strike (also known as the French Waiters Strike) when more than 10,000 hospitality workers walked off their jobs. The group found support among Columbia students, including not only Wohlstetter and his soon-to-be wife, Roberta, whom he had met at Columbia, but the future philosopher Morton G. White.

The LRWP soon found itself under investigation by the Federal Bureau of Investigation for subversive activities. Sociologist Paul Jacobs, who claimed to be a card-carrying LRWP member like the Wohlstetters, recounted to Ellsberg[12] that the records of the group were lost when Field, moving files surreptitiously from an office in a horse-drawn lorry—this was 1934, after all—became involved in an accident at a busy intersection after his horse died. Afraid that he would be charged with the accident and that his radical activities would land him in an even greater jam, Field fled the scene, leaving all the files, publications, and membership rolls to be disposed of by

New York City sanitation. The LRWP barely survived the 1930s, with Field ultimately dropping out of politics to join a California real estate firm run by a former acolyte.

Although Wohlstetter sometimes obliquely referred to his radical past, he never publicly disclosed his membership in the LRWP (and, of course, with the records that would have revealed that membership rotting in a landfill, he never had to). His daughter, Joan, could not confirm or deny her father's membership, although she discounted it, saying her father was never much of a joiner. She did acknowledge that everyone in her father's circle was a radical of one sort or another at the time, adding that Wohlstetter claimed he had been named "Enemy No. 1" by the Communist Party in the 1930s because of his opposition to its Stalinist orthodoxy.[13]

Glazer, who knew both Wohlstetter and Jacobs at the time, stated in an interview that "everyone knew that Albert was a member of a radical group, we just didn't know which one."[14] In his memoirs, White also refers to having been introduced to the LRWP by Wohlstetter. Group headquarters were north of Union Square, in a bare second-floor loft, where members would meet to hear lectures on Marxism.[15]

Wohlstetter's past certainly explains his lifelong friendship with former Trotskyite writers James T. Farrell and Saul Bellow and with radicals such as the Schwerins and Mary McCarthy.[16] However, even more important was the lasting impression that the old Bolshevik worldview left on Wohlstetter's work. Leon Trotsky, who had gone into exile after a power struggle with Joseph Stalin, was a believer in the imposition of Communist ideals by force.[17] Wohlstetter believed the Soviet Union was a monolithic system intent on world conquest, and he based his strategic decisions on that opinion—one widely shared by people at RAND, not to mention the American public at large. All the same, Wohlstetter's insistence, long after the facts suggested otherwise, on the protean willfulness of the Soviet

Union and its unbridled desire for a nuclear confrontation certainly carried more than a whiff of the old radical boxed in by old, unacknowledged beliefs.

After graduating from Columbia as a mathematical logician— giving up his attempt to become a lawyer as "a sort of diversion"— Wohlstetter went to work at the National Bureau of Economic Research. During World War II, he moved to the War Production Board and to the National Housing Agency, then managed his brother's electrical generator plant. After the war, Albert Wohlstetter wound up as vice president of the General Panel Corporation of California, a factory that sold and constructed homes based on a modular system created by the architect Walter Gropius, one of the founders of the Bauhaus art movement. Soon the home-factory enterprise began to founder, as its modules did not conform to standard American construction codes. All the while, Wohlstetter was longing to return to the kind of mathematical research work he had conducted in college.

One evening, while on a walk in Santa Monica with Roberta, he ran into several old colleagues from back East, McKinsey and two other mathematicians, Olaf Helmer and Abe Girshick. They told him they had recently begun to work at a new place called RAND, located at an abandoned newspaper plant in downtown Santa Monica, and immediately tried to recruit Wohlstetter to join them. Girshick promised Wohlstetter he would have the time of his life. Wohlstetter demurred; he felt too great an obligation to General Panel. He had given his word that he would try to refinance the company loans so the operation could stay afloat.

However, Roberta thought RAND would be fun, so the trio prevailed on Hans Speier, the new head of the Social Sciences Division, to hire her to do book reviews. After a few months, Roberta was fired because of budget issues, and then she had to pretend to be someone else to get a job as an analyst until they appreciated the quality of her work and she could reveal her identity. When General Panel finally was dissolved, its brilliant design systems folded up and stored for the time in the future when prefabricated housing would become popular again, Wohlstetter applied to and was hired at RAND.

By the early 1950s, RAND's reputation as the arsenal of ideas for Cold War warriors that Leo Rosten had warned John Williams and Collbohm about had become, if anything, even more pronounced. There were rumors that it was involved in flying saucers, in experimental trips to the moon, in creating devastating weapons that could destroy the world in an instant. To counter that ghoulish aura, RAND allowed a *Fortune* magazine writer to profile the organization. John McDonald's piece was the first in a series of hagiographical articles that credited the think tank with all but single-handedly saving mankind from impending doom.[18] In a series of ads years later in *Scientific American,* RAND heralded its researchers as the heirs to a long line of intellectual inquiry that began with Galileo and passed through Descartes, Edison, and Einstein before culminating in flinty administrator Frank Collbohm.[19] By the end of the decade, in the public eye RAND was everything that was intellectual and cutting edge. RAND was jazz on a summer day as yet another technological top-secret miracle was cooked up in the back lab—RANDites were the unflappable harbingers of a cool new world.

In 1951, Wohlstetter began working at RAND as a consultant to the Mathematics Division. He wrote some methodological studies, but soon he grew bored with mathematical logic and wanted to tackle real-world issues. He got his chance in May when Charles Hitch approached him with the kernel of the idea that would become the basing study: "How should you base the Strategic Air Command?"

As head of the Economics Division, Hitch was empowered to carry out Williams's vision of interdisciplinary approaches to problem solving. Hitch's bailiwick included the Logistics Department, which applied techniques of quantitative analysis to the maintenance and supply operations of the Air Force; the Cost Analysis Department, which sought to streamline the procurement processes of the Air Force; and the Economics Department, which applied cost-benefit analysis to national defense programs.[20] Given his background in statistical analysis and his experience in quality control of armaments during World War II, Wohlstetter seemed an ideal candidate to conduct the study for SAC.

Wohlstetter, however, was considerably less than enthused by Hitch's offer. His reply, after Hitch explained all the technical requirements, was typical of the strategist's mandarin manner. He told his superior that the assignment looked like a rather dull logistics problem, and he was not interested. Nevertheless, the following weekend, he found himself going over the possibilities inherent in a basing study.

Wohlstetter became intrigued by the dynamic problems of the project. Some strategists in SAC invariably would want the bases close to Soviet targets, for ease of sorties and lower costs. Others would want the bases far from the enemy regardless of the greater costs. As Wohlstetter said, "If you were close to him, why there was just a good chance he would also be close to you. So he would be getting in a lot of whacks . . . It struck me that in the abstract there was no way of resolving this."[21]

Moreover, Wohlstetter reasoned that the study would teach him about nuclear war in a very concrete way. He had been appalled by the dropping of the atomic bomb on Hiroshima, thinking it reprehensible and unnecessary, and thus had a predisposition to find a way to limit attacks on cities during any kind of nuclear exchange. As Bernard Brodie had discovered, this attitude went against the grain of Air Force thinking, especially that of General Curtis LeMay, head of SAC since 1948.

LeMay's "Sunday punch" all-or-nothing strategy was the official military response to any kind of Soviet aggression on U.S. bases or American allies in Europe. However, since for most of his life Wohlstetter had deliberately ignored military and strategic policy matters, he took on the study without any knowledge of traditional strategic bombing analysis. He might have been new to the organization, but he was already developing what became the RAND operational ethos, that a researcher was at liberty to arrive at whatever conclusion the facts might warrant.

The following Monday, he informed Hitch he had changed his mind: he would be happy to undertake the study after all. Soon Wohlstetter was devoting practically all his days and nights to exploring the report's vast scope.

Wohlstetter's basing study was charged with examining the period from 1956 to 1960, when SAC expected to have about 1,600 B-47 bombers with a combat radius of 1,700 miles, 300 vintage B-36 bombers with a 2,950-mile radius, and perhaps a wing of 3,060-mile B-52s and 720 KC-97 flying tankers.[22] Most of the bases, thirty-two in all in 1951, were close to the Soviet Union, sited with the express intention of being as close as possible to the enemy. In the tradition of World War II operational analysis, where what counted was penetration into the enemy zone, losses of bases and equipment were expected in a war. Bombers would fly from the United States to overseas bases, take on bombs, wing to their targets, drop their loads, then return to the same advance bases for refueling and reloading.

Wohlstetter's work in government and manufacturing made him conversant with technical requirements, enabling him to understand how the different elements of the basing system worked. He eventually amassed such a wealth of detail that colleagues, observing him trooping up and down the corridors of RAND seemingly drunk on the streams of information, wondered whether Wohlstetter would be able to subdue all his knowledge into a comprehensible, useful study.[23] Eventually he hired a part-time secretary, whom he paid out of his own pocket until Hitch discovered it and insisted that RAND bear the whole cost.[24] Wohlstetter also recruited two young economists, Henry "Harry" Rowen and Fred Hoffman. He assigned them the classical work of bombing campaign analysis—reviewing extant airplane penetration tactics, figuring alternative flight paths and possible attrition rates for each alternative. They also helped determine the cost of the various basing proposals.

Wohlstetter's thinking was deeply affected by the work Roberta was conducting at the same time, a study on the Japanese surprise attack on Pearl Harbor from the perspective of the known intelligence available prior to the attack. Andrew Marshall, an analyst in the Social Sciences Division of RAND, had suggested the idea to Roberta in 1951. She would spend seven years on the study, finishing it in 1957. The Air Force immediately classified the document as top secret and kept only two copies, storing them in a vault. Ironically, Roberta did not have high enough security clearance to keep a copy of her own work. It wasn't until five years later, when RAND analysts had migrated from the think tank to high government positions, that she managed to have it declassified.[25] Published under the title *Pearl Harbor: Warning and Decision*,[26] the book received copious accolades, garnering the prestigious Bancroft History Prize and earning Roberta a reputation as the preeminent historian of the attack.*

Roberta's thesis, that so-called noise or superfluous information crowded out warning signs of the deadly incursion, dovetailed with Albert's predisposition to believe the Soviets would strike preemptively if they saw a chance. And when Wohlstetter examined the situation strategically, he saw danger everywhere.

SAC had thirty-two bases in Europe and Asia with minimal pro-

---

* Assistant Secretary of Defense Paul Wolfowitz cited the work during his first appearance before Congress after the World Trade Center attack on 9/11. Wolfowitz was familiar with the text, having been a student of Albert Wohlstetter and an intimate of the family.

tection against a surprise Soviet attack. Should such an attack materialize, Air Force plans for retaliation were deficient to the point of uselessness. Buildings, warehouses, and other facilities at the bases were concentrated by design to minimize construction costs, even though this greatly increased their vulnerability.[27] SAC's radar defenses could be easily circumvented by low-flying Soviet bombers that deviated from the predicted avenues of attack—what Wohlstetter sarcastically referred to as "the Western-preferred Soviet strategy." The bombers themselves were highly vulnerable, parked out in the open, in close proximity to one another without any kind of protection such as fortified hangars. Finally, the assumption by Air Force planners that bomber groups would have time to assemble their wings, fly to the location of the nuclear bombs, load, and then deliver them with only the half hour of warning a radar system might give proved untenable. Wohlstetter and his team estimated that the Soviets would need only 120 tactical nuclear bombs of 40 kilotons to destroy up to 85 percent of SAC's European-based bomber fleet.[28]

Wohlstetter saw no reason why the Soviets wouldn't take their chances and strike first. He saw the Soviet situation of the time as analogous to that of pre–World War II Japan: both were rising empires with subprime technology desperate to become top dogs, ready to risk retaliation so long as they could deliver a crushing blow to the forces that stood in their way. In the case of Japan, it had been the American fleet that threatened Japan's desired hegemony over the South Pacific. In the case of the Soviet Union, it was American forces prepared to halt Soviet tanks from rolling into Western Europe.

Wohlstetter and his team were appalled by the implications of their findings. To assure top secrecy, their study, R-244, was labeled an "S" document, which meant it was to be excluded from the usual list of RAND publications, lest some publicity-hungry congressman or benighted bureaucrat reveal that the crown jewels of SAC were scattered like pearls before swine. Proposals for safety measures that needed to be urgently carried out were not committed to paper. Wohlstetter even refrained from making comments at a conference where RAND scientists, comforted by their ignorance, publicly speculated on the best way to attack U.S. defenses, without realizing that their speculations could come true all too quickly if nothing was done about it soon.[29]

Ironically, Wohlstetter's warnings about the vulnerability of SAC bases were borne out domestically by the summer weather. On September 1, 1952, a tornado slammed into Carswell Air Force Base in Texas, with gusts up to 125 miles per hour. The storm collapsed hangars, totaled a B-36 bomber, and put eighty-one other aircraft out of commission; it also damaged electrical circuits, exposing the base to a dangerous fire risk.[30]

Wohlstetter used this near disaster in his presentations, pointing out that had a Soviet forty-kiloton bomb exploded anywhere near the base, even if the explosive missed by 9,000 feet, it would have caused winds of a similar force. Moreover, the intense heat and radiation from the blast would have killed most people. He created an extensive series of recommendations, including that SAC's bombers be based in the United States and only land overseas to refuel, that the bombers be dispersed in several locations, and that SAC build bomber shelters sufficiently hardened to withstand nuclear explosions.

Late in 1952 Wohlstetter and his team sailed into Washington, D.C., armed with their charts, their numbers, and their absolute conviction that they were all that stood between SAC and its destruction. They would wind up giving their presentation ninety-two times to different groups of officers in the Air Force without much progress. Only at the end did they realize that the main obstacle to their crusade was General LeMay. His reaction to Wohlstetter's proposal for bomber shelters exemplified his attitude toward the whole study: "Piss on shelters."[31]

LeMay was opposed to the idea of additional protection for the bomber force out of principle. When bombers were lost, it meant that newer, better airplanes were ordered to replace them. Besides, LeMay was inclined to strike a preemptive blow to the Soviet Union if there was ever any indication that the Soviets were massing their forces for an attack. Finally, there were political considerations. By agreeing to RAND's recommendations, LeMay would be losing authority to the Air Force; SAC, although nominally part of the Air Force, took orders only from the Joint Chiefs of Staff. There was no way the gruffly independent LeMay would be anybody else's man.

In desperation, Wohlstetter and his team made an end run around LeMay. In August of 1953, using RAND's contacts, they arranged for a direct presentation to General Thomas D. White, the acting Air Force chief of staff. They convinced White of the pressing need for change, and White promised he would see that their suggestions were considered by the Air Force council for implementation. When later that month the Soviet Union announced it had set off its first hydrogen nuclear bomb, the news added urgency to the study. By October 1953, the Air Force signed off on most of Wohlstetter's recommendations.[32] In April 1954, Wohlstetter, Rowen, Hoffman, and R. J. Lutz put their full briefing in a top-secret study, R-266, "Selection and Use of Strategic Air Bases." The report wryly noted the changes already being implemented by referring to previous SAC plans as the "formerly programmed system."[33]

LeMay continued pushing for a different solution to the vulnerabilities that he refused to admit. When Colonel Ed Jones, an Air Force planner in Tampa, came up with a plan that would have B-47 bombers fly out of the United States fully loaded, refuel in the air over Iceland, proceed to their targets in the Soviet Union, and recover in overseas bases, LeMay jumped on the idea. The Jones plan gave LeMay a way to address the weak points of SAC without surrendering control or decision making to outsiders. Calling it the Fullhouse Concept, it became Air Force policy. The plan's intent was "to limit the importance of the overseas areas as pre-strike bases and [reduce] their role to principally that of en route aerial refueling bases and post-strike support."[34]

Undaunted, Wohlstetter took his basing study one step further and came up with a concept that would become indelibly marked in American history: fail-safe. No longer would war planners operate in the dark or blame snafus for unwanted excursions. Nuclear attacks would always be deliberate, never accidental. Essentially, fail-safe was a simple idea with huge ramifications. Just as the basing study was the product of Wohlstetter's insight that proximity is a two-way street, so fail-safe was the result of his realization that not everything in life goes as planned.

Wohlstetter asked himself: How do you stop planes sent to bomb Moscow by mistake? There must be a way to recall bombers if a mission is canceled. Given that so many lives—and the future of the planet itself—depended on absolute certainty in bombing targets, Wohlstetter argued for a series of checkpoints at which nuclear-armed bombers would receive confirmation of their target attack. If they did not receive such confirmation, the mission would abort by default.

> Bombers, flushed by some serious yet not unambiguous warning, [would] return to base unless they are specifically directed to continue forward. If the alarm is false, the bombers will return to base even if there is a failure in radio communications. If the alarm was in response to an actual attack and some radio communications should fail, this failure would mean only a small percentage diminution of the force going on to target.[35]

The fail-safe concept was adopted by the Air Force and to this day is credited with having saved the world from possible nuclear catastrophe on several occasions. One recent instance played out in 1979, when a telephone-operator mistake led to the transmission of a wrong message that the United States was under nuclear attack. Ten fighters from three separate bases were scrambled and sent airborne; they were recalled when the error was found. In 1980 a failed chip in a minicomputer led to yet another transmission that the Soviets were attacking the United States with nuclear weapons. In that case, had the failure not been discovered in time, nearly a hundred B-52s would have been launched, the president roused from the White House, and preparations-to-strike signals sent to ICBM crews.[36]

Wohlstetter's triumphs with the basing study and fail-safe not only earned him the respect and admiration of fellow analysts at RAND but also gained him entry to the top strata of government that very few military analysts enjoyed. His work had pointed out a fatal deficiency in the nation's war plans, and it had saved the Air Force several billion dollars in potential losses.[37] When a few years later he presented his updated version of the basing study, R-290, "Protecting U.S. Power to Strike Back in the 1950s and 1960s," at the Pentagon, he didn't have to undertake an odyssey through ninety-two offices: he personally briefed Defense Secretary Charles Wilson, accompanied by General White and General Nathan Twining, chairman of the Joint Chiefs of Staff.[38]

R-290 WAS A PARTICULAR triumph for RAND. The report elaborated on the tactical uses of a brilliant new idea by Bruno Augenstein, one of the most prominent physicists at the think tank. Augenstein had proposed a formula for manufacturing hydrogen bombs that would make them far more lightweight, and thus capable of being used for the missile heads of the less-than-accurate ICBMs of the time. It wouldn't matter if the missile fell as much as three miles away from its intended target—the increased power of the "super" would destroy everything within a thirty-mile radius and thus trump the relative inaccuracy of the rocket. Augenstein's recommendation, when implemented, made intercontinental missiles viable instruments of war, fulfilling RAND's original raison d'être.*

Not only had RAND become a true martial *académie,* a school of scholars developing wondrous weapons of war, it had finally succeeded in making viable the most coveted weapon of the postwar period, the intercontinental ballistic missile.

RANDites were not content to concoct new thunderbolts; they also wanted a voice on how and where to hurl them. From a collection of experts gathered to tackle specific projects for the Air Force, by the mid-1950s RANDites had undergone a transformation as unexpected as the fields of green glass left in the sand dunes by the first atomic blast at Alamogordo. The geeky scientists of RAND became the brains that guided the brawn of SAC and the Air Force, leading the country's leaders to a new level of uncontested military primacy. They appointed themselves the wise men of all things nuclear, in the process creating the brand-new discipline of nuclear strategy. Yet their work in this field would not be without discord. Soon there developed major disagreements between the suave Wohlstetter, who accepted the tragic inevitability of limited nuclear wars, and the tortured father of the discipline, Bernard Brodie, who sought by all means possible to avoid ever having to fight a nuclear conflict.

Brodie had been deeply affected by his participation in a massive study on the hydrogen bomb, so top secret it would not be declassified until 1995. Recruited by Hitch in 1951 to collaborate with him and physicist Ernst Plesset on "Implications of Large Yield Weapons" for the Air Force, Brodie examined the effects of the weapon and the possibility of defense against it, as well as Soviet ac-

---

* The missiles were originally called IBMs until the company of the same name protested and the Pentagon grudgingly changed the acronym to ICBM.

quisition and use of the hydrogen bomb and American offensive deployment of the "super."

The analysts assumed that the weapon used would be a five-megaton fusion bomb—that is, one with the explosive power of ‚250 of the type of bombs used in Nagasaki—the kind being constructed at that moment in the Lawrence Livermore National Laboratory. They concluded that the H-bomb would demolish all structures within a seven-mile radius from the force of the blast and its ensuing firestorm. Unsheltered people within a fifty-five-square-mile area would die immediately, and even those in shelters within a thirty-square-mile area from the point of impact would perish. There would be a 50 percent survival rate for people at the edge of each respective area.[39]

It was obvious that thermonuclear weapons would be "killers and fantastically destructive." The authors concluded that although "large scale reciprocal use of atomic and thermonuclear weapons against cities would not fall short of national suicide for both sides," they still urged the quick stockpiling of the weapons. In their view, Russia was simply too unpredictably belligerent for the United States to do otherwise. "We may lose our ability to deter the Soviet Union from aggression and indeed may lose our chance of national survival if we do not develop thermonuclear weapons at the most rapid rate possible."[40] The study was widely distributed in national security circles and President Truman was briefed on it. It was appropriately received in an administration that had increased defense spending from $13.5 billion to $48.2 billion in 1951 out of a belief that the Soviet Union was implementing its master plan for world domination.[41]

Brodie's conclusion was unavoidable: although deterrence through the use of nuclear weapons was unavoidable, nuclear war was inconsistent with any rational political objective. To Brodie this was a wrenching realization, for he had been one of the pioneers of the study of nuclear war. Yet with both the United States and the Soviet Union feeling compelled to continue developing these vastly murderous weapons because of the very dynamics of their political systems, there was always the risk that someday, somehow the jinni would escape from the bottle and obliterate 10,000 years of civilization in a flash. How to reconcile that contradiction?

Brodie's solution was twofold. On a policy level, he advocated even harder for deterrence through the building of bigger and deadlier nuclear weapons, in tandem with a plan for civil defense that would ensure the dispersal of cities and population, urging that "new industrial centers should be built away from current heavy concentrations." He also pushed for selective dispersal of critical military installations and building up reserves of military equipment and supplies, as well as constructing reinforced civilian shelters that could withstand the impact of nuclear explosions. All so that if the Soviets were to attack, the United States would conserve the capacity and manpower to retaliate.

On a personal level, Brodie entered into a period of prolonged psychoanalysis, extolling the virtues of therapy to all who listened at RAND. Analysis became almost de rigueur among *bien-pensant* RANDites, mirroring the fascination that Freud held for a Western society grappling with the aftermath of World War II and the anxieties of the new Cold War. Nathan Leites and Roberta Wohlstetter were psychoanalyzed to help with writer's block,[42] while Brodie extended his fascination with Freud into an internally circulated RAND memorandum that drew an analogy between nuclear war strategy and sex. He compared his plan of withholding fire after a first-round nuclear response to allow time for a response to withdrawal before ejaculation. He also likened SAC's favorite Sunday punch to a quick and messy climax. (Herman Kahn would famously borrow this analogy and tell an assembly of SAC officers, "Gentlemen, you don't have a war plan, you have a *war-gasm!*"[43])

Brodie's years of intense reflection and psychoanalysis in the 1950s resulted in the best-known work of his entire career, *Strategy in the Missile Age,* in which he advocated the use of tactical nuclear weapons, giving each side a chance to come to terms before proceeding to a wider, more deadly attack. In the end, though, Brodie's vision was bleak, and in his writings he admitted he could not discern any way in which the two superpowers would avoid a conflict that, once started, inevitably would result in the death of millions.

Beginning in the fall of 1952, Brodie, Andrew Marshall, Hitch, and others formed an informal group they called the Strategic Objectives Committee. Meeting at lunchtime and after hours, they argued about the best way to deploy the enormous nuclear arsenal the United States was accumulating. Between 1953 and 1955, the American nuclear stockpile rose to nearly 2,000 bombs—without counting the addition of dozens of hydrogen bombs and their multi-megaton impact. Following SAC's preferred Sunday punch playbook, in case of a conflict with the Soviet Union, SAC planners expected to annihilate three-quarters of the population in each of 188 cities in Russia. Total casualties would be in excess of 77 million in the Soviet Union and Eastern Europe alone.[44]

To avoid the mass catastrophe envisioned by SAC planners, RAND's Strategic Objectives Committee put forward a concept then gaining traction among nuclear strategists: counterforce. Broadly defined, counterforce meant having a reserve nuclear force, also known as second-strike capability, to be able to respond to a surprise attack. Counterforce also incorporated a concept suggested by Brodie, who believed that nuclear attack plans should spare cities and concentrate instead on military targets. As a corollary, counterforce contemplated using force in graduated attacks, giving the opponent sufficient time to declare a truce and come to an agreement before the next wave of nuclear missiles was unleashed. The concept soon led many RAND analysts to believe that limited nuclear wars not only could be waged but could also be won. Although at first rejected by SAC and LeMay, within a few years counterforce would become the accepted nuclear strategy of the U.S. government. Its effects would be felt all the way through Vietnam and the continuing Cold War, until the final collapse of the Soviet Union.

By the late 1950s, RAND's political triumphs cemented the dominance of the Economics Department and of the numerical, rational, and empirical approach to reality that would come to define the think tank for decades. The Soviet publication *Pravda* at this time famously called RAND "the academy of science and death," but a much better moniker would have been the academy of numeric rationalism. At first, Williams and Collbohm had brought in the social sciences to round out their theories of war; they felt they needed experts on the human factor. However, with the triumph of the hard sciences, RANDites turned the concept of human knowledge on its head. Instead of complementing the numerical approach with the softer disciplines of history, social sciences, and anthropology, the economists made them mere adjuncts of the hard sciences, traducing them into numbers, choices, and decision patterns through modeling and systems analysis. This meant the growing marginalization of Brodie, who ironically had been among the first to argue that war after Hiroshima would never be the same. His reasoned, historical-based approach to issues, with emphasis on motivation and gradual escalation of conflicts, was in opposition to the analytical approach of Wohlstetter and his followers, who consciously limited their focus on the enemy's capabilities, while assuming the Soviets capable of endless perfidy.

At RAND, counting, parsing, and enumeration beat out tale-telling, psychology, and interpretation. This would have vast consequences. RANDites posited a new view of human existence: everything of importance in human existence can be traduced into numbers, which serve humanity to keep track of its main driving force, which is self-interest. Since self-interest, according to Kenneth

Arrow, is material consumption of goods, then the best kind of government that liberal democracies can promote is that which spurs unrestrained consumption. RANDites therefore established the foundation of a new rationale for Western liberal democracies, one based on the uncontested primacy of the individual consumer—both of goods and politics.

Concurrently, Wohlstetter's success, and his charismatic personality, transformed the mathematical logician–cum–nuclear strategist into the RAND house guru by the end of the 1950s. While he was already given to orotund statements and unflagging self-confidence, his achievements fired him up to pursue all the different interests that attracted him. And there were so many interests! During conferences, he would frequent the best and most expensive restaurants to sample as many cuisines as possible, observing that life is like a meal book with a limited number of tickets and it is everyone's responsibility to use as many tickets as possible before the book expires.[45] At his modernist aerie, he staged classical music concerts, played by amateur musicians culled from the ranks of RAND. He hosted banquets for top diplomats, collected art and LPs, had his picture taken for Sunday supplements—in short, there was nothing he apparently could not do. Even when he didn't speak a foreign language, he dissembled so well that native speakers at times could be fooled into believing he did. A true Renaissance man, he funded his many interests by his unending study of American military vulnerability— that is, he found a racket and exploited it all his life.

Not everyone at RAND thought as highly of Wohlstetter as he did of himself. Some of his contemporaries viewed him as arrogant, imperious, and condescending. David Novick, head of the Cost Analysis Department, the man who originally hired Wohlstetter as a consultant, accused him of falsifying the figures to his basing studies and had him fired. (Wohlstetter denied the charge and Hitch rehired him.)[46] Once, after Wohlstetter imparted his wisdom to his coterie, one of his colleagues left Wohlstetter's house with a bitter taste in his mouth, sniping, "You'd think he was reciting from the Sermon on the Mount up there!"[47] All the same, younger RAND analysts began to ape Wohlstetter's taste for art and gourmet cooking; most of all they imitated his blithe self-confidence, acting as though no one was or could be as smart or gifted as they were. Humility, always viewed as a weakness in RAND circles, was in even scarcer supply during Wohlstetter's heyday.

For his part, whether consciously or not, Wohlstetter seems to have encouraged a kind of filial idolatry. Never having had a son, he surrounded himself with younger men whom he could mentor in the ways of the strategy world. They would come to pay obeisance in his all-white office—white shag carpet, white furniture—the dazzling glare of his accomplishments eclipsing the groundbreaking work of the many other gifted researchers at RAND.

At the close of the decade, General Arnold and Collbohm's dream of an intellectual powerhouse was uncontested reality. RAND had amassed the grandest collection of brainpower in one institution since the Manhattan Project—among others, mathematicians John von Neumann, John Nash, and George Dantzig; computer pioneers Willis Ware, James G. Gillogly, and Allen Newell; economists Kenneth Arrow, Thomas Schelling, Herbert Simon, and Harry Markowitz; physicists Edward Teller, Bruno Augenstein, Ernst Plesset, Harold L. Brode, and Samuel Cohen. Wohlstetter stood atop them all by virtue of his closeness to power, the most influential in the rarified circle of nuclear mandarins.

Yet within that circle there was another analyst who would symbolize if not the anti-Wohlstetter perspective, at least a divergent path not taken by Wohlstetter and his cohorts. He also happened to be the man who exemplified both the intellectual daring and the moral callousness of RAND in the eyes of America and the world in the late 1950s and early 1960s: Herman Kahn.

6

The Jester of Death

HERMAN KAHN WAS what most RAND analysts, by dint of their belief in their intellectual superiority, never deigned to be: a showman. And his shtick was death. Death by the millions, the tens and hundreds of millions. It is with Kahn that RAND becomes, in the popular mind, the place where people think the unthinkable. As Kahn liked to ask, "If 180 million dead is too high a price for punishing the Soviets for their aggression, what price would we be willing to pay?"[1] Are you better dead than Red? And if humanity does survive a nuclear war, will the survivors envy the dead?

In an age of plainspoken chain-smokers with slender builds—the average American male was five foot nine, barely registering 160 pounds—Kahn stood out for his girth and his loquaciousness. Like John Williams, Kahn was almost as wide as he was tall—six feet and 300 pounds—and he could extemporize for hours on his favorite topics: civil defense and thermonuclear war. His were riveting performances, as Kahn, looking like the Pillsbury doughboy, prattled humorously about the end of the known world. People laughed in spite of themselves, and sometimes, after his seminars, threw up from shock and fear. Roberta Wohlstetter called him a fragmentation bomb,[2] while more than one nuclear disarmament maven commented that Kahn's lectures were the best argument ever for a nuclear freeze—though that was never Kahn's intention, having long advocated a preemptive nuclear war. He was from RAND, and RAND people were the prime practitioners of realpolitik in America's intellectual world. To them, facts, no matter how distasteful, were facts. Moral and humane considerations should never interfere with policy analysis. No wonder then that famed film-maker Stanley Kubrick based the main character in his movie *Dr. Strangelove or: How I learned to Stop Worrying and Love the Bomb,* with his doomsday machine and his never-ending supply of morbid one-liners, on the exuberant and irrepressible Kahn. (He cribbed so much material from Kahn's work that Kahn demanded royalties, to which an incensed Kubrick responded, "That's not how it works, Herman!")[3]

Jewish, like Wohlstetter and Bernard Brodie, Kahn was born in New Jersey and grew up in the Bronx. Although his father was religious, Kahn never professed any faith, but he remained an ardent supporter of Zionist causes throughout his life. After his parents divorced when he was ten, Herman moved with his mother and his brothers, Morris and Irving, to Southern California. They lived in the Jewish district of Los Angeles, where the family endured hard times; twice his mother was forced to apply for public assistance.[4]

After graduating from Fairfax High in 1940, Kahn studied physics at University of California at Los Angeles. His voluble (if not histrionic) personality was already in full bloom when he was ordered to take a mental aptitude test by the Army Reserve Corps prior to induction in 1943.

Kahn was told that no one had ever finished the Army IQ test, so he crammed for it by deconstructing any aptitude test he could find. When his turn came, he ripped through the entire exam in half an hour, then left and collapsed in dramatic exhaustion, heaving and perspiring profusely, only to pick himself up and dash back to the examination hall a few minutes later, clamoring, "I made a stupid arithmetic mistake on question 132. I want to change it! How can I be so stupid?" He was gratified to learn later that he had achieved the highest score ever for that test.[5]

Following service in the Pacific theater, Kahn returned to Los Angeles and enrolled for a master's degree at the California Institute of Technology. Strapped for cash after his mother's sudden death, and having to support his younger brother, Kahn took out a real estate license. However, his friend and fellow physicist Sam Cohen— the future inventor of the neutron bomb—had just been hired by RAND and got Kahn a job there. Kahn would remain at the think tank from 1947 to 1961.

At first, Kahn was assigned to a project for developing a nuclear-powered airplane, an idea that would prove unfeasible. Within a year, though, he had joined the RAND team designing the "super"—the top-secret H or hydrogen bomb. Most of the work was conducted at the newly opened University of California's Lawrence Livermore National Laboratory near San Francisco; the frequent travel to the Bay Area was a boon to the gregarious Kahn, so exuberant that colleagues wondered how he was ever cleared for his high-ranking Q security status at RAND.[6]

Because of the highly confidential nature of their work, the physicists at RAND worked in an area separated by thick glass doors from the rest of the building—just as the original RAND people had done at Douglas Aircraft. The reclusiveness grated on Kahn, who could not resist roaming the corridors, introducing himself to people whom he didn't know outside the top-secret area, and besieging those he did know with questions, comments, and plans. He would almost in-variably return from his sojourns down the bifurcating halls of RAND with two or three new projects to work on and a handful of books and publications to scribble on during breaks from his bomb creations. Newly married to his former research assistant, Rosalie Jane Heilner—whose political inclinations he once lovingly described as "to the right of the John Birch society"—Kahn was by all ac-counts ecstatic with his new position. His honeymoon at RAND lasted until the FBI began to investigate him in the early 1950s.[7]

Kahn had passed two previous security screenings without much difficulty, but that was before his marriage to Heilner, whose two older sisters were reportedly Communists.[8] Now it turned out that an FBI informant had also denounced Kahn, claiming he was a member of an alleged Communist front, the Committee for the Pro-tection of the Foreign Born. A liberal, a member of the American Civil Liberties Union and the Americans for Democratic Action, Kahn was also a known anti-Communist who felt that Communists should never work on government security projects. Although he was soon cleared to work with top-secret documents, his high-ranking Q clearance—a prerequisite for his work on the hydrogen bomb—was suspended while the FBI investigated further.[9]

Kahn would have J. Edgar Hoover to thank for his disengage-ment from hard science, a process that would turn the irrepressible transplant from New Jersey into a member of the most exclusive circle in RAND, that of the nuclear analysts. Men like Wohlstetter, Brodie, Charles Hitch, and economist Thomas Schelling, a late ar-rival to the club, would become his peers, his competitors, and, at times, his fiercest critics.

Kahn, who had struck up a friendship with RAND researcher Andrew Marshall,[10] at first was drawn to game theory. The two published a book on the "Monte Carlo method," a mathematical construct for analyzing chance, as applied to bombing raids on So-viet defenses.[11] Kahn's random walks through the halls of RAND put him in the path of Wohlstetter, who at the time was busy constructing the massive edifice of facts, insight, and speculation that would become his basing study. Kahn became a sort of junior associate to Wohlstetter's project, which soon grew by leaps and bounds, commandeering the time and assistance of practically all the experts in the organization. Kahn found his true métier, however, when he was assigned to give lectures to Air Force officers on systems analysis and its role in national defense.

In retrospect, it is clear why someone with Kahn's ebullient personality was a natural for live presentations. His gift was gab; his patter was comparable to that of later stream-of-consciousness hip comics like Mort Sahl and Dick Gregory (he was never risqué enough to match Lenny Bruce). Even his closest colleagues, however, were stunned by the ease with which Kahn transformed himself into what Jewish comedians would have called a *schpritzer.* Tapped to give a presentation on systems analysis to junior Air Force officers, he had the stiff military men roaring with his puns, analogies, and not-so-subtle put-downs: "You see, ideally, what we would like to do is to get the models of your bombers, send them over Russia, see how many get shot down, how many get through, let them run over their bombing runs, then come back. But you can't get cooperation in doing this."[12]

Borrowing liberally from Brodie's writings and from Wohlstetter's basing study, Kahn latched onto the concept of civil defense as the answer to the Soviet nuclear threat. If out of a U.S. population of 200 million, let us say 30 million died in a nuclear war, then 170 million survived! And if the number of casualties could be brought down to 10 million through the widespread use of shelters—in places like mine shafts, caverns, and fortified bunkers—why, there would still be plenty of Americans left to rebuild the country!

Kahn was so taken by his inspiration that he urged the Eisenhower administration to initiate a massive program of civil defense shelters around the country. For a mere $200 billion, he argued, the country could make sure there would be an American waving the Stars and Stripes after the last mushroom cloud cleared. Not only would the shelters physically protect citizens, but they would also prove a deterrent to Soviet aggression. If the Kremlin knows that our citizens have little to fear from a nuclear war, and that there will still be enough of us standing to launch a counterattack, the Soviets will have less of an incentive to attack at all.

The Eisenhower administration's reaction to Kahn's scheme was tepid at best. Kahn was appointed to yet another committee to study the problem, but his vision of a massive shelter construction program never got off the easels he used in his presentations. The official policy of the administration might have remained massive retaliation, but Eisenhower preferred to concentrate on disarmament, having come to believe that neither side could—or would—survive the devastation of nuclear war. By the mid-1950s, Eisenhower began reaching out for some kind of compromise with the Soviets to reduce the size of both countries' nuclear arsenals.

Undaunted, Kahn took his message to the public at large. In 1959, he asked for leave from RAND and joined Princeton's Center for International Studies, where he worked for a semester. Then he began to speak on civil defense to community groups, universities, and foreign affairs organizations around the country. Whereas most speakers contented themselves with one- or two-hour lectures, Kahn gave two- and three-day presentations, using a plethora of slides, charts, drawings, and projections to hammer his many points home. His graphs, showing the number of casualties under diverse wartime conditions, bore captions such as WILL THE SURVIVORS ENVY THE DEAD? and TRAGIC BUT DISTINGUISHABLE POSTWAR STATES. He divided the possibility of war into sections and subsections, contingencies and subcontingencies, and ladders of aggression escalation, all the while joking about the possibilities of death on a scale that had never been conceived, much less declared in public before.

Never much of a writer, with the help of collaborators Kahn compiled transcripts of his talks, which he edited down to a large, informal, yet apparently amoral and decisively infuriating book. He called it *On Thermonuclear War,* in homage to Carl von Clausewitz's military classic *On War.* His confreres in RAND's nuclear analysts club—with their scorn of public exposure and their rational, precise use of language, figures, and statistics—were contemptuous of the work when Kahn submitted it to RAND management for release authorization. Most of the analysts felt Kahn had cribbed from everyone and given credit to no one.[13]

Kahn had handed a copy to Wohlstetter for review. Bruno Augenstein was in Wohlstetter's pristine, all-white office when Kahn peeked in and asked his erstwhile mentor for his response.

"There's only one thing to do with this, Herman," replied Wohlstetter, tossing the manuscript back. "Burn it."[14]

Kahn did no such thing, of course, but pressed RAND management to authorize the work's release. Collbohm was critical of the book, not only for bowdlerizing the doctrines that so many had spent years elaborating at RAND but for being inimical to the interests of the Air Force and the SAC. Collbohm finally gave his consent to publication, as there was no classified information in it and it was not an official RAND document.

The 652-page tome was an immediate success when published in 1960 to widespread, controversial reviews; more than 14,000 copies sold during the first two months. To a world familiar with hopeless talk of total annihilation if nuclear bombs were used for war, Kahn's pragmatic views were unexpectedly bracing and clearheaded—or repulsive and pornographic, depending on the reader's political persuasion.

Like Brodie, Kahn espoused limited war, denying that the threat of massive retaliation brought about deterrence. In his book, he concocted a so-called doomsday machine, one that would automatically release enough nuclear bombs to wipe out all life on Earth if the

Soviet Union engaged in some forbidden practice. He likened that contraption to SAC war plans, calling them both absurd as they offered no flexibility in response to a Soviet attack. Kahn borrowed Brodie's concept of a nuclear reserve force, which Wohlstetter had appropriated and dubbed second-strike capability; Kahn also used the recommendations of Wohlstetter's basing study, the dispersal of bombers and military personnel, as well as the hardening of hangars and missile silos. Finally Kahn threw into the mix the RAND notion of counterforce—that is, going after specific military targets instead of cities in a nuclear war.

Kahn saved his most colorful, riveting descriptions for his visions of civil defense and life during and after a nuclear exchange. Blithely assuming that the federal government and the economic system would survive by people hiding in backyard shelters, evacuation centers in fortified mine shafts, and deep caverns, he declared that the vaunted effects of radioactive fallout were highly exaggerated. Certainly there might be some genetic mutations as a result, but those mutations already existed at rates higher than most people suspected—and in any case, humanity would eventually adapt and survive. Since the most noticeable effect of fallout would be radiation sickness, he urged the widespread distribution of radiation counters, so anyone could tell whether their neighbor in the shelter is truly sick or just having a fit of nerves. "You look at his meter and say, 'You have received only ten roentgens, why are you vomiting? Pull yourself together and get to work.'"[15]

Kahn suggested that food be labeled according to its contamination level, with the degree of contamination expressed in five different grades, from less to more poisonous. "The A food would be restricted to children and to pregnant women. The B food would be a high-priced food available to everybody. The C food would be a low-priced food also available to everybody. Finally, the D food would be restricted to people over forty or fifty . . . [for] most of

these people would die of other causes before they got cancer." E
food would be for animals.[16]

Many people were shocked by the apparent callousness of *On
Thermonuclear War.* Although sympathetic to the squeamish, Kahn
felt such trepidations were a waste of time and intellectual energy. In
an era when humankind teetered on the brink of the most destructive conflict ever imagined, it was essential for Americans to know
that they could definitely survive if thermonuclear war broke out.
That knowledge alone was enough to make them stronger and safer.

A comparison to Nazi death camps was about the only insult not
hurled at Kahn when his book was published—even though just
such a comment was originally included in a savage critique ap-
pearing in *Scientific American* (judiciously, it was edited out), where
mathematician James Newman called the book "a moral tract on
mass murder: how to plan it, how to commit it, how to get away
with it, how to justify it."[17] Other publications were equally harsh,
with the *New Statesman* calling it "pornography for officers."[18] Curiously, the conservative *National Review* panned it, saying the work
was not tough enough on the Soviet Union.[19]

Some of the loudest praise came from pacifists and advocates
for nuclear disarmament, including the philosopher Bertrand Russell, who believed Kahn unwittingly illustrated the impossibility of
peace through nuclear weapons. Socialist Party presidential nominee
Norman Thomas concurred with Russell's assessment, writing in
the *Saturday Review,* "Mr. Kahn deserves attention from those of
us who believe that universal disarmament . . . is our sole valid hope
of a decent existence for our race."[20]

Collbohm tried to impose conditions on Kahn's return to
RAND, but Kahn, flush with his success, made a final break with
the organization. He moved with his wife and three children to New
York and with a million-dollar grant from the Rockefeller Foundation, set up the Hudson Institute, his own competing think tank.

There he originated "futurology,"[21] a doctrine that held that capitalism and technology had an unlimited future and that the destiny of humankind was to populate outer space.

In spite of his growing reputation as an unorthodox thinker, and with dozens of books published on a host of subjects, Kahn would never match the success of *On Thermonuclear War*. He died in 1983, working on a new edition of the book, still intent on proving the old RAND doctrine that only those who are willing to die are prepared to live in the nuclear age. He could not anticipate how the tides of history would leave him and his theories of nuclear war by the wayside, even while his former friends in RAND's coterie of strategists adapted to the new technological currents and prospered in the pitiless world they had created.

7

In RAND's Orbit

AN EERIE, OTHERWORLDLY beeping transfixed all of America the evening of October 4, 1957. The radio transmissions of *Sputnik I,* the world's first orbiting artificial satellite, could be heard throughout the land by anyone with a cheap shortwave receiver. Steady and piercing, the signals were a clear sign to Americans that the United States had lost its vaunted technical superiority to the Soviet Union—and that the Communists just might bury us, as shoe-pounding Soviet premier Nikita Khrushchev had threatened at the United Nations. To add insult to injury, the two-foot-wide, 184-pound sphere flew so low it could be seen by the naked eye in most of the country—as bright as the star over Red Square.[1]

That night, when *Sputnik I* flew over a bewildered America, Senate majority leader Lyndon Baines Johnson was hosting a barbecue at his Texas ranch on the Pedernales River. Hearing the news over the radio, he tuned in and listened to the satellite's cryptic transmission. He would write in his memoir, "Now, somehow, in some new way, the sky seemed almost alien. I also remember the profound shock of realizing that it might be possible for another nation to achieve technological superiority over this great country of ours."[2]

The launching of *Sputnik I* was no surprise to the Eisenhower administration, although its timing certainly was. For years, the United States and the Soviet Union had been in a race to be the first to send a satellite into outer space for the so-called International Geophysical Year, an international scientific research effort to study astronomical phenomena. The sponsoring organization, the Comité Spécial de l'Année Géophysique Internationale, had decided that July 1, 1957, to December 31, 1958, would be the period of emphasis, in part because of a predicted expansion of solar activity. The American effort, code-named Project Vanguard, was behind schedule and overbudget when the Soviet news agency TASS announced the successful launching of *Sputnik I* from a base in the desert of Kazakhstan in Central Asia.

Soon a wave of hysteria swept the country. In the popular imagination, Soviet technology was a ray gun aiming straight at the heart of America. Many feared the Russians would be as merciless as the Martians in the newly released movie of H. G. Wells's *The War of the Worlds*, only the Soviet menace wasn't science fiction, it was fact. Physicist Edward Teller, the father of the H-bomb, said America had just lost a battle more important than Pearl Harbor, while congresswoman Clare Boothe Luce called the launching "an intercontinental space-age raspberry to the American way of life."[3]

Even the staid *New York Times* raised the alarm in an editorial: America was lagging "in a race that is not so much a race for arms or even prestige, but a race for survival."[4] Other newspapers blamed a do-nothing Eisenhower administration, which they claimed refused to spend the funds necessary to assure American technological superiority. Democrats, who for years had been chastised for being soft on Communism and national defense, saw in *Sputnik I* an opportunity for political payback and were quick to pounce on the apparent ineptitude of the president. They accused Eisenhower of wanting to play golf rather than tend to the nation's business. Democratic governor of Michigan G. Mennen Williams wrote a doggerel poem about it:

> Oh little Sputnik, flying high
> With made-in-Moscow beep,
> You tell the world it's a Commie sky
> and Uncle Sam's asleep.
>
> You say on fairway and on rough
> The Kremlin knows it all,
> We hope our golfer knows enough
> To get us on the ball.[5]

LBJ was not far behind when it came to drawing a bead on the Eisenhower administration. On November 25 he opened a series of hearings by the Senate Armed Services Committee to look into the glaring failure that *Sputnik I* represented. The conclusion, as might have been expected, blamed the fiscally conservative Republican administration, which the committee said had mismanaged the country's space resources. "The simple fact is that we can no longer consider the Russians to be behind us in technology," said George E. Reedy, one of Johnson's aides. "It took them four years to catch up to our atomic bomb and nine months to catch up to our hydrogen bomb. Now we are trying to catch up to their satellite."[6]

The Eisenhower administration's top scientific voice, James R. Killian, head of the Massachusetts Institute of Technology and the president's special assistant for science and technology, called the incident "an affront to my national pride."[7] Killian had been in charge of a committee formed a few years earlier to suggest measures that would reduce the danger of a Soviet sneak attack on the United States and its allies. That panel had recommended that the nation's ICBM program be accelerated and that work be sped up on the development of a radar-evading, high-altitude jet that would be able to detect Soviet military capabilities—what would come to be known as the U-2 plane.[8] Eisenhower had authorized the development of the U-2, but he kept it and the results of its observations top secret. Nonetheless, even that flying eye in the sky had been of little use in detecting this latest perceived threat to American power.[9]

At RAND, the news was equally alarming, even if it represented a kind of poetic justice. As far back as 1946, in its very first project completed for the Air Force (the 324-page "Preliminary Design of an Experimental World-Circling Spaceship"), RAND analysts had noted

> one can imagine the consternation and admiration that would be felt here if the U.S. were to discover suddenly that some other nation had already put up a successful satellite. Since mastery of the elements is a reliable index of material progress, the nation which first makes significant achievements in space travel will be acknowledged as the world leader in both military and scientific techniques.[10]

No one in the Air Force or anywhere in government had heeded RAND's prophetic call to use rockets to send up satellites and place space stations in orbit. Now the day that RAND had predicted had dawned. RAND analysts, tsk-tsking all the time, collectively rolled up their sleeves and once again—and certainly not for the last time—set themselves to work.

Besides the satisfaction of righteousness, RAND also received ample compensation for its farsightedness. Eisenhower-driven budget cuts had hit RAND hard—but now close to $2 million that had been subtracted from the Department of Defense contract with RAND was immediately restored and another $4 million added for the fiscal years 1959 through 1961. *Sputnik I* became a spigot of research funds for RAND, which conducted dozens of studies exploring the technical and political consequences of its launch.[11]

Politically, *Sputnik I* placed President Eisenhower in a quandary. Since his reelection in 1956, he had been reluctant to expend more funds on national defense, particularly in the area of nuclear weaponry. The reason was easily explained: the former general was exceedingly pessimistic about the prospect of surviving a nuclear war, regardless of whether the Soviets attacked military targets or civilian areas. "It would literally be a business of digging ourselves out of the ashes, starting again."[12] He believed the Army's greatest job would be to keep order in the country after a nuclear exchange; for years he resisted deploying large numbers of soldiers to areas outside the continental United States to keep them in reserve in case the unthinkable occurred during his watch.

This reluctance played to Eisenhower's frugality and to his defense policy, the New Look doctrine. Put into effect at the start of his administration in 1953 as a conscious effort to pare down Truman's profligate defense expenditures, New Look committed Eisenhower to using nuclear weapons to deter Soviet aggression anywhere in the world. His National Security Council plan 162/2 also emphasized a long-term planning approach to defense that would be calibrated to the American economy. Above all, Eisenhower was determined to avoid having to pay for another Korean War, which had caused a national recession. However, in 1954, reluctant to intervene to stop the French defeat at Dien Bien Phu in Vietnam, Eisenhower developed a "new" New Look, one that emphasized a flexible response to local conflicts. For the first time, the United States approved the use of tactical nuclear weapons for local conflicts in limited wars, in what was called "flexible response." Although it

was only a step from there to RAND's notion of counterforce—and
the idea that nuclear wars were winnable—Eisenhower emphasized
that U.S.-Soviet disarmament talks were the way out of the atomic
dilemma.

To silence critics of his defense posture, Eisenhower made use
of an already existing committee headed by RAND chairman H.
Rowan Gaither. The Security Resources Panel, also known as the
Gaither Committee, had been set up in the wake of Albert Wohlstetter's R-266 study in order to analyze the problems of national defense. The panel constituted a perfect example of the confluence of
the military, industry, and academia that Eisenhower would warn the
country against. Many of them were affiliated with RAND—and
most important, they all shared the RAND belief that the Soviet
Union was a far more powerful enemy than the Eisenhower administration wanted to contemplate.[13]

Wohlstetter, Herman Kahn, and Andrew Marshall were advisers to the blue-ribbon body. The group included Richard Bissell, of
the Central Intelligence Agency, who would become notorious for
his role in the failed Bay of Pigs invasion of Cuba; Frank Stanton,
chairman of CBS; James R. Killian of MIT; General James H. Doo-
little, of the Tokyo raid, who worked for Shell Oil; Dr. Ernest O.
Lawrence, of the Radiation Laboratory of the University of California at Berkeley, where the H-bomb was developed; John McCloy,
of Chase Manhattan Bank and future president of the World Bank;
and Admiral Robert B. Carney of Westinghouse Electric; as well as
several RANDites providing technical advice.[14] The committee chairman was Robert Sprague, president of Sprague Electric, a company
that had developed and manufactured crucial components for
weapons systems, including the atom bomb.[15]

Sputnik I spurred the Gaither Committee into raising an even
louder alarm over the prevailing problem of national defense—for,
even though it turned out to be merely an observation satellite, what
if it had been a weapon? Worse, what if this was just a test run be-

fore Moscow pressed its technological advantage and attacked the United States? What defense could the United States have? In its report, the Gaither Committee urged the Eisenhower administration to quickly build shelters to protect civilians during nuclear war, as had been advocated in previous studies by organizations such as the Rockefeller Foundation and Massachusetts Institute of Technology. The National Security Council put a price tag of $44 billion[16] on the ✓ project—almost as much as the entire Defense Department budget during the height of the Korean War.[17]

The tone of the report was made even more cutting by the unexpected illness of Gaither, who would die of cancer within months. The man picked to write the final draft was Paul Nitze, the driving force behind the eschatological NSC-68 memorandum, which had predicted a cataclysmic American-Soviet clash in 1954. Now, three years after the foretold doomsday date had come and gone, Nitze took the same alarmist tack in the Gaither Committee's report.

Deterrence and Survival in the Nuclear Age warned that "we have found no evidence in Russian foreign and military policy since 1945 to refute the conclusion that [Soviet] intentions are expansionist and that her great efforts to build military power go beyond any concepts of Soviet defense." It stated that the Soviet Union possessed material for at least 1,500 nuclear weapons and that Moscow most likely had built more ICBMs than the United States. Because defense programs currently planned would not provide enough protection for civilians in case of a Soviet attack, national protection would fall "primarily upon the deterrence provided by SAC."[18] Seeming to borrow a page from Roberta Wohlstetter's Pearl Harbor study (perhaps supplied by Albert Wohlstetter), the report declared that SAC was highly vulnerable to what RAND analysts had long called "a bolt from the blue." It recommended improvement of the nation's radar system, the construction of widely dispersed hardened shelters for SAC, greater aerial reconnaissance, and a series of civil defense measures and shelters.

Many of these measures had been advocated in previous studies by RAND, such as defense systems analyses by E. J. Barlow and James Digby. That was not surprising, given that RAND analyst Marshall was a member of the panel; that Kahn was an adviser; that RAND engineer Edward P. Oliver served as its official technical adviser; and finally that Gaither, one of RAND's founding fathers, was the chairman. All the same, the committee's (and RAND's) expectations that the nation's long-standing problems of apparent vulnerability would quickly be redressed were misplaced.

From personal experience, President Eisenhower believed that military incursions were never quite a "surprise," that a degenerating political situation always presaged an attack, as happened with Pearl Harbor. Moreover, Eisenhower, who never believed *Sputnik I* constituted a serious military threat, was opposed to the concept of civilian shelters. He wrote that even if thirty or forty million people survived a nuclear war in them, "there wouldn't be enough bulldozers to scrape the dead off the pavement."[19] Finally, he felt he could rely on the results of the secret U-2 overflights of the Soviet Union (which were being overseen by Bissell). Never having rejected outright the idea of a preemptive attack, Eisenhower believed he would receive enough warning from his spy planes to be able to wipe out practically the entire Soviet air force if need be. Finally, Eisenhower, a plainspoken Kansan, detested hype, and hype is what he felt the Gaither Committee was feeding him.

Instead of adopting the recommendations, the Eisenhower administration attempted to bury the top-secret report. At a meeting with Gaither, whose cancer was for the moment in remission, Eisenhower agreed that in the next four years the country would have to start spending more money on defense, but he declined to do so during his administration, ignoring the recommendations of Senator Johnson's committee hearings.

Eisenhower took issue with the report's comment that the country could survive the decimation of half of the population in a nuclear war, pointing out that the measures advocated by Gaither would serve little purpose, for "there is in reality no defense except to retaliate."[20] The president believed SAC was more defensible than the committee argued, since overseas bases could always provide shelter for bombers, and that the rest of the free world would gladly help contain an expansionist Soviet Union.

The following day, Eisenhower met with about fifty of the committee's staff scientists to thank them for a job well done. He told them it was a very interesting work and added, "You recommend spending a billion dollars for something in there. You know how much a billion dollars is? Why, it's a stack of ten-dollar bills as high as the Washington Monument!"[21] He sent them home with a clear message: if he objected to a billion-dollar item, how could they ever expect him to approve the $44 billion the report asked for?

About a month later, in December of 1957, frustrated by the administration's neglect of the Gaither Committee's recommendations, the deputy head of the committee, William Foster—who was also the chairman of the Olin Mathieson Chemical Corporation, makers of Winchester rifles and ammunition—hosted a momentous dinner at his Georgetown manse. The group included some of the most influential figures in national politics and media of the late 1950s—among them Vice President Richard Nixon, CBS president Frank Stanton, Laurence Rockefeller, Nitze, pollster Elmo Roper, and John Cowles of the Cowles newspaper chain, which sponsored the reformist Cowles Commission.

This dinner party can be seen as a template for the kind of informal power brokering that years later resulted in the rise of neoconservatism and the revival of the Cold War, culminating in the presidencies of Ronald Reagan and George H. W. Bush. Heretofore, the strategists at RAND and their allies, the foreign policy hawks, had triumphed over the institutional inertia of the Air Force and had trumped General Curtis LeMay in reorganizing SAC. Now that their national security recommendations were blocked at the highest echelons of the Republican administration, they turned their guns on the GOP itself, aiming for regime change at the White House.

Nitze had hoped he could use the dinner to convince committee leaders to go public with the report's conclusions. Sprague, who had replaced the ailing Gaither, officially declined to go to the press. Yet two days later, on December 11, the *New York Times* carried a story about the dinner. Less than two weeks after that, the *Washington Post* outdid its traditional rival, emblazoning its front page with the headline ENORMOUS ARMS OUTLAY IS HELD VITAL TO SURVIVAL. The lead paragraph warned of "the Nation moving in frightening course to the status of a second-class power," declaring that the still-top-secret Gaither report "portrays a United States in the gravest danger in its history" from the almost immediate threat of a "missile bristling Soviet Union."[22]

Almost immediately Democratic politicians jumped on the Gaither bandwagon, demanding to see the classified report and castigating Republicans for placing the lives of Americans in such clear and present danger. The administration's position was not helped by the failure of Project Vanguard, the American reply to *Sputnik I.* Two Vanguard rockets malfunctioned and exploded seconds after liftoff, even while the Soviets proceeded to put *Sputnik II, III,* and *IV* into outer space. The Soviet advantage in rocketry expanded, in the nervous public's view, into Soviet superiority in armaments as well.

The notion of a "missile gap" became a burning political controversy for the Eisenhower administration, which was seen as sitting on its hands, wasting time while the Soviets outgunned and outfoxed America. There was a growing desire for a new kind of activist government, a muscular democracy that would stand up to the Soviet threat and restore American supremacy in the world. By 1958, the issue became an item in the upcoming presidential campaign, with Massachusetts senator John Kennedy harping in his speeches, "We have to get this country moving again!"[23]

A frustrated Eisenhower ordered an investigation to uncover where the notion of a missile gap had developed. He found its origin in faulty Air Force intelligence estimates of a bomber gap from the mid-1950s. At the time, there had been discrepancies in simultaneous reports prepared by the Air Force and the Central Intelligence Agency on the number of Soviet Bison bombers in existence. Battle had broken out between the two agencies, with the Air Force fiercely defending its higher numbers, as that meant more money, more planes, and, therefore, more power. At first, CIA director Allen Dulles was reluctant to endorse his own people's estimates, since the Air Force had traditionally been the main source for the data on which the CIA based its numbers. With the launching of *Sputnik I,* Dulles was able to explain the discrepancy as an American misinterpretation of a covert effort by the Soviets to divert their manufacturing capacity away from bombers to the kind of missiles that had placed *Sputnik I* into orbit. This conspiratorial assumption made perfect sense in view of the boastful declarations of Khrushchev that, in the future, manned bombers would be found only in museums. Soviet missiles would rule the sky. By bureaucratic legerdemain, then, the bomber gap became the missile gap.*

Late in 1957, analysts' reports that the Soviet Union would have 500 bombers by the end of 1962 or, with a crash program, as early as 1961 were changed. The National Intelligence Estimate, a compendium of foreign intelligence findings prepared by the CIA for the president, stated instead that the Soviets would have 500 ICBMs. The correction was cold comfort, since the United States was expected to have only twenty-four ICBMs in 1960 and sixty-five by 1961.

---

* This concert of confusion was due in large part to the lack of reliable human intelligence on the ground as to what Soviet plans were. The United States did not have enough spies to ferret out facts so it relied on photographs, scientific deductions from observable data, and assumptions. Often all of these, as with the missile gap alarm, proved to be plain wrong.

    In 1958, extrapolating information from flight photographs
✓ taken by U-2s, the Air Force arrived at the (erroneous) conclusion
that the Soviets had enough ICBMs to destroy almost all of the SAC
bases if the Soviets decided to stage a preemptive nuclear war.[24]
However, doubts about the figures continued to swell within the intelligence community. CIA analysts argued that if the Soviets had all
these missiles, they should be testing them, yet from atmospheric
analyses of launchings, readings from secret radar installations in
Turkey which detected Soviet moves, as well as photographs taken
by spy planes, it was evident that the number of Soviet ICBMs in
operation was radically smaller than what the Air Force argued. A
push for smaller figures also came from analysts in the Navy and
Army, who put the number of working Soviet missiles at closer to
50. These conflicts were reflected in the National Intelligence Estimate of 1960, which put forth no definitive estimate of Soviet nuclear missile forces, but instead offered a hodgepodge of figures. The
Soviets would not have 500 missiles until 1963, perhaps even later.
By 1960, they would have only 50 ICBMs, and maybe only 35
would be operational. By 1961, they would have from 175 to 270,
by 1962 from 325 to 400, the figures all covering a broad range of
options.

    The stymieing effect of these conflicting predictions on national
defense policy was compounded by two other factors: Democratic
senator Stuart Symington's publicizing of leaked material about the
supposed missile gap, and a change in the CIA's confidential document distribution rule.

    Symington, who had been the first secretary of the Air Force in
1947 when it split from the Army,[25] harbored presidential ambi-
tions. A senior member of the Armed Forces Committee, he had a
pipeline to Air Force numbers through his former assistant, Colonel
Thomas Lanphier, a World War II hero working for Convair, the
manufacturer of Atlas ICBMs. Symington requested a personal
meeting with CIA chief Dulles to review the supposed missile gap.

Dulles handed Symington figures on the actual numbers of Soviet missiles tested. The numbers were in such contradiction with the estimates from the Air Force that Symington, at a second meeting, insisted the CIA was feeding the wrong numbers to the administration for political reasons. Dulles, who had concluded that the Air Force estimate had mistakenly relied on observations of mislabeled intermediate and not intercontinental missile test firings, refused to concede the point.

When Symington went public with his criticism, the administration found itself in a bind: it could not rebuff Symington's attacks without disclosing classified information, leaving only the weak argument that the administration was privy to military secrets and that it knew what it was doing. It was as though Khrushchev were writing the Democrats' political campaign themes.[26]

Compounding the bureaucratic bungling, in 1958 the Eisenhower administration implemented a change in the rules on the release of official estimates: henceforth military contractors, like RAND, would no longer receive official government figures. That meant that the last official estimate RAND obtained contained the highly inflated figures put out by the Air Force of 500 Soviet ICBMs by 1961. Critics such as Symington—with their eye on the White House—charged the Eisenhower administration of deliberately ignoring the Soviet threat. When, by 1959, the administration apparently refused to do anything about the supposedly growing Soviet menace in spite of the Sputnik program and the missile gap, RAND analysts began to go outside their usual policy circles to, as Wohlstetter phrased it, prevent America from resuming its "pre-Sputnik sleep."

The disarray inspired Wohlstetter to compose a carefully written warning against willfully blind politicians leading to possible holocausts, which he titled "The Delicate Balance of Terror." The article, published in 1959 by the influential magazine *Foreign Affairs,* was a historic event, comparable to the famous "X" memorandum from Moscow in which Ambassador George F. Kennan conceived of containment.[27] More than any other writing up to that time, Wohlstetter's essay prompted a reexamination of American-Soviet relations, laying the groundwork for the constant escalation of the nuclear race that would result in each side having enough armaments to destroy the world thousands of times.

In his article, Wohlstetter decried the Eisenhower administration's belief in a so-called automatic balance of terror, which in its simplest terms meant that the mere existence of nuclear weapons in the hands of the United States and the Soviets was enough to keep the world secure, since any nation that tried to use them would be committing suicide. This, he insisted, was wrong and highly dangerous.

Wohlstetter painted himself an errant knight, lance in hand, tilting against the powers that be. He labored to convince the world that it was not a mere windmill he attacked but a ferocious giant that needed to be vanquished for the survival of Western civilization. His warning echoed the fundamental arguments of his basing study:

> We must expect [in the 1960s] *a vast increase in the weight of attack which the Soviets can deliver with little warning, and the growth of a significant Russian capability for an essentially warningless attack. As a result, strategic deterrence, while feasible, will be extremely difficult to achieve, and at critical junctures we may not have the power to deter attack* (italics in original).[28]

To those who believed that a thermonuclear war would mean extinction for the aggressor as well as the attacked, Wohlstetter reminded them of the Russian example during World War II:

> Russian fatalities in World War II were more than 20,000,000. Yet Russia recovered extremely well from this catastrophe. There are several quite plausible circumstances in the future when the Russians might be confident of being able to limit

damage to considerably *less* than this number—if they make sensible strategic choices and we do not. On the other hand, the risks of *not* striking might at some juncture appear very great to the Soviets, involving, for example, disastrous defeat in peripheral war, loss of key satellites with danger of revolt spreading—possibly to Russia itself—or fear of an attack by ourselves. Then, striking first, by surprise, would be the sensible choice for them, and from their point of view the smaller risk.[29]

Wohlstetter framed his arguments on quantitative grounds. Not for him the wide sweep of historical analogies and comparisons of Brodie or the ecstatic visions of postnuclear survival of Kahn. Wohlstetter advocated a new version of deterrence, elaborating on the concept of second-strike capability that he had originated at RAND—namely, that what truly counts in a nuclear exchange is the capacity to survive with enough firepower left to retaliate.

In the last year or two there has been a growing awareness of the importance of the distinction between a "strike-first" and a "strike-second" capability, but little, if any, recognition of the implications of this distinction for the balance of terror theory . . . Such assumptions suggest that Soviet leaders will be rather bumbling or, better, cooperative. These are best called "Western-preferred Soviet strategies." However attractive it may be for us to narrow Soviet alternatives to these, they would be low in the order of preference of any reasonable Russian planning war.[30]

While advocating the use of ICBMs, Wohlstetter considered the parallel spread of intermediate range ballistic missiles (IRBMs) a fool's errand; they served as propaganda, but did nothing to increase security in the Western alliance. The main reason for that uselessness was their closeness to the Soviet Union and the ease with which they could be attacked, not to mention the coordination needed before pushing their launch button. (Unlike manned bombers, which could follow a fail-safe policy, a missile, once launched, was hard to stop, much less to recall.)

Wohlstetter also warned that the Soviets saw IRBMs as a form of encirclement, and a preparation for a first strike by the United States—which, we must remember, had not been ruled out by Eisenhower. This observation is corroborated by the story of Khrushchev staring out of his vacation home in Crimea at the Black Sea and asking his guests what they saw. When they answered, "Nothing," he replied, "I see U.S. missiles in Turkey aimed at my dacha."[31]

In his article, Wohlstetter advocated the development of nonnuclear armaments and modern technology, which would render a nuclear response unnecessary, anticipating the Revolution in Military Affairs (RMA) implemented in the 1990s:

> I would conjecture that if one considers the implications of modern surface-to-air missiles in the context of conventional war in which the attacker has to make many sorties and expose himself to recurring attrition, these weapons would look ever so much better than they do when faced, for example, with the heroic task of knocking down 99 percent of a wave of, say one thousand nuclear bombers. Similarly, advances in anti-tank wire-guided missiles and anti-personnel fragmentation weapons, which have been mentioned from time to time in the press, might help redress the current balance of East-West conventional forces without, however, removing the necessity for spending more money in procurement as well as research and development.[32]

Wohlstetter also pointed the way to the development of Star Wars, the antimissile defense system advocated by the Reagan administration in the 1980s and pursued by successive Republican administrations:

> If we could obtain a leakproof air defense, many things would change. A limited war capability, for example, would be unimportant. Massive retaliation against even minor threats, since it exposed us to no danger, might be credible. Deterring attack would also not be very important.[33]

Wohlstetter's genius was to marshal numerical arguments and wed them to a broad and consistent, if extremely pessimistic—that is, "realistic"—view of history. He assumed that the people on the other side thought like RAND analysts; it was the mirror-imaging problem of intelligence agencies, the presumption that when the other side weighs the risks and possible benefits, it comes to the same rational conclusion as your side does. Wohlstetter was attributing to the Soviet leadership a level of monstrosity that had rarely been seen in history; outside of RAND and Pentagon contingency plans, no nation has ever *deliberately* sent twenty million of its people to their death in war for possible political gain.*

A point to consider is whether a society that is not controlled by a single ruler, as the Soviet Union was under Stalin or Germany under Hitler, is even capable of sacrificing millions of its citizens in this kind of venture. A purely quantitative analysis misses the historical fact that collective-leadership governments, like the Soviet Union's in 1959 under Khrushchev, no matter how authoritarian, cannot afford to take those chances as the leadership will quickly splinter into opposing factions. Only absolute rulers—or a nation under attack—may take such risks.

One might well counter that Japan, under a collective leadership,

---

* I am indebted to Daniel Ellsberg for this observation.

did stage just such a surprise attack as Wohlstetter envisioned. That argument is superficially plausible but fundamentally specious. Japan did not mean to strike a knockout blow or to annihilate the entire population of the United States (or even that of Hawaii) but only to disable the American Pacific fleet on the mistaken assumption that the United States would be incapable of retaliating in time to stop the Japanese consolidation of conquered territories in Southeast Asia.[34] Emperor Hirohito certainly did not anticipate his country's destruction because of the sneak attack on Pearl Harbor. One can only speculate what course Tojo's war cabinet might have chosen had it known the United States was prepared to use nuclear weapons in case of aggression.

Wohlstetter's was a self-fulfilling prophecy; whether proffered sincerely or not, his pessimistic worldview helped to create a world in which the worst was always possible. It would profit him for the next four decades in a variety of ways—through the commissioning of books and articles, government panel appointments, consulting work, and university positions. Yet perhaps someone like Wohlstetter was necessary to bring a modicum of urgency to what otherwise could have been a fatal case of Pollyannaism. If planners at the top levels of government do not thoroughly prepare for all eventualities, they are shirking their responsibilities. But on the other hand (and this business always requires more hands than Shiva), some historians have suggested[35] that the assumptions made by both sides eventually would have made the question of nuclear warfare collapse of its own weight had it not been for prophets of doom like Wohlstetter. Wohlstetter, of course, would have vigorously rejected that argument. From his point of view, it behooved someone with his knowledge to anticipate the worst eventuality, so that once ready for it, it might not happen at all. We must prepare for war, so that we might have peace, said the Roman emperor Augustus. It's an ancient argument, and Wohlstetter always feared the casus belli.

In the event, Wohlstetter's exhortations to prepare for catastrophe quickly became the rallying cry for a new generation of war planners and politicians. Lusting to break through the superannuated restraints of the Eisenhower administration, they would succeed beyond their greatest expectations—and bring the world to the brink of nuclear conflagration.

PART 3

8

A Delicate Dance

THE CALL to Albert Wohlstetter came from deep in the Kennedy campaign, from someone who knew that the internal political friction between RAND management and its top strategic analysts was grating raw. Frank Collbohm was always sticking up for the Air Force and the Eisenhower administration, while the coterie of experts that gathered around the Wohlstetters—brilliant economists, physicists, mathematicians like Alain Enthoven, Fred Iklé, Daniel Ellsberg—yearned for a new direction, a different way of thinking. So Wohlstetter was not at all surprised when the contact was made—by a graduate of both Wells and Smith, no less.

Deirdre Henderson, then twenty-five years old, was an aide to Jack Kennedy. Henry Kissinger, while director of the Defense Studies Program at Harvard, had recommended her to the senator's office. Though she had been a research assistant at first, Henderson's knowledge of defense and security policies quickly made her Kennedy's liaison to the Professors for Kennedy, a group of mostly young intellectuals who felt the country needed a new start. She was also the Kennedy campaign liaison with the so-called Brain Trusts of the Harvard and Boston area, working closely with Professor Archibald Cox—later to become a special federal prosecutor during Watergate—and with Theodore Sorenson, Kennedy's main speechwriter and consigliere. Henderson's job was to obtain information, position papers, and intellectual support for what would soon be called the New Frontier.[1] She had met Ellsberg while he was on leave from RAND at Harvard finishing his Ph.D. Ellsberg, in turn, had put her in touch with Wohlstetter.

Wohlstetter had already noticed that Kennedy had appropriated many of the issues he had brought up in "The Delicate Balance of Terror." Combining Wohlstetter's ideas with the apocalyptic warnings of columnist Joseph Alsop[2] and others, Kennedy seized on the supposed missile gap to jawbone the Eisenhower administration's national security policies—or lack thereof. Although Wohlstetter had disdained the idea of a missile gap, which he suspected did not exist, he was very pleased by the play his ideas were receiving in the Democratic Party.

For one thing, Wohlstetter was less than fond of the Republican candidate, Vice President Richard Nixon. He had been disgusted by Nixon's red-baiting Senate campaign against Helen Gahagan Douglas. Besides, Wohlstetter was as frustrated as the rest of his fellow RANDites with the general lassitude of the Republican administration. That was why, when Henderson showed up at his compound on Woodstock Road, he welcomed her as warmly as he knew how. They sat in his downstairs den, the giant Japanese symbol of prosperity, a red paper carp, hanging from the ceiling; when she asked whether he would be willing to advise the Kennedy campaign on national security matters, Wohlstetter replied in all sincerity that he would be delighted to do so.

Although Henderson kept wandering back to the issue of the missile gap, Wohlstetter did his best to steer her away from the subject, concentrating instead on what should be the real key security issues for a new administration. Not that he wanted to avoid altogether talk of a missile gap—after all, he recognized a good political line when he heard it—it was just that things were, well, more complicated than a partisan attack could ever be. He did promise to enlist the aid of others at RAND, thinking specifically of Harry Rowen, Charles Hitch, and Ellsberg, the sort of fellows who could be entrusted to keep a secret. However, it would have to be done very discreetly. RAND was still a creature of the Air Force, and Collbohm was an Eisenhower loyalist. Besides, Wohlstetter was already in hot water with Collbohm over Bernard Brodie.

To Wohlstetter, the controversy seemed so trivial it barely merited mention, but Brodie had been so incensed he had practically demanded an apology. To think it was all because of wine! Wohlstetter had been puzzled when Collbohm called him into his office to talk about a complaint Brodie had lodged. Wohlstetter never really got along with his superior, finding him sometimes less than rational. He would automatically become supercilious when confronting Collbohm, as if out of spite.

Collbohm showed Wohlstetter a letter from Brodie, complaining that visiting French dignitaries were neglecting Brodie's invitations to dinner. They preferred instead to frequent Wohlstetter's soirees because he served expensive wines and food. Brodie felt that he was missing out on important contacts and sources of information, and that his own contributions were being denigrated by Wohlstetter's dinner parties.

At first Wohlstetter thought Collbohm was joking. After all, Wohlstetter did not charge RAND for his food and wine, even though Vice President J. Richard Goldstein told him they were legitimate expenses and he should put in for reimbursement. Realizing the intensity that shone in Collbohm's eyes, Wohlstetter simply

replied, "Frank, I like wine. And as it happens, so do a lot of French-
men, especially French wine, and so I don't think that is the reason
they come to see me. But if so, I can't really help it. Why don't you
buy Bernard some better wine?"

Wohlstetter felt no need to reciprocate Brodie's ill will. He considered Brodie a sensible man who was writing for the public but
who was not at the center of things at RAND. The crux of RAND's
work was recommendations on policy, and there Brodie was so absent as to be nonexistent. Yet it was apparent to Wohlstetter that
from now on he would have to do something to divert Brodie's ire
or, at the very least, shelter himself from it. Perhaps the challenges
of a new administration might do the trick. Or maybe he could hand
Brodie the opportunity to write that book on nuclear strategy
Wohlstetter had been offered. Brodie would have to go to Europe to
do some research, and that would certainly get him out of Wohlstetter's hair for a while. In the meantime, Wohlstetter had more important things to think about—like his daughter's party.

IT WAS SUPPOSED to be a simple little pool party, but somehow,
like always, events had gotten out of hand in the Wohlstetter household. Joan had wanted to invite friends from Hollywood High, some
of the kids she took Spanish with. Most other fourteen-year-olds
did not have their own pools and she certainly could use some company—it wasn't that much fun to swim all by your lonesome on a
warm spring day.

But then Albert decided he wanted to show off the mosaic Joan
had made by the pool, near the Mondrian-like alternating colored
panels of fiberglass hiding the pool equipment and the changing
rooms. So he invited a few of *his* friends and added to the menu of
hot dogs, chips, and burgers some food more appropriate for adults,
such as canapés, terrines, and Sancerre. Of course they had to have
some grown-up music, too, and Joan again had to suffer through
Albert and Roberta doing the paso doble in the now emptied den

as a prelude to the entertainment, as though they were still in that dance troupe they belonged to when they were young.

Fortunately, Joan's parents were done with their fancy stepping before her guests arrived, and once the adults showed up with their single malt whiskeys, French wines, and Russian vodka, she was more or less left to her friends. Until the moment when Albert, glass in hand, made a toast to her artistic gifts and poured a small libation on her work to propitiate the gods of artistic inspiration. That was embarrassing, yet, like everything else about her dad, oddly endearing.

Joan would never forget all his letters from the many high-security places he visited in his travels, accompanied by wondrous illustrations, as though Ludwig Bemelmans, instead of drawing Madeline, had become a nuclear strategist. With him, she could always expect the unexpected. Still, that day she was surprised by the conversation her dad wound up having with one of her classmates, Richard Perle.

Richard had heard about her dad already, and when Albert went around introducing himself to her friends, Richard engaged him in a conversation about nuclear disarmament. Albert was so taken by the boy's inquisitiveness that he went to the den, got out an issue of *Foreign Affairs,* and gave him a copy of "The Delicate Balance of Terror," telling Richard he should read it if he really wanted to know about the country's military weakness. He would later tell acquaintances that the boy's questions made more sense than the ones all the so-called Pentagon experts had asked him.

"So what about Kennedy, Mr. Wohlstetter?" asked Richard.

Wohlstetter smiled and changed the topic.[3]

9

Whiz Kids Rule

ON THE NIGHT of January 17, 1961, in his farewell address before handing over power to the Democrats, President Eisenhower gave what would become the defining speech of his administration—the warning against the military-industrial complex.

Mortified by the way the Gaither Report had leaked, and how the so-called missile gap had grown to be a decisive presidential campaign issue, Eisenhower warned of an ominous threat to American liberty:

> In the councils of government, we must guard against the acquisition of unwarranted influence, whether sought or unsought, by the military-industrial complex. The potential for the disastrous rise of misplaced power exists and will persist . . . only an alert and knowledgeable citizenry can com-

pel the proper meshing of the huge industrial and military machinery of defense with our peaceful methods and goals, so that security and liberty may prosper together.[1]

In the penultimate draft of his speech, Eisenhower had referred to the military-industrial-*congressional* complex, but reportedly crossed out the last portion in deference to legislators. After all, they might be the last guarantors of traditional America, one where there was "no armaments industry [where] American makers of plowshares could, with time and as required, make swords as well."

However, as Eisenhower noted at the end of his speech, he was handing over power in three days to a successor—and that man, John Fitzgerald Kennedy, was in essence a product of the military-industrial complex. In fact, it could be argued that given the slim margin of his victory over Nixon, Kennedy owed his presidency to his RAND advisers and the issue of the missile gap. Throughout his campaign, Kennedy harped on America's weak defenses by using information provided by RAND researchers and wise men, whereas Nixon, constrained by government secrecy, could never directly challenge Kennedy's assertions.

With Kennedy's accession to the White House in 1961, RAND was finally able to break the chains that bound it to the Air Force. The Democratic Party, with its muscular liberalism, signified a radical departure from the flabby Republican circles that called the shots with Eisenhower and kept RAND under their thumb. Moreover, Kennedy's deliberate use of the nation's intellectual elite to provide gravitas to the country's youngest president constituted an open invitation for the Santa Monica mandarins to seek their fortune back East. Therefore, it came as no surprise that when Charles Hitch met the new secretary of defense, Robert McNamara, it was love at first sight.[2]

McNamara, with his fierce grasp of graphs, charts, and equations, whose very appearance—his rimless glasses, dark suits, and slicked-back hair—seemed more hawkish than owlish, was the perfect match for the soft-spoken but supremely self-assured vicar of calculations from RAND. They both firmly believed that numbers could save the world.

McNamara was confident in his ability to reshape the recalcitrant military, dominated by parochial political interests. Traditionally Congress decided on a certain amount to spend on defense, and the different branches of the military then fought among themselves as to who would get the lion's share. Once the pot was divided, the branches by and large were free to spend the money on whatever projects they saw fit. Even seasoned Pentagon observers such as Bernard Brodie seemed used to it, only wishing wistfully that there was a way to put an end to the custom.

That old way of thinking was about to meet a swift death. Not only did McNamara have specific marching orders from President Kennedy to reform the Pentagon but he came to the job with a history of whipping large organizations into shape, making them leaner and more efficient. At forty-four, McNamara was the youngest president ever of Ford Motors, having been promoted to the post months before the 1960 election. A liberal intellectual from northern California, a member of the NAACP and the ACLU, McNamara worked in Detroit but lived in the nearby college town of Ann Arbor, Michigan. He thought nothing of coming home after twelve-hour days to help his wife host salons with the intellectual elite then to finally bed down with a nice fat tome on the latest political issue.

World War II irrevocably altered McNamara's course in life, as it did for so many others of his generation. Volunteering for the Army, he joined the Statistical Control Office of the Army Air Corps, where as part of a Harvard Business School group he worked on applying new management theories to increase efficiency in warfare. Among his many accomplishments, he helped General Curtis LeMay increase the flying hours of his 21st Bomber Command in Japan by 30 percent.

After the war, McNamara and nine other junior officers formed a group to offer their management expertise to businesses needing new techniques. Henry Ford II, who had recently inherited control of the automotive giant from his grandfather, hired the group. McNamara and his band of experts became known as the Whiz Kids, as they mercilessly cut, slashed, and trimmed, bringing the creaking Detroit giant into the modern era while increasing profits, efficiency, and popularity. McNamara even helped design Ford's first compact car, the Falcon. He was the manager who could do no wrong.

Following Kennedy's election, liberal economist John Kenneth Galbraith suggested McNamara for the top job at the Pentagon. Kennedy, who wanted to centralize power and modernize the armed forces, had the efficiency wizard over for an interview. At the president-elect's home in Georgetown, McNamara proved reluctant, telling Kennedy flat out, "I am not qualified."

"Who is?" replied Kennedy, ironically.

When McNamara insisted that he had not kept up with military affairs since the war and that he wasn't sure he knew how to be a secretary of defense, Kennedy replied that there wasn't a school for presidents either, but after meeting President Eisenhower, he knew he was up to the job.[3] At last, McNamara accepted, but on condition that he be exempt from the usual Washington folderol social life, and that Kennedy allow him to pick his own staff. When Kennedy gave his consent, McNamara hunkered down in a suite at the Shoreham Hotel for a week with hundreds of index cards to select his crew.[4]

Galbraith again intervened, suggesting that McNamara interview Hitch. McNamara did not know the RAND analyst, but after reading the book Hitch coauthored with Roland N. McKean, *Economics of Defense in the Nuclear Age*,[5] he was hooked. In the book, Hitch compiled a series of ideas that had long been discussed at RAND, in essence advocating the same kind of statistical analysis, price comparison, and program-based management control through rational decision-making systems that McNamara had utilized to rework the Ford Motor Company. That is to say, McNamara had been a practitioner of RAND's systems analysis even before he knew the existence of the term, much less the discipline. When McNamara offered him a position, Hitch too was initially reluctant to accept, but was likewise persuaded with the promise that he could select his own underlings to implement his ideas. Named assistant secretary of defense, comptroller, he immediately called on former RAND analyst Alain Enthoven to head the newly created Office of Systems Analysis as deputy assistant secretary of defense.[6]

A serious-minded Roman Catholic who treated the subject of national defense with the utmost devotion, Enthoven was one of Wohlstetter's acolytes, having worked with him on a RAND follow-up study to R-290 on SAC vulnerability.[7] Enthoven had joined RAND in the late 1950s but soon left the think tank for the Pentagon out of frustration with RAND management.

> I have lost patience with the whole climate that fosters the treatment of subjects of the utmost gravity and complexity in a slick 45-minute briefing . . . My favorite caricature of RAND has Herman Kahn finishing a two-hour briefing full of important and exciting new ideas only to have one prominent member of the management say, "Why is your fly open?" while another says, "You'll have to cut it to a half hour."[8]

Enthoven had been working at the Pentagon's research and engineering directorate for a year when he joined up with Hitch. They saw their mandate as nothing less than to reshape the way the entire Pentagon conducted its business—it was to be a revolution, shaped by the doctrines developed at RAND. Who better to implement it than the people who had originated systems analysis?

Within days Hitch and Enthoven asked dozens of people at Santa Monica to come join them, specifically to help define the Defense

Department budget and to analyze the implications of its decisions over the next five years. In spite of misgivings that this could be to the future detriment of the Air Force (RAND was still receiving 90 percent of its research program budget from Air Force contracts), Frank Collbohm went along with the plan. Fourteen consultants from the Economics Division alone, along with ten new hires loaned to the Office of the Secretary of Defense, soon set up shop at the RAND office in Bethesda, Maryland.[9]

Simultaneously with Hitch's reworking of the Pentagon budget, another member of Wohlstetter's elite circle, Henry Rowen, was joining the upper ranks of the Kennedy administration. Rowen had taken a year off to work on a book at Harvard. While there, he met Paul Nitze, whom Kennedy had named assistant secretary of defense for international security affairs as a reward for running his national security staff during the presidential campaign. Finding that Rowen's aggressive views on national defense matched his own, Nitze appointed him as his deputy in the area of European security.[10]

Strangely enough, Wohlstetter never accepted any official position with the Kennedy administration, although he was in constant contact with the RAND strategists, especially Rowen, who often solicited his advice. Sadly, the one RAND analyst who would have dearly loved to work for the New Frontier, Brodie, was never tapped. He waited for the call that never came, then, in anger, turned his sights on the man he was certain had orchestrated his exclusion from the magic circle: Wohlstetter.[11]

Meanwhile, dozens of other RAND analysts were "loaned" for different periods of time to the Department of Defense—among them Ellsberg, who would go on to work as special assistant for Nitze's successor, John McNaughton, in 1962.

Ellsberg's journey of political transformation parallels, in reverse, the one undertaken by the neoconservatives. Like Brodie, Kahn, Wohlstetter, and so many influential strategists at RAND, Ellsberg was a secular Jew—his parents were devout converts to Christian

Science. A brilliant and original economics professor at Harvard, he wrote several seminal articles on decision theory, the abstract analysis of making decisions under uncertainty; he was also a first lieutenant in the marines, who enjoyed the service so much that for a while he contemplated a professional military career. He thought of himself as a Truman Democrat: a social liberal on domestic matters and an aggressive anti-Communist warrior abroad.[12]

Loquacious, temperamental, and endlessly inquisitive—as well as helplessly digressive—Ellsberg married at age twenty and had two children before he was twenty-five. In 1958, following Wohlstetter's recommendation, he was hired at RAND as an economic theorist, more or less at the same time as Enthoven. Like his future Pentagon colleague, the twenty-seven-year-old Ellsberg was so convinced of the possibility of a nuclear war that he declined to enroll in RAND's pension plan, seeing no future in it.[13]

Ellsberg's dedication to the RAND ethos did not go unperceived. Hailed as a brilliant and innovative thinker, he fell in with the nuclear strategists that gravitated around Wohlstetter, whom he came to see as a father figure. Ellsberg also became fast friends with Rowen, Wohlstetter's collaborator on the basing study. Ellsberg was the golden boy of RAND management, which was grooming him as the best hope for the future of the think tank.

Under McNamara, RANDites had full access to all corridors of power in the Pentagon, without the constraints imposed by Collbohm or a suspicious Air Force. In the last few months of the Eisenhower era, when Collbohm realized that Wohlstetter's circle was aiding the Kennedy campaign, he had reorganized the departmental structure within RAND, creating new divisions and transferring the old power to hire, fire, and budget from division heads to a management council that was mostly beholden to him. This had clipped the wings of the strategic analysts around Wohlstetter, yet now, as McNamara's emissaries, they actually had authority over the very same Air Force people who had lorded over them previously. They wasted no time in exercising their power, using the guise of objective rational analysis to force their will on the Pentagon.

Helped by David Bell, Kennedy's budget director, Hitch and Enthoven chopped, sliced, cut, and rearranged the Defense Department, taking particular aim at the Air Force. Within months, hallowed LeMay projects such as new B-58 and B-70 bombers and various missile systems had been scrapped by the young, crew-cutted, sack-suit-wearing, pipe-smoking intellectuals who came to be known as "McNamara's Whiz Kids," in homage to the group that reshaped Ford. To many of these RANDites, LeMay and SAC were little short of hidebound Neanderthals, unwilling to adapt to the new times, which demanded flexibility, accountability, and thrift. To add insult to injury, the RAND people favored the Navy's Polaris submarine program, and advocated augmenting the Army's conventional forces. The Whiz Kids knew they were almost universally despised by the Air Force, but they didn't care, even joking when flying to Army headquarters at Fort Leavenworth about how LeMay might well blow their plane out of the sky if he knew how many of them were together in one place.[14]

It wasn't just the cuts that hurt; it was the Whiz Kids' confrontational style that got under the skin of the Air Force brass. At one point in a heated discussion about nuclear war, Enthoven bellowed, "General, I have fought as many nuclear wars as you have." While getting an unwanted lecture from another Air Force general, Enthoven flatly stated, "General, I don't think you understand. I didn't come for a briefing; I came to tell you what we have decided."[15]

Financially, RAND profited from the takeover of the Pentagon by the Whiz Kids. The Office of the Secretary of Defense cut a number of new, lucrative contracts with RAND, and the Air Force, pressured by McNamara, expanded its outstanding contract with RAND. By the summer of 1961, Collbohm's Management Committee—having seen the light of McNamara's interests—was requesting ideas from the corporation's departments on new projects to submit for funding to the Office of the Secretary of Defense, including such previously disdained arenas as limited war studies, research on arms control, and political area studies (particularly those focusing on Africa and Latin America—civil defense and Cold War studies).[16]

All the same, the rancor against RAND ran deep and was long-lived. Twelve years later, Air Force general Bernard Schriever would still complain about McNamara's Whiz Kids:

> His staff would go charging around all over the country. They would go into our command, talk to people in the command at all levels, go into industry in the various companies, talk to people in these companies at all levels. Most of the time we didn't even know what they were wondering about. In no circumstances were we ever provided with copies of their reports when they came in, so we didn't even know what the hell was going on up there.[17]

The Air Force considered RAND's successful incursion into the Pentagon nothing less than treason. LeMay, now head of the Joint Chiefs of Staff, was furious that the outfit he had nurtured and protected was turning against its parent. He despised McNamara and the Whiz Kids, and would go around telling his friends in the Air Force, "I ask you: would things be much worse if Khrushchev were Secretary of Defense?"[18]

In response to this RANDite attack on their heretofore sacrosanct bailiwick, military leaders created their own set of systems analysts to come up with figures to justify the weapons they wanted. They learned the language of "cost effectiveness" and "plausible scenarios," as well as the mechanics of inquisitive "murder boards," the infamous presentations of RAND staff members where projects were argued and dissected to exhaustion and often ridicule. Initially the military's attempt to ape the RAND methodology was shaky, the calculations laughable, but eventually officers learned how to game the mechanics of RAND's systems analysis—how to twist a premise and apply a set of constrained parameters that, when properly joined to impressive graphs, calculations, and equations, arrived at the desired preordained conclusion.

RAND stopped being the only think tank in an advisory role to the military. The Army came up with its own proprietary think tank, and so did the Navy; even the Air Force gestated a more closely held outfit, the Aerospace Corporation. None of these, however, had the clout or reputation of RAND, mostly because few of them were involved in the same long-range, what-if kind of planning that had made RAND's reputation.

All the same, RAND was lumped in with other think tanks in a series of Air Force–inspired articles in general publications like *Life, Look,* and the *Saturday Evening Post.* They popularized the concept of "defense intellectuals," people who believed "modern war could be settled on a chessboard in an ivy-covered Great Hall"— that is to say, RANDites.[19] Critics chastised them as feckless academics accountable to no one, imposing their elitist ideology on an unsuspecting public. Think tanks became a target of congressional investigations and, ultimately, Congress moved to reduce the Pentagon's think tank budget, including RAND's.[20]

Arguing that acceptance of non–Air Force projects diluted the attention and resources of RAND, Secretary of the Air Force Eugene Zuckert then attempted to put conditions on the kind of "outside" work he would allow RAND to conduct, limiting it to 20 percent of the total. This demand divided the group within RAND still beholden to the Air Force after the eventual departure of the Whiz Kids. The situation was exacerbated when the Air Force threatened to cut off all funds if RAND failed to do its bidding. At that point even Collbohm rebelled, and in a heated exchange he thundered to

Air Force general counsel Max Golden that RAND was ready to cancel all its contracts with the Air Force and close up shop altogether if it insisted on those conditions. Collbohm was so worked up that three times during the talk he got up to leave. Finally Golden, realizing his bluff had been called, told Collbohm, "Unlike RAND, we cannot afford the luxury of jeopardizing the national interest and, with a gun to my head, I am authorized to go along with the terms of the old negotiation."[21]

The Air Force's counterrevolution had failed. Not only would RAND analysts continue to reshape the Pentagon, making it leaner and more efficient, but eventually RAND's language of systems analysis and program budgeting would become the lingua franca of the entire government. Most important, its theories on war making, deterrence, and relations between the West and the Communist camp would become enshrined doctrine during the Kennedy administration and change the way America viewed the world.

10

The Art of Science

In the spring of 1960, the young engineer Paul Baran learned firsthand the horrific implications of his new assignment at RAND. If he failed, if he miscalculated, the United States might well have no future at all. To wit: if the Soviets unleashed a surprise nuclear attack on the United States, how could Strategic Air Command authorize a counterstrike if all its communications systems were blitzed? To use Albert Wohlstetter's terminology, how would the United States have a viable second-strike capability if it did not have a way to communicate with the remaining missiles?

It was this kind of problem that had prompted Baran, once a design engineer for Minuteman missiles at Hughes Aircraft in El Segundo, to join the pencil pushers at RAND up the coast in Santa Monica. He was deeply concerned.[1] Like so many at RAND in the late 1950s and early 1960s, he was convinced that the future of civilization might well depend on his calculations. As Wohlstetter had pointed out, a small group of Soviet bombers on a sneak mission could conceivably wreak severe damage on the nation's nuclear arsenal. Not only that, the effects of nuclear explosions in the ionosphere would knock out all long-range, high-frequency radio communications. If one also assumed that the attack destroyed the central switching nodes of the telephone system, there would be no workable command, control, and communications system left to get American missiles in the air.

A native of Poland who had immigrated with his parents to America when he was two years old, Baran had been deeply affected by the unpredictability of history, how everyone's life was affected by the weakness or strength of national defense.[2] Baran's response to the missile communication challenge ultimately would point the way to what we know today as the Internet.

Baran had long been intrigued by studies of so-called neural nets—that is, decentralized patterns of thought in the human brain. This complex network of neural interconnections enables an extraordinarily flexible response to physical challenges. If one system is under stress, then another comes to the rescue. When the command to lift a hand, for example, cannot be routed through the normal nerve pathway, the brain reroutes the command through a parallel, analogous channel temporarily hijacked for that purpose.[3]

Taking as his cue an observation by Frank Collbohm on the abundance of low-frequency AM radio stations around the country, Baran devised an ingenious plan that would get American ICBMs in the air by utilizing AM radio antennas as the alternative nerve centers, or control nodes, for communications throughout the country. In the event of an emergency, SAC would be able to commandeer the antennas to transmit commands to the missiles. The Air Force quickly adopted Baran's recommendations and established just such a network of dual-use antennas that transmitted secret attack signals, which were carried from node to node and could not be heard over the radio.

Although gratified by his success, Baran wanted to improve upon it; he wanted the system to go beyond simple "go, no-go" orders. To do that, given the noise produced by inefficient analog circuits, he would have to find a way to encode the messages digitally.

The early 1960s was an era in which most people barely knew the meaning of the word "digital," much less used it in daily conversation. All radio and telephone signals were analog—that is, they sent data via continuous variable electric currents and voltages, creating the need for central switching nodes in the telephone system, which at the time, in most places in the country, was owned by the monopoly AT&T.* Those nodes received a signal, amplified it, then sent it on its way to the ultimate recipient. The problem was that the farther away the recipient was from the sender, the greater the distortion (or noise) as the signal was repeatedly amplified by successive nodes—just as a movie on a videocassette copied from a copy of a copy ends up barely watchable and blurry. (This explains, for those with long memories, the echolike effect of telephone calls from overseas.)

Digital, by contrast, is binary, which means that all the information is sent out in long sequences of positives and negatives, or ones and zeros, as in a computer. Noise and distortion from distance have little effect on the data, making high-quality transmission possible.[4] A digital signal could also be rerouted, if need be, through redundant circuits, without the need for amplification and consequent distortion.

Baran's brilliant breakthrough was not just to digitize the messages but also to divide them into "packets." These were discrete bundles of data bearing information about the recipient, origin, length of time it had been in the network, and the sequence order

---

* Coincidentally, Wohlstetter's brother, Charles, became a multimillionaire by buying up small, local telephone systems and stringing them together into large, regional ones. Eventually he created a national behemoth called Continental Telephone.

in which the packets were reconstituted to make a comprehensible whole.[5] Each packet contained its own routing information; like a DNA molecule, each replicated itself correctly whenever there was a transmission error. The packets automatically searched for the most convenient pathways and automatically reconfigured once the message reached its destination.

No longer would there be need for a node or a switching station or even a direct phone line. If direct communications between Washington and the missile silos in Wichita were destroyed, the packets would search out whatever phone line was available, from the United States to Australia to China to Hawaii to Canada to Wichita, all in the fraction of a second that it would take for the electrical signal to be transmitted. The whole world, then, would be like a brain and the telephone wires the central nervous system—the neural net.

Baran tried to convince AT&T of the viability of his idea. The phone company told Baran, however, that even if his digital system could be built, AT&T would not create something that would be its own worst competitor.[6] Instead, the creation of a worldwide packet switching system fell to the Air Force, and then to the Defense Department, with the Pentagon's Advanced Research Projects Agency (ARPA) devising the ARPANET to link data banks and scientists in 1966. Ironically, ARPANET adopted the architecture developed by British scientist Donald Davies, who had independently come up with his own version of the network. Over the years, ARPANET would shed its military coloration and become the Internet we now know.

BARAN WAS the victim of ill timing. He had come up with a digital system before the world was ready to go binary. It was not the first or the last occasion in which RAND would find itself in the vanguard of scientific innovation, all for the sake of national security.

In the early 1950s, John Williams traveled to the East Coast to convince IBM it should build RAND a computer to help with the overwhelming amount of calculations needed for its Air Force projects. Calculators at that time were incapable of handling the myriad variations of a given exercise in RAND's newly invented systems analysis. For instance, when Edward Paxson was given the job of designing the "best" bomber for an attack on the Soviet Union, he had to take into account the performance of the planes, the expected losses, target coverage, logistics, and auxiliary needs such as protective fighters, as well as the phasing of the funds for research, procurement, and operations. The interrelation of these variables involved massive computation.[7] IBM refused to design a computer to handle all these requirements, so RAND engineers opted to build their own.

RANDites dubbed their machine the JOHNNIAC, after the Princeton Institute for Advanced Study machines—which included the ILLIAC, SILLIAC, WEIZAC, MANIAC—as well as in honor of a RAND consultant, mathematician John von Neumann. Renowned computer wizard Willis Ware was the JOHNNIAC's hardware designer. For years after its creation, only about ten computers in the country could match the JOHNNIAC's capacities. The machine contained a number of groundbreaking features, including punch-card input and output devices; it was also configured to give easy access to its eighty vacuum tubes for servicing. The elementary computers of the time could not operate for more than a few hours without interruptions; to keep its moving parts cool and functional, RAND engineers kept the basement room where the JOHNNIAC was stored at a constant fifty-five degrees Fahrenheit. Sardonic researchers quickly dubbed the machine the Pneumoniac. Over the years engineers continually improved the JOHNNIAC, exchanging its storage tubes for the first commercially produced magnetic core memory, coupling it to 140 column-wide high-speed impact printers, and putting in a swapping drum to support multiple users in what amounted to one of the first online time-sharing systems.[8]

One of the seminal uses of the JOHNNIAC at RAND was in the development of computer software for linear programming. This refers to the calculations needed to find the optimum value for a multivariable function governed by a system of linear equations. For instance, given a set of requirements for a soldier's diet—such as number of calories, proteins, and vitamins, and within the range of foods available at a particular time and place, and within a particular budget—how do you arrive at the best result? In the late 1940s, RAND's George Dantzig developed what he called the "simplex method" to arrive at such optimum result. He conceived of expressing the set of all possible solutions as a polyhedron, examining each vector until it became clear which worked best. The simplex method, when coupled with the JOHNNIAC's computing power, enabled RAND researchers to solve quickly and efficiently a variety of problems in military procurement, industrial processes, and management planning.

The JOHNNIAC, however, was not advanced enough to help in the formulation of what would be RAND's bestselling publication, *A Million Random Digits with 100,000 Normal Deviates*.[9] The book was, as its title equivocally states, a compilation of numbers chosen by a fancy electronic roulette wheel rigged up by RAND engineers. This sort of chance numeration was crucial for RAND studies on probability. In fact, a nuclear submarine commander kept a copy of the book with him to chart courses during evasion maneuvers. The title was odd enough that reportedly it caused the New York Public Library to file the book in its psychology section. *A Million Random Digits* went through three printings by 1971 and was reprinted again for our age of anxiety in 2001.

RAND's calculation ability proved invaluable for the infrared detection of Soviet rockets, as well as for what was arguably RAND's greatest known—which is to say, declassified—contribution to American national security (besides the work of Wohlstetter): the development of the ICBM as a weapon of war by RAND physicist Bruno Augenstein.

Williams hired Augenstein away from Purdue University in 1949 to work on the hydrogen bomb. At RAND, Augenstein studied the results of the detonation of the first Soviet hydrogen bomb and discovered that Russian scientists were using lithium as fissile material. This allowed the Soviet bomb to be much lighter in weight than the American weapon; Augenstein then came up with the idea of packing several of these lighter hydrogen bombs onto a missile head. Although the intercontinental missiles of the early 1950s were not accurate enough to serve much military purpose when delivering ordinary atomic bombs, their lack of precision was almost immaterial when the warhead packed a series of deadlier hydrogen bombs, with a much wider radius of destruction.

In 1954, Augenstein made his proposal in a memorandum that is widely considered one of the most important documents on missiles of the time. He also briefed a Department of Defense committee chaired by von Neumann, already a RAND consultant. Based on Augenstein's numbers and von Neumann's forceful advocacy, the Air Force implemented Augenstein's recommendations.[10]

In the wake of Augenstein's presentation, the Department of Defense asked RAND to conduct the systems engineering on the project. Knowing this would change RAND from a think tank to an applied science outfit, Collbohm turned down the job. The work instead was carried out by an upstart company called Ramo-Wooldridge.[11] In retrospect, this constituted a momentous decision, for RAND thereby passed up the opportunity to become an engineering and aerospace giant, such as Ramo-Wooldridge became under the name TRW. For Collbohm and RAND, the life of the mind was too intoxicating to give up for mere profit—an odd choice for an organization that would rewrite history through the twin prisms of self-interest and the dollar sign.

Within the organization, Augenstein's success represented the acme of importance of the Physics Department to RAND's internal dynamics. The highly classified nature of the work, and its limited income potential for continued government sponsorship, would soon pressure RAND to develop other fields that could create new sources of revenue. For a while, the exploration of outer space promised to be the solution. RAND's affinity for rocketry was already manifest at the very birth of the think tank, as seen in its first project, the "Preliminary Design of an Experimental World-Circling Spaceship," which took the notion of space travel out of the realm of fantasy. However, it wasn't until after *Sputnik I,* more than ten years later, that RAND scientists got the green light to fully develop its ideas about space.

In September 1954, the Science Advisory Committee of the Office of Defense Mobilization, prodded by the findings of Wohlstetter's basing study, had begun studying the possibility of a surprise Soviet attack for the Eisenhower administration. James Killian, president of the Massachusetts Institute of Technology and confidant of RAND director Collbohm, headed the committee. His right-hand man was Edwin Land, president of the Polaroid film and camera company. A trim, dark-haired man whose almond-shaped eyes never quite masked a certain melancholy, Land was called both a genius and a showman. He invented polarizing film and Polaroid instant film, becoming vastly wealthy in the process. He was also intimately involved in government-sponsored scientific research. Killian had named him chairman of the committee's Technological Capabilities Panel, which focused on the problem of strategic intelligence.[12] He drafted most of the Killian committee's report, "Meeting the Threat of Surprise Attack," which warned Eisenhower,

We must find ways to increase the number of hard facts upon which our intelligence estimates are based, to provide better strategic warning, to minimize surprise in the kind of attack, and to reduce the danger of gross overestimation or gross underestimation of the threat. To this end, we recommend adoption of a vigorous program for the extensive use of the most advanced knowledge in science and technology.[13]

A greatly impressed President Eisenhower authorized further exploration of means to obtain more intelligence on the Soviet threat.[14]

Already, in a highly classified project for SAC in the early 1950s, RAND researchers had come up with the notion of sending hundreds of unmanned hot air balloons to spy on the Soviet Union. This was in response to a 1949 U.S. Navy effort, code-named MOBY DICK, which had sent a number of observation balloons flying over the USSR. Ever in competition with its sister branch, the Air Force had commissioned RAND to set up its own larger secret spy-balloon operation. RAND scientists originated Project GOPHER, which launched more than 500 high-altitude balloons laden with cameras from Turkey and sites in Western Europe, hoping air currents would send them into Soviet territory. The plan called for large cargo planes called C-119 Flying Boxcars to snatch the balloons with their precious spy cameras in midair. Astoundingly, it worked. Forty of them were, in fact, brought back; their pictures covered about two million square miles of Soviet territory.[15]

In 1952, when the Soviets found the remnants of an American spy camera in their territory, most Project GOPHER operations were called off. But not before possibly—and inadvertently—triggering a nationwide mania. Some historians speculate that the widespread reports of UFOs in the Southwest in the 1950s, particularly near Air Force bases in Nevada, were just random observations of balloon tests over the desert. Unfortunately, this theory has never been corroborated, as many of the details of those experimental flights are still classified.

The termination of Project GOPHER prompted the Eisenhower administration to order modified bombers to carry out reconnaissance overflights of the Soviet Union; however, a number of these flights were shot down in incidents that came close to provoking international crises. When the Killian report came out, the Air Force decided to try another tack. This time the balloons would fly at greater altitudes, higher than 70,000 feet, on the fringes of outer space. They would drift over the Soviet Union and be recovered somewhere in Japan or Alaska. The Air Force dubbed the project GENETRIX. SAC teams, along with RAND researchers, launched the balloons from bases in West Germany, Scotland, Turkey, and Norway.

To forfend any possible complaints from the Soviets lest the spy balloons be captured again, the Eisenhower administration concocted a cover story: the balloons were to chart jet streams as part of the survey project called the International Geophysical Year.[16] Meanwhile, Eisenhower secretly approved two convergent plans: development of the high-altitude U-2 spy plane as well as a RAND design for a nuclear-powered reconnaissance satellite.

To give these efforts further cover, President Eisenhower announced what came to be called the Open Skies Doctrine at a summit conference in Geneva with Soviet premier Nikita Khrushchev on July 21, 1955. Eisenhower stated that the "absence of trust" between the superpowers and the presence of "terrible weapons" provoked fears of a surprise attack. He proposed facilities for aerial photography of the other country, as well as mutually supervised reconnaissance overflights to allay those fears.

Before the day had ended, though, Khrushchev refused Eisenhower's Open Skies Doctrine, viewing it as an intrusion of his country's airspace. As he told the president in a conversation in a corridor, "This is completely unacceptable to us, because this is inspection without disarmament."[17] Undaunted, on his return to the United States Eisenhower announced plans for "small, unmanned Earth circling satellites." In effect, Eisenhower had set Khrushchev up. By refusing to consent to the mutual overflights, Khrushchev had inadvertently given the United States the excuse to establish the principle of "freedom of space," the notion that outer space belongs to all nations. Freedom of space became a cardinal principle of international law and would be incorporated in international treaties during the 1960s.

One of the "small, unmanned Earth circling satellites" that Eisenhower had in mind when he announced the Open Skies Doctrine in Geneva was the RAND proposal for a nuclear-powered space vehicle. Called Project Feedback, the unmanned satellite was designed to photograph the Earth's surface and beam its reconnaissance observations via a television camera. The satellite would deliver images to a resolution of 100 feet while operating 300 miles above the Earth.

Project Feedback was formally proposed by RAND on March 1, 1954, almost at the same time that a Defense Department study group on guided missiles informed the Air Force that ICBMs were technically feasible—and could be in operation within six years. By the end of 1954, the military had approved development, on parallel tracks, of the RAND satellite and the ICBMs.

The Air Force assigned the RAND design for a nuclear-powered satellite to Lockheed Aircraft, which labeled it the WS 117L.[18] It was a visionary project, yet those very innovative properties provoked skepticism about its viability. For one thing, the Air Force was still wary of proposals using nuclear power. Project Feedback was reminiscent of RAND's last project with just such an energy source, a nuclear-powered jet. The Air Force had declined to develop that aircraft since the amount of radiation emitted by the reactor would have proven fatal to any pilot.[19] With regard to the nuclear-powered satellite, an additional concern was its incorporation of a television camera; television technology was still in its infancy and could not be relied on for accuracy and secrecy of broadcasting. Photographic cameras would prove more accurate and reliable.

By late 1957, the WS 117L was missing its deadlines and encountering technical difficulties. Shocked by that year's *Sputnik* launch, and wanting to quickly resolve the problem of how to conduct reconnaissance over the Soviet Union, the Killian committee urged President Eisenhower to scratch the RAND nuclear satellite idea. In its place, he approved a new, covert system that combined aspects of both Project Feedback and of the balloons used earlier in the decade. Called CORONA, the project involved sending satellites into orbit on the back of missiles; it became the pioneer of all subsequent satellite reconnaissance programs.*

CORONA would still send a camera-laden observation satellite using an ICBM converted into a space launcher. However, instead of transmitting the images by television, as RAND had envisioned, the satellite would orbit the globe and eventually drop to earth, to be recovered like the GENETRIX balloons. The president's order specified that the CORONA project be directed by the Central Intelligence Agency—which at that point had been conducting successful U-2 reconnaissance overflights of the Soviet Union for close to two years. ARPA would execute the CIA's orders, with RAND scientists still supervising.

It was a perfect match of CIA secrecy, ARPA technological know-how, and RAND scientific inspiration. There was only one problem: the program literally could not get off the ground. Beginning in 1958, the first twelve CORONA missions—launched out of today's Vandenberg Air Force Base in central California—were dis-

---

* Legend had it the project was dubbed CORONA after a stumped aide looked down at his Smith Corona typewriter and came up with the name in a hurry.

mal failures. A short interval of one month between launches hardly gave project engineers enough time to correct problems before making another attempt. But the Eisenhower administration was under enormous pressure to determine once and for all the true tactical capabilities of the Soviet Union. The missile gap had become a political football, and even within the administration there were widely ranging estimates as to the Soviets' true strength.

The thirteenth CORONA mission, launched on August 10, 1960, was the first successful flight. It carried no film, however, only diagnostic instruments. The fourteenth CORONA mission crowned all the years of effort: it returned with sixteen pounds of film and more coverage of the Soviet Union than all prior U-2 flights combined. For the next twelve years, until its replacement by newer satellites, CORONA provided the backbone of American intelligence on Soviet designs, playing the equivalent of the Enigma intercepts of World War II.

CORONA images eventually improved to a resolution of six feet, allowing the United States to photograph practically every inch of the Soviet Union (and most countries of the world as well). It opened up new horizons for analysts, who before had to rely on outdated maps and secondhand information from unreliable agents on the ground. With CORONA, analysts discovered the location of Soviet cities they had only heard of before; they observed antiballistic missile placements, the deployment of forces along the Chinese border; the nuclear plants and streets and fields of the Soviet Union; even the amount of fruit hanging from a tree in a given year's crop.

During the major crises of the Cold War, CORONA gave the U.S. government a precise idea of the strength of the Soviet enemy. CORONA images also covered the Six-Day War between Israel and the Arab nations, the Soviet invasion of Czechoslovakia, and even the remains of the Gulag Archipelago. As President Johnson would say, "We've spent 35 to 40 billion dollars on the space program.

And if nothing else had come out of it except for the knowledge we've gained from space photographs, it would be worth ten times what the whole program has cost."[20]

RAND's participation in the space program went beyond CORONA; RAND also played a decisive part in the creation of the National Aeronautics Space Agency (NASA) by developing a new system for estimating development costs that aided enormously in the preparation of budgets.

In the early 1950s, when the Air Force assigned RAND to conduct studies on initial versions of the ICBMs, as well as jet fighters and jet bombers, there were no quick methods for estimating nonrecurring costs associated with research, development, testing, and evaluation. This had become a problem, as the Pentagon, faced simultaneously with a shrinking Defense Department budget and hikes in the cost of new technologies, demanded effective cost control measures. RAND analyst David Novick came to the rescue.

As the head of the Cost Analysis Department, founded in 1950, Novick and his group redefined the art of cost analysis, so much so that the literature of cost analyses in the 1950s and 1960s is dominated by RAND contributions. Building on a type of statistical estimate of the cost of airplanes on long production runs called "a learning curve," RAND's analysts developed what they dubbed cost estimating relationships. These allowed for high-level comparisons of aircraft cost as a variable of such factors as speed, range, and altitude, giving a clear view of development cost trends. Predictive equations made it possible to estimate quickly and accurately the cost of new systems. RAND eventually extended these techniques to all phases of aerospace systems. Rocket scientists such as Wernher von Braun, who had little cost-data history for the enormous rockets then being planned, used the RAND techniques to gather data for estimating the costs of rocket liftoff weights and their appropriate budget.[21]

In 1958, the House Select Committee on Astronautics and Space Exploration asked RAND to prepare a guide to the uses and characteristics of space systems.[22] Later that year, following the creation of NASA by President Eisenhower, the Air Force encouraged RAND to "keep its hand" in space matters and do research work for the new agency. RAND managers had begun to chafe under Air Force restrictions and, wanting to diversify their sources of revenue, eagerly accepted this recommendation.

RAND at first failed to convince NASA administrators of the think tank's suitability for space work because of long time delays in delivering contracted studies. It wasn't until 1960 that RAND work finally met with NASA approval, when the think tank conducted a crash study on the public policy problems associated with communications satellite development. Unlike previous assignments, RAND turned this one around in a matter of weeks, which prompted NASA to order another short-term study, analyzing the possible use of nuclear-powered rockets. This report also was completed with alacrity but NASA officials were less than happy with the tone of RAND's conclusions, which they felt would make it hard for the agency in "selling their program."

RAND revised the report to modify the tone, but the accommodation stuck in the craw of many RAND scientists, who felt their reputation for objectivity had been compromised. To avoid the problems of short-term task-specific projects, RAND sought a long-term contract with NASA similar to Project Air Force, but their efforts were to no avail. It would take the death of a president and the unleashing of the most unpopular war in American history, under the guidance of RAND advisers, before the think tank achieved its goal of diversification away from the Air Force.

11

A Final Solution to the Soviet Problem

THE FIRST CONCRETE, and perhaps most benign, result of the RAND influence in the Kennedy administration was a change in the nation's general nuclear war plan—called the Single Integrated Operational Plan (SIOP).[1]

President Eisenhower had ordered SIOP during the last year of his administration as a response to the uncoordinated proliferation of nuclear weapons in the U.S. Armed Forces. Although it centralized command of all the nuclear weapons—the Navy's Polaris missiles, and the other nuclear arsenal of the Navy fleet and of the Army units—the SIOP strategy was nothing less than the old Sunday punch of the 1950s. Labeled SIOP-62, for the first year in which it would become operational, the plan contemplated responding to an impending Soviet invasion of Western Europe with a U.S. nuclear force of 1,459 bombs, packing a total of 2,164 megatons—even if the Soviets did not employ any nuclear weapons. They would be directed at 654 targets, military and urban, in the Soviet Union, China, and Eastern Europe. If the United States fired a preemptive first attack, as was official policy in case of a perceived Soviet threat, then the entire American nuclear arsenal force would be unleashed. That would mean 3,423 nuclear weapons, totaling 7,847 megatons. It was estimated that 285 million Russians and Chinese would die in this holocaust and that perhaps 40 million more would be severely injured.[2]

Nor was that the limit of the carnage. The Joint Chiefs of Staff estimated that another 100 million or more would die in Eastern Europe. Fallout also would claim 100 million lives in neutral countries surrounding the attacks—places like Finland, Austria, and Afghanistan. Ultimately, there could be yet another 100 million deaths in NATO countries, depending on which way the nuclear fallout blew. In total, up to 600 million people—the just and the sinners, the bystanders and the ignorant—would perish because of an automatic response to a perceived threat. Needless to say, no thought was given to the effect such massive bombing would have on the global climate.[3]

Strategic Air Command briefed McNamara on SIOP-62 on February 3, 1961, just two weeks after John F. Kennedy's inauguration. General Thomas White, the Air Force Chief of Staff, led the presentation to McNamara; his deputy secretary, Roswell Gilpatric; and a retinue of other top Department of Defense civilians. The SAC officers had hoped to impress McNamara with their dazzling display of charts, numbers, and statistics, but McNamara was far from pleased with what he saw. He was able not only to comprehend instantly the gist of any presentation but to synthesize, analyze, and compare the given data to previous analyses, and he immediately pointed out the enormous duplication of destruction in the plan, with some targets destined to be hit four to ten times; he also openly criticized the underestimation of Soviet casualties and industrial destruction.[4]

McNamara was particularly aghast when General White, in a semihumorous aside, said, "Well, Mr. Secretary, I hope you don't have any friends or relations in Albania, because we're just going to have to wipe it out."[5] That is, the Albanians, like hundreds of millions of people in Eastern Europe, the Soviet Union, and China, would be annihilated merely because they happened to live under Communist rule.

McNamara left SAC headquarters determined to change the nation's nuclear policy. He convinced President Kennedy to forswear initiating a nuclear war.[6] Yet some other kind of plan had to be drawn up in case the nuclear specter became a dreadful eventuality. But what? His answer came a few weeks later, when he received a crucial briefing by RAND analyst William Kaufmann on counterforce, a concept new to McNamara.

Alain Enthoven and Charles Hitch arranged for the talk by Kaufmann on February 10, 1961. A former student of Bernard Brodie's at Princeton and a colleague of Albert Wohlstetter's, Kaufmann had elaborated on Brodie's original concept of a no-cities targeting plan. Essentially, the plan called for delivering nuclear weapons to known Soviet military targets instead of population centers. Kaufmann also built on Wohlstetter's second-strike concept by proposing a calculated response—the American nuclear counterattack would be carried out in steps, gradually increasing in intensity so as to give the Soviets a chance to halt before further escalation occurred. The briefing was one that Kaufmann had given to the Air Force dozens of times over the previous years, without much consequence. He had prepared charts, tables, and graphics for a four-hour conference, but McNamara grasped the concepts so quickly Kaufmann was done within an hour.[7]

McNamara seized on Kaufmann's proposal incorporating counterforce and second-strike capability, believing it offered a new way to utilize the nation's nuclear arsenal by giving the president flexibility in response to Soviet moves. Atop a to-do list of 96 items that came to be known as the 96 Trombones—a conflation of the idea of McNamara's aides being known as his band, the lyrics to an old operetta song,* and the "76 Trombones" number from *The Music Man*—McNamara ordered his assistants to prepare "a draft memorandum revising the basic national security policies and assumptions, including the assumptions relating to 'counterforce' strikes . . ." Their work, with Kaufmann as consultant, would form the basis of the new nuclear policy.[8]

McNamara turned over Project Number 1 of his 96 Trombones to Paul Nitze, who then handed it over to Harry Rowen. Rowen in turn gave it to Daniel Ellsberg, since the former marine was one of a handful of civilians who had closely studied the military's war plans. Ellsberg saw this as his chance to make the nation's nuclear response more precise and effective, not to mention more rational, for to him the general nuclear plan in existence seemed ludicrous and insanely murderous, even in the face of Soviet aggression.

Kaufmann's plan had assumed that the call to pull the nuclear trigger was a considered decision, made at the highest level of government—by the president or the secretary of defense. Ellsberg knew better. In the late 1950s, RAND had loaned Ellsberg to the forces of the Commander in Chief Pacific to study the problems of nuclear control and command. He learned then that in spite of all public declarations to the contrary, Eisenhower had delegated to commanders in major theaters the authority to start a nuclear attack under certain circumstances, such as a communications breakdown with Washington (which happened frequently back then) or the incapacitation of the president (which had occurred twice when Eisenhower suffered heart attacks). Not only that, some of the four-star commanders who had this authority had in turn delegated it to their subordinates, which meant that the capability to order a nuclear

---

* I am the only German in McNamara's band, etc. . . .

attack was much more widespread and susceptible to possible error or abuse than suspected. The nightmare of a deranged local commander calling in a nuclear strike, the basis of so many science-fiction movies and thrillers, was not far from reality after all—especially before Wohlstetter came up with the concept of fail-safe. (All the same, Kennedy later reauthorized this delegation of power, which was reaffirmed by President Johnson in 1964.)

In his draft, Ellsberg repeatedly emphasized that the United States would not hold the people of Russia, China, or Eastern Europe responsible for the actions of their governments. Therefore, the American response in case of war would seek to minimize the number of civilian casualties. The plan called for refraining from indiscriminate attacks on population centers "while retaining U.S. ready residual forces to threaten those targets" if needed. Ellsberg also emphasized the absolute necessity of a continuing command control center for U.S. forces, as well as the need for weapons to be held in reserve for a counterattack, both of which had been omitted in the extant nuclear war plan.[9]

In May of 1961, the month before SIOP-62 was to be adopted as official policy, McNamara sent Ellsberg's plan to the Joint Chiefs of Staff as the basis of a new operational plan for 1963. Ellsberg meanwhile repeatedly urged the national security leaders in the administration—McGeorge Bundy at the National Security Council, Walt Rostow of the State Department, and Gilpatric—to rewrite the definition of a general war so that a conflict with the Soviet Union did not degenerate into nuclear war. Ellsberg's efforts met with success, and early in 1962, McNamara made the new counterforce policy public in a speech at the University of Michigan.[10]

This new measure for facing crises would be put to the test soon enough—in fact, within weeks. In the summer of 1961, all of the RAND ideas of counterforce versus massive retaliation faced a real-life challenge when, for a brief interval, the American government gave serious consideration to unleashing preemptively the nation's nuclear arsenal on the Soviet Union. The springboard was that most contested of cities, Berlin.

An island of American influence in a sea of Communist oppression, the former capital of Germany had been divided into a Communist East and a democratic West after World War II, mirroring the division of Germany. Mass defections from East Germany to West Germany plagued the East German authorities for years. By 1958, two million people had migrated to the West, with close to 10,000 still escaping every month—many of those through Berlin. Stalin had blockaded the city in 1948 to force the U.S. allies out, but after a massive 300-day airlift thwarted his plan, the Soviet Union signed an agreement allowing free access to Berlin. Before Kennedy's election, Soviet premier Nikita Khrushchev had been making noises about restricting the movement of troops and supplies to Berlin again, under the pretext of signing a final peace treaty with East Germany and making the Communist regime there responsible for all traffic in and out of Berlin—therefore choking the Western-controlled part of the city.[11]

Khrushchev repeated the threat at a June 1961 meeting in Vienna with President Kennedy. At the time, Kennedy was still trying to find his legs politically following the debacle of the Bay of Pigs. Originally authorized by Eisenhower as a CIA undercover operation, the April 1961 invasion had aimed at deposing Fidel Castro's Communist regime with a force of 1,200 American-trained Cuban exiles. When confronted by superior Cuban forces and a refusal by President Kennedy to provide needed U.S. military support, the exile invaders went down to defeat, giving Castro his first major victory against the United States and a gigantic black eye to the Kennedy administration.[12]

That failure, compounded by Kennedy's youth and inexperience in world affairs, made the Crimean peasant that lurked within Khrushchev believe the American president was in way over his head. Khrushchev proceeded to lecture Kennedy, warning of war if the United States and its allies did not withdraw from West Berlin by December. Kennedy responded defiantly, "Then there will be war, Mr. Chairman. It's going to be a very cold winter."[13]

One thing that did not much concern Kennedy was the size of Khrushchev's much-vaunted atomic arsenal. Just weeks after the inauguration, the CIA had informed McNamara of the secret U-2 spy plane conclusions: the so-called missile gap favoring the Russians did not exist. When McNamara blurted out at one of his first press conferences that if there was a gap, it was actually in favor of the United States, an immediate scandal ensued. The *New York Times* ran the story on page one and newspaper editorials across the country excoriated the new administration for its deceit, while in Congress there were calls for McNamara's resignation and a rerun of the presidential election. McNamara offered to resign but Kennedy refused the offer, telling him, "We all put our foot in our mouth once in a while. Just forget it. It'll blow over."[14]

However, while the Kennedy administration knew that the Soviet boasts of nuclear superiority were a Potemkin village, it was painfully aware that Soviet combat strength superiority in East Germany was the real thing. Several Soviet divisions surrounded Berlin, and U.S. military forces there had just enough ammo and provisions to withstand a conventional conflict for eighteen days.[15] If the Russians decided to blockade West Berlin, the plan by the Joint Chiefs of Staff was for the United States to send a handful of brigades down the autobahn from West Germany to break the Soviet stranglehold. If the Soviets or their Warsaw Pact allies resisted, the next step was the all-out nuclear strike of SIOP-62.

Back in Washington, Kennedy received sharp advice from Truman's secretary of state, Dean Acheson (Kennedy had appointed career diplomat and Rockefeller Foundation president Dean Rusk to preside over Foggy Bottom).[16] In Acheson's view, the Berlin crisis was nothing less than an excuse by Russia to test America's will. If

Kennedy backed down on Berlin, the Soviets would feel that they could attack American interests elsewhere with impunity. The United States would be seen as incapable of or unwilling to honor its commitments to other countries, for fear of using its nuclear forces. Acheson suggested that Kennedy order a massive buildup of conventional forces to send a message to the Soviets that America would not be pushed around—although Acheson ruefully acknowledged this move might result in a nuclear war.[17] Secretary of State Rusk, who had accompanied Kennedy to Vienna, seconded his predecessor's recommendation, and made plans to meet with European foreign ministers and the NATO Permanent Council later that summer.

On July 25, 1961, Kennedy followed Acheson's advice, asking Congress for a $3.3 billion supplement to the appropriations bill, with half of the money earmarked for an increase in conventional forces; he also upped the Army's strength from 875,000 to 1,000,000 troops and ordered an array of other measures to augment the nation's war readiness.[18] To avoid the possibility that a confrontation over Berlin might lead to a nuclear war for which the country would be unprepared, Rowen ordered a contingency memorandum to be drafted, elaborating on the Kaufmann counterforce/no-cities ideas that Ellsberg proposed for SIOP-63.[19]

The memo, written by National Security Adviser Carl Kaysen,[20] offered the new and dismayingly tantalizing possibility of eliminating the Soviet nuclear arsenal altogether. Analysis of photographs taken by reconnaissance satellites had disclosed that the once-feared Soviet missile force was even smaller than anyone had dared to hope. The National Security Council deduced that the Soviets actually had only four land-based operational intercontinental ballistic missiles capable of striking the United States. A preemptive counterforce first strike against Soviet installations would therefore most likely result in the permanent destruction of the Russian nuclear

land-based missile threat, at a cost of a few million Soviet lives.*
The memo warned, however, that if some Soviet bombers and
submarine-based missiles survived the attack and the Soviets struck
back, from two to fifteen million Americans might die.

The memo inflamed tempers throughout the administration. Ted
Sorenson, Kennedy's main speechwriter and chief White House
counsel, screamed at Rowen's assistant, who brought him the memo,
"You're crazy! We shouldn't let guys like you around here." A leftist staffer on the National Security Council, Marcus Raskin, who
would found the Institute for Policy Studies and go on to renown as
a fierce opponent of the Vietnam War, asked, "How does this make
us any better than those who measured the gas ovens or the engineers who built the tracks for the death trains in Nazi Germany?"[21]

Even Paul Nitze vetoed the proposal. What if all the weapons
were not taken out? he asked. What if they were aimed at Washington or New York? Could the country really afford to lose those
cities and what they meant to civilization?[22] Moreover, the study
recognized that there was no certainty as to the location of all the
short- and medium-range Soviet missiles, of which there were hundreds, which could rain down on American allies. The number of
European casualties could be in the tens of millions. No, the plan
was not acceptable. Besides, the Soviets had already acted in their
own inimitable way to bring the crisis under control: in August
1961, they had built the Berlin Wall and effectively halted the mass
migration that created the problem.[23]

The crisis gradually defused, thanks in no small part to Kennedy's
tough but flexible posture—a lesson that would serve him well in

---

*   For decades afterward Soviet leaders dedicated themselves to achieving nuclear parity with
the United States to avoid this kind of preemptive attack. Recent research suggests that with
the fall of the Soviet Union, the United States is again in a position of nuclear supremacy,
where it could, if it chose, eliminate the nuclear arsenal of Russia *and* China with a preemptive first strike. See "The Rise of U.S. Nuclear Supremacy," *Foreign Affairs* (March/April
2006).

later negotiations with Khrushchev. In October, after he established direct communications with Kennedy seeking accommodation on the issue, Khrushchev waived his self-imposed deadline on Berlin. To reinforce the need for negotiations, Gilpatric gave a speech in late October 1962 hinting that the United States knew the limits of Soviet missile strength. He cautioned that any enemy move that brought American nuclear retaliatory power into play would constitute a death sentence for the Soviet Union.

Cowed by the American firmness, Khrushchev allowed the movement of troops and supplies into West Berlin to return to normal. Nevertheless, if ever there was a moment when the RAND theories of counterforce could have had their optimum real-life application, it was during the Berlin crisis. Even during the Cuban Missile Crisis a year later, when the Kennedy administration found Russian SS-4 and SS-5 medium-range nuclear-armed missiles pointed straight at the mainland, there was no thought of a preemptive nuclear strike on the Soviet Union. True, at one point, there was talk of a U.S. invasion of the island, and a possible air strike on the Cuban nuclear missile sites to disable them beforehand, but even then no one in Kennedy's inner circle gave serious consideration to the kind of full-fledged nuclear wipeout envisioned by the Kaysen memo. Instead, Kennedy imposed an embargo blocking further Soviet weapon deliveries to the island. After a tense standoff with Khrushchev, Kennedy pledged not to invade Cuba and, in exchange for the withdrawal of the Soviet missiles, withdrew some obsolete NATO missiles from Turkey so Khrushchev could save face before the Politburo.[24] As in so many RAND war games, nobody in the U.S. government had the gumption, madness, or suicidal urge to pull the nuclear trigger.

Vietnam, however, was another madness altogether.

12

An Irresistible Force

THE CAPTURED GUERRILLA was adamant. He told his RAND interrogators that not only was he proud to lay down his life for the Vietcong, the loose coalition of Communist-led forces that controlled most of the South Vietnamese countryside, but he would gladly do it again if he could. Small, spare, and unfailingly polite, the prisoner did not regret one single revolutionary action. His face was bruised and his nose smashed from the beating he had taken at the hands of the South Vietnamese Army, but still the prisoner showed nothing but contempt for the government in Saigon.

His was a story that Anthony Russo and other RAND researchers heard time and again in South Vietnam in 1965. Originally a mere distraction in a backwater of the American foreign policy horizon, the Communist insurgency in Vietnam had become President Johnson's obsession. He did not want to lose the war, no matter the cost. The Defense Department had contracted RAND to

carry out a study on the motivation and morale of the forces opposed to the U.S.-backed regime, so Russo and his RAND colleagues had been trekking through South Vietnam since late 1964.
Accompanied by University of Saigon scholars and translators, for
months they recorded hundreds of interviews with guerrillas. Although at first taciturn, concerned that they would be tortured, the
prisoners opened up when they were assured that Russo only was
interested in their beliefs. The Vietcong invariably described themselves as patriots leading a war of national liberation.

The struggle had begun with the French, the Vietcong said; it
would continue until all the American forces were gone and North
and South Vietnam were reunited, as North Vietnamese leader Ho
Chi Minh wanted. The Vietcong weren't fighting just for a little plot
of land. They wanted better education for their children, greater economic opportunity, equality regardless of social class, and justice.
They fought for freedom from the foreign imperialists and their pup-
pets, the corrupt Saigon government officials. And no, it didn't matter how many Vietcong were killed; if they died, others would take
their place. Even if the struggle lasted a hundred years, the Vietcong
would never surrender.

The analysts thanked the prisoner, and then went outside the interrogation room for a cigarette break. The blare of Saigon traffic
muscled into the old French colonial office building on rue Pasteur
that had become RAND headquarters. Smoke wreathed about the
giant banana trees growing in the courtyard as the men contemplated what they had just experienced for the umpteenth time. Russo
turned to his assistant.

"Our government is wrong, totally wrong, in what it's telling us
about the war."[1]

A SEARCH FOR righteousness was not RAND's contracted task in
Saigon. Questioning the morality of policy was not the mission either. The assignment was to analyze and implement the Vietnam

policy of Kennedy's successor, President Lyndon Baines Johnson. RAND had been hired to study the nature of the insurgency, to find out what motivated the Vietcong so they could be neutralized. This type of counterinsurgency work was paying many bills at RAND. Almost a quarter of RAND's total funding was now coming from Department of Defense contracts, as well as from research studies conducted for NASA. About 70 percent of RAND's income still came from the Air Force—but that amount was diminishing every year.[2] The RAND divisions that were thriving under the new marching orders were the long-neglected social sciences, which now took the spotlight away from the Economics Division—much like economics had stolen the spotlight from physics and physics in turn from the Mathematics Division, in a natural progression away from the work that had been RAND's original raison d'être.*

RAND's surge to Third World studies had started in 1959, when the Pentagon commissioned research on how to deal with a series of leftist insurgencies. Cuba, Guatemala, Venezuela, Colombia, Congo, Laos—at the time it seemed there was no end to the spread of fierce anti-American uprisings in what had been U.S. protectorates. The Defense Department, which for years had concentrated on total war with the Soviet Union in Central Europe, needed a new paradigm to help America manage this latest threat. RAND at first encouraged the change in direction and hosted a conference of experts to discuss possible solutions to the problem of insurgencies. RAND determined that one way to defeat the insurrectionists was by endorsing military takeovers in the endangered countries, since the armed forces could assist in rapid modernization, transmit industrial and secular values, and might even be solicitous of the

---

* Of course, it could be argued that in essence these divisions amounted to distinctions without differences, given that the numerical approach of rational choice had made the social sciences an unacknowledged adjunct of the Economics Department, with its emphasis on game and set theory.

poor. "Military modernization" and the tacit acceptance of military coups came into vogue in the Pentagon; American analysts hailed Third World military classes as champions of progress that would bring their nations into the twentieth century. Not coincidentally, those classes would also strongly support American interests and values, in exchange for generous American aid. These tenets applied very nicely to the South Vietnamese military-backed government of 1965.[3]

RAND's turn to Third World studies had also come about as a corollary of counterforce. William Kaufmann had recognized that since the strategy of massive nuclear retaliation was not credible in all instances, the United States might be "nibbled" to death by non-nuclear attacks from the Soviet Union and China on the periphery of the free world. The concept of counterforce was backed by critics of the LeMay Sunday punch, like Army General Maxwell Taylor, who said that to retain credibility America would have to come up with what he called a "strategy of flexible response" to attacks, since the United States couldn't very well be expected to unleash a nuclear rain over a Chinese border incursion in, let's say, northern Burma.[4]

The theory of limited response dovetailed with President Kennedy's fascination with a speech Soviet premier Nikita Khrushchev had given early in January of 1961. In that speech Khrushchev stated that in spite of his country's desire for "peaceful coexistence" with the United States, Communists were ready to engage capitalists in a contest for the hearts and minds of peoples throughout the world. Khrushchev singled out what he called "wars of national liberation" as arenas where the two competing systems could go toe to toe, and that the USSR would always be ready to aid "wholeheartedly and without reservation" countries that chose the path to socialism.[5] A few days later Kennedy would reply in his famous inaugural address, pledging that the United States would "pay any price, bear any burden, meet any hardship, support any friend, oppose any foe to assure the survival and the success of liberty."[6]

Kennedy distributed copies of Khrushchev's speech to the top-ranking members of his administration and made frequent reference to it until his death. Cuba's embrace of communism and the sudden proliferation of Socialist revolutions in former European colonies where the East and West vied for predominance—such as Laos and the Belgian Congo—weighed heavily on Kennedy's mind. He was convinced that with Western Europe in a virtual standoff, the Third World would be the next theater of battle in the Cold War.

This was also the thinking of Albert Wohlstetter, who exerted considerable influence on government policy through the good offices of his protégé Harry Rowen, who had been hired to run the Department of Defense's Office of International Security Affairs. Through Rowen, Wohlstetter—and by extension RAND—capitalized on Kennedy's increasing preoccupation with Third World conflicts. RAND vice president J. Richard Goldstein noted, "We convinced ourselves that we did have, or at least should have, a unique combination of skills necessary to tackle this clearly interdisciplinary problem."[7]

The consequence was a series of RAND studies on limited wars and counterinsurgency operations, as well as work dealing with NATO policy, logistics problems, and support systems. RAND also analyzed several historical events, such as the successful antiguerrilla campaign by British forces in Malaysia after World War II and the Quemoy Islands affair. Albert and Roberta Wohlstetter wrote two insightful essays on Cuba, "Notes on the Cuban Crisis" and "Studies for a Post-Communist Cuba,"[8] stemming from advice Albert had given to the Kennedy administration on dealing with Fidel Castro. (Not surprisingly, Wohlstetter concluded that Castro was an unstable—which is to say, irrational—personality full of guile who could not be trusted, and recommended that the embargo of the island continue and that the United States be ready to encourage an anti-Castro movement on the island, if it ever came up, but not to expect one either.)[9]

The Vietcong Morale and Motivation Study that Russo was involved in had been commissioned by Robert McNamara's office to investigate the driving force behind the determination of Vietnamese Communist guerrillas. Two consultants, anthropologist John C. Donnell and political science professor Joseph J. Zasloff, headed it.[10] When Donnell and Zasloff presented preliminary results to Rowen and his new boss, John McNaughton, in 1965, they emphasized that the Vietcong saw themselves as waging a war against imperialists for the independence of Vietnam.[11] They neither were Communist zealots nor were they animated, like some Asian version of Mexican Zapatistas, by a simple desire for land. They were patriots, and they were in the war for the long haul. It was then that Rowen turned to McNaughton and exclaimed, in an echo of Russo's observation, "John, I think we're signed up with the wrong side—the side that's going to lose this war."[12]

The conclusions of the Vietcong study echoed analyses RAND had conducted years earlier. In 1962, at a symposium on counterinsurgency held at RAND's Washington office, a group of military experts who had been heavily involved in fighting guerrilla campaigns in places such as Kenya, Malaysia, and French Vietnam, warned that the most effective guerrilla fighter was the one who was committed to the cause. Major Edward Lansdale—who, ironically, would become heavily involved in the American pacification effort in Vietnam of the mid-1960s—explained that educated, motivated activists constituted the core around which a successful insurgent movement revolved. These were not roving bandits or just plain bad guys, they were men of principle who were willing to die for a cause—and unless the conditions that gave rise to their discontent changed, the guerrilla campaign would go on until they all died or the central government fell.[13]

All the same, the Johnson administration disregarded Donnell and Zasloff's warnings. By then the United States was escalating the conflict, not reexamining the assumptions for the American presence in Vietnam. In approaching RAND, Johnson was trying to find a way to defeat the Vietcong, not to understand them. Elected by a landslide vote in 1964 with a promise that he wouldn't be sending American boys to do the job the Vietnamese ought to do, by the end of 1965 President Johnson deployed an extra half a million American soldiers to South Vietnam. The situation was no longer as deceptively clear as it had been in 1962 when McNamara had toured the country and stated, "every quantitative measurement . . . shows that we are winning the war."[14]

In fact, the United States at that point was finding itself in an increasingly untenable spot. Vietcong strength by 1965 was more than 170,000 men, and North Vietnamese troops were enlarging the Vietcong contingents, supplying communications experts, ordnance technicians, and other specialists. Hanoi had also opened the Ho Chi Minh trail—once a narrow twisting path through the jungle—into a virtual highway ferrying in modern equipment and supplies. Moreover, even though Operation Rolling Thunder, a relentless bombing campaign against North Vietnamese targets, had been unleashed, the Communist enemy showed no intention of even coming to the table for peace talks. For the North it was victory or death. As Paul Warnke, the assistant secretary of defense, later would ruefully admit, "We anticipated that they would respond like reasonable people."[15]

In spite of the growing chaos in South Vietnam, some RAND reports signaled that perhaps with enough money and dedication, the American effort would eventually pan out. Charles Wolf, Jr., head of the Economics Division, wrote perhaps the most prominent of all, *Insurgency and Counterinsurgency: New Myths and Old Realities*.[16] He made recommendations for rewards for information and defection, encouraged amnesty programs, and presented a persuasive case that control of the food supply just might persuade Vietnamese peasants to go America's way. His conclusions were far from being universally accepted, and soon RAND analysts were dividing into pro– and anti–Vietnam War factions.

The sense of mission that earlier had animated the think tank began to dilute, as analysts pondered whether killing poor peasants seeking social justice in far-off corners of the world was really in the national interest of the United States. Prominent among the doubters was a German exile, Konrad Kellen, a political scientist who was the RAND coordinator of the Vietcong study. The study's conclusions about the fierce patriotism of the captured enemy left him deeply pessimistic about the efficacy of American policy in Southeast Asia. From 1965 on, he advocated a unilateral withdrawal from Vietnam, saying the war was unwinnable and that the Vietcong perhaps could be annihilated but never subdued. He formed part of a growing number of analysts within RAND—including Daniel Ellsberg—who grew more anguished every year over the conflict, even going so far as to send an open letter to the *New York Times,* urging the Johnson administration to end the American military involvement in Vietnam.[17] A few days later, the prowar faction within RAND sent its own letter to the *Times,* countering the arguments made by Kellen, Ellsberg, and the others.[18]

Equally controversial views came from another exile, an Eastern European named Leon Gouré. A specialist on the Soviet Union, Gouré was blinded by his fierce anticommunism. His 1962 work, *Civil Defense in the Soviet Union,*[19] erroneously warned that a vast Soviet civil defense system he had detected presaged a sneak nuclear attack by the Kremlin. After a visit to Vietnam in 1965, Gouré took a portion of the data gathered by Donnell and Zasloff and interpreted it to mean that South Vietnamese peasants blamed the Vietcong for causing the U.S. bombing campaigns and the ensuing mayhem. Therefore, Gouré urged greater and wider bombing attacks as a means of demoralizing the enemy. His prescription was warmly received by the Air Force, as well as by Frank Collbohm and other conservative members of RAND. They believed in the domino theory, which argued that if one country in a region turned Communist, soon all its neighbors would likewise fall to the Soviets like dominoes in a row. The double irony of Vietnam would be not just what Leslie Gelb of the *New York Times* wrote—that the first real domino to fall was American public opinion[20]—but that the countries that did fall like dominoes into the Socialist camp afterward—Cambodia, Laos, and Burma—did so as a result of the failed American intervention in Vietnam.

Many prominent RAND analysts dismissed Gouré's methods as intrinsically biased, a case of someone twisting the facts to suit his beliefs. Gustave Shubert, who had replaced Charles Hitch as head of the Economics Department, accused Gouré of "picking, maybe at random hours or days of the week, excerpts from the interviews that supported a point of view—and that point of view was that bombing, and to some extent shelling, resulted in increased hatred for the Viet Cong and not for the Americans, and therefore, the more, the better."[21] The animosity between the pro- and antiwar groups was so bitter that fistfights broke out in management sessions.[22] RAND was faithfully mirroring the country—in this case, mirroring the divisions tearing it apart.

The entire handling of the war in Vietnam from 1961 to 1967 can be seen as another application of the RAND notion of limited conflict—lifted out of the playbook of war against the Soviet Union. One of the main instigators was Thomas Schelling, a future Nobel Prize–winning economist who belonged to Wohlstetter's cadre of nuclear analysts. While at RAND, Schelling had written *The Strategy of Conflict,* in which he argued that war is always a bargaining power and that the bargaining power comes from the capacity to hurt.[23] When President Johnson and McNamara decided to step up the pressure against North Vietnam, they opted to follow Schelling's precepts. According to historian Fred Kaplan, on May 22, 1964, President Johnson received a memo from National Security Adviser McGeorge Bundy. "An integrated political-military plan for graduated action against North Vietnam is being prepared under John McNaughton at Defense," Bundy wrote. "The theory of this plan is that we should strike to hurt but not to destroy, and strike for the purpose of changing the North Vietnamese decision on intervention in the south."[24]

McNaughton was the assistant secretary of defense in charge of the Vietnam desk at the Defense Department. He approached Schelling, a friend and former colleague from Harvard, for advice on how to handle the escalation. McNaughton—who, incidentally, was Ellsberg's boss—thought a bombing campaign would be the best vehicle to inflict enough pain to grab Hanoi's attention. What sort of campaign should it be? How hard should the United States hit, and how would Washington know that it had Hanoi's attention? How could America ensure that North Vietnam wouldn't simply resume its activities after the bombing ceased?

The men pondered the situation for an hour but could not come up with answers to any of the questions. Schelling warned McNaughton, though, that if the campaign was launched, it should not last more than three weeks. At the end of that period either Hanoi would sue for peace—or nothing would ever come of it. Operation Rolling Thunder began on March 2, 1965. It had no apparent effect on North Vietnam or the Vietcong, which continued trying to overthrow the American-backed Saigon regime.

The U.S. government was saying, in effect, we will avoid the major population centers in our bombing (that is, Hanoi) and the North Vietnamese dikes, which if damaged could have killed millions.[25] We will proceed one step at a time in a deliberate escalation of the war effort, we will not invade North Vietnam, and we will wait for the enemy to respond to our messages and ask for a halt, since they will have obviously learned that there is no rational way out other than a negotiated peace. It was a policy of deliberate stalemate, to be achieved by the careful, escalated, clinical infliction of pain—that is, torture—until Ho Chi Minh cried uncle, since "the costs of fighting to him outweighed the costs to the United States and consequently that the advantages of terminating the conflict were greater than the advantages of continuing it."[26] The failure of that policy, and the tragedy it caused, is a moral burden that RAND has never acknowledged.

It is true that RAND, with its Vietcong study, attempted to fulfill its moral responsibility of speaking truth to power by explaining Vietnamese behavior—giving the lie to Secretary McNamara's subsequent apology that the absence of a credible explanation for Vietnamese behavior was the main impediment to peace.

> Our government lacked experts for us to consult to compensate for our ignorance . . . I knew of only one Pentagon officer with counterinsurgency experience in the region—Colonel Edward Lansdale, who had served as an adviser to Ramon Magsaysay in the Philippines and Diem in South Vietnam. But Lansdale was relatively junior and lacked broad geopolitical expertise . . . We also totally underestimated the nationalist aspect of Ho Chi Minh's movement. We saw him first as a Communist and only second as a Vietnamese nationalist . . . We failed to analyze our assumptions critically. The foundations of our decision making were gravely flawed.[27]

Yet this self-serving apologia from McNamara, coming almost twenty years after the fact, does not let RAND off the hook. By supplying the theoretical structure of counterforce as a means of achieving strictly political aims (no one ever claimed that Vietnam was going to drop a nuclear bomb on American soil), RAND was as responsible as those who put counterforce into effect. It would have taken a decisive intervention on the part of RAND to stop the intellectual justification of the war, something that some individual analysts did—such as Ellsberg and Kellen—but that RAND itself, as an institution, did not wish to do. Although other members of the so-called Establishment at the time, like the Ford Foundation and

Harvard and Columbia, eventually denounced the war, to the end RAND did not.

RAND found itself bound by the power of the purse wielded by its patron, whether it be the Air Force or the Office of the Secretary of Defense. Then again, taking a moral stance on any particular policy issue goes against the core principles of RAND. No one expects Fritz to tell Dr. Frankenstein that making monsters out of dead bodies is a bad thing. The helper is there to harvest the brain of a dead man so the mad scientist can make the monster.

It is hard to make yourself understood when the enemy not only speaks a different language but has a different set of goals and expectations. As an observer commented when counterforce arguments were first made during the Cold War, what were Americans supposed to do, hop in a helicopter with a bullhorn and fly over enemy territory shouting, Had enough? Surrender? Tragically, that is exactly what U.S. forces would do in South Vietnam. American helicopters dropped millions of pamphlets on bombed-out zones, urging Vietcong fighters to give up. In the last week of August 1966 alone, more than forty-five million leaflets were dropped over Vietcong-held areas and North Vietnam.[28]

But as student demonstrators chanted at the time,

> *Ho, Ho,*
> *Ho Chi Minh*
> *NLF is going to win!*

For the Vietcong and the North Vietnamese there was no solution but victory, regardless of pain.[29] The result of willful American blindness, when coupled with President Johnson's desire to "nail that coonskin to the wall"[30] and not be the first American president in the twentieth century to lose a war, would result in fits of madness like the famed "Five O'Clock Follies," the press briefings in Saigon when the U.S. military spokesman would state the number of enemy dead and wounded as proof that the United States was winning the war.[31] This would devolve, at its murderous extreme, into the horror of Operation Phoenix, a notorious campaign that culminated in the outright execution of tens of thousands of Vietnamese.

The main RAND character in Operation Phoenix was Robert W. Komer, a man of fierce passions and keen intellect. Komer was known as "Blowtorch Bob," a nickname given to him by U.S. ambassador Henry Cabot Lodge, who said that arguing with Komer was like having a blowtorch aimed at the seat of your pants. Yet, with his normally mild demeanor, horn-rimmed glasses, and briar pipe, Komer could also pass for what spy novelist John le Carré called an "intellocrat."[32]

As a National Security Council staffer in the mid-1960s, Komer was involved in the planning of a successful military coup against the Socialist regime of President Kwame Nkrumah in Ghana, West Africa. In 1966, as the U.S.-led war in Southeast Asia escalated, President Johnson named Komer special assistant in charge of the "direction, coordination, and supervision of all U.S. non-military programs for peaceful construction relating to Vietnam."[33] Komer's mission was to win control of the hearts and minds of the Vietnamese through pacification, a program that in theory used information, propaganda, and judicious amounts of force to accomplish its objective. When Komer told Johnson that he didn't have much experience in the field, the president replied, "Well, maybe what we need is some fresh meat."*

Future CIA director William Colby would later describe Komer as "statistics crazy and aggressively optimistic," urging Vietnam experts to set measurable goals and standards of achievement for the

---

* In an interview years later, Komer was still amazed at Johnson's choice of words. "That's what he said. Not fresh blood but fresh meat."

conflict instead of settling for broad philosophical discussions. Komer, who shared the RAND devotion to numerical rationality, was also someone whose antennae were supremely sensitive to Johnson's needs. And what Johnson needed at the time were figures to back up his claims that America was winning. An aide to Johnson said that if Komer had been asked how many people were influenced by Vietcong propaganda, he would have replied within "13 hours and 20 minutes" with a top-secret cable "definitively stating: 2,634,201.11."[34]

Komer arrived at the U.S. embassy in Vietnam in 1967 as second in power only to then Ambassador Ellsworth Bunker. Within days, Komer was restructuring the civilian command side of the U.S. effort in Vietnam. Designated to be General William C. Westmoreland's deputy for Civil Operations and Revolutionary Development Support, Komer persuaded South Vietnamese president Nguyen Van Thieu to establish a special program to capture or kill the leadership of the Vietcong command infrastructure. It was named Phoenix, a loose English language translation of the name of a Vietnamese mythological bird called Phung Hoang that could fly anywhere.[35]

Operation Phoenix gathered information from Vietnamese intelligence agencies, using CIA assassination squads known as Provincial Reconnaissance Units to scour the Vietnamese countryside. After years of fighting, the identity of Vietcong cadres, that is to say the leadership of the Vietcong at the local level, was common knowledge in their villages. With Colby as his right-hand man, Komer set a quota for the program: 3,000 Vietcong cadres "neutralized" every month.

Technically, none of the people captured in Operation Phoenix was marked for assassination, since in theory captured prisoners were to lead authorities to other guerrillas after they talked. In practice, it was a case of shoot first, ask questions later. Corrupt Saigon officials perverted the process to some degree, blackmailing innocents and demanding bribes so as not to arrest those who should be taken in. As noted by *New York Times* correspondent Neil Sheehan in his Pulitzer Prize–winning account of the Vietnam War, *A Bright Shining Lie,* "In the rush to fill quotas, [Saigon officials] posthumously elevated lowly guerrillas killed in skirmishes to the status of VC hamlet and village chiefs."[36]

Thousands were killed, tortured, or swallowed by the maw of the South Vietnamese prisons. The torture tactics included rape, electrical shock, water torture, beatings, hanging from the ceiling— and ultimately execution. In 1971 Barton Osborn, an Operation Phoenix agent, testified before a congressional committee, "I was following through on a reported (VC) suspect that one of my agents had identified. The man was interrogated at the Marine counter- intelligence complex and I was invited to witness it. As I entered the hooch, the man was being taken out, dead. He died from a six inch dowel pushed through his ear and into his brain . . . I never knew an individual to be detained as a VC suspect who ever lived through an interrogation."[37] During that same hearing, Colby would testify that 28,527 Vietnamese had been killed during the life of Operation Phoenix.

However objectionable on moral grounds, in terms of the hard numbers that people like Komer favored, Operation Phoenix was a success. Vietcong forces were pushed out of their traditional refuge in the Mekong Delta, and South Vietnamese forces were able to re- gain control over areas that had not seen a Saigon presence in more than five years.[38] For his efforts, Komer would be appointed U.S. ambassador to Turkey in 1968 by Johnson. Recalled by President Nixon, he joined RAND, where he wrote studies on NATO and the need for rapid deployment forces in the Persian Gulf.[39] He would later be named undersecretary of defense for policy by President Carter, practically the last of the Vietnam-era warriors to serve in a Democratic administration.

RAND's role in Vietnam did not stop at the theoretical or pol- icy level. RAND conducted research in 1965 and 1966 on the utility of the F-5A jet (the Skoshi Tiger) as a counterinsurgency aircraft. A RAND team wrote the test plan, spent six months analyzing the plane's combat effectiveness, and then prepared most of the final report put out by the Air Force. The study concluded that the simple, light jet fighter was highly suitable for the conflict, and the aircraft were turned over to the South Vietnamese Air Force, which would fly them until the fall of Saigon in 1975.[40]

As the 1960s began to draw to a close, though, RAND commenced to extricate itself from the controversial morass that was Vietnam. A project code-named Camelot was the unlikely catalyst.

Camelot was a secret study commissioned by the Army on the prospects of radical revolutions in Latin America.[41] When authorities in Chile accidentally uncovered the study in 1965, it caused widespread international embarrassment, particularly since neither the Chilean government nor the American ambassador to Chile knew of its existence. Chilean students protested, and the government in Santiago filed a formal protest with Washington. Following the scandal, Secretary of State Dean Rusk set up a special group to review the viability of research projects involving foreign countries handled by outside contractors like RAND.

Annoyed by the lack of coordination in his administration, President Johnson declared, "I am absolutely determined that no sponsorship of foreign-area research should be undertaken which in the judgment of the Secretary of State would adversely affect United States foreign relations."[42] He then issued a directive covering the Office of the Secretary of Defense, all the defense agencies, and the Joint Chiefs of Staff, ordering that a single representative from the State Department review all contracts on behavioral and social studies, opinion surveys, and economic studies at all levels of government. No more would the Whiz Kids be able to pick up the phone and ask a former colleague at RAND to investigate this or that particularly interesting aspect of military research. All requests would have to go through channels they no longer controlled.

Not that there were that many Whiz Kids left by the end of 1965. Hitch had accepted an offer to become the president of the University of California system, and Rowen had moved on to the Office of the Budget, while Kaufmann and Schelling[43] had returned to academia. Even Alain Enthoven would soon depart government office, although not before commissioning a report on the war in Vietnam from the Office of Systems Analysis—staffed largely by current RAND members and RAND members on leave. The study concluded that American bombing was counterproductive and there was no prospect of a military solution to the conflict anytime soon.[44]

The earlier departure of the Whiz Kids from RAND to the federal government, as well as the increasing popularity of systems analysis—and its cohort in government parlance, the Planning, Programming, and Budgeting System—had also strongly affected RAND. Staff members felt that systems analysis had played itself out; "the idea has lost much of its novelty and today everyone is doing it."[45] Many rued the absence of those the RAND people called "mavericks," like Herman Kahn, Edward Paxson, and Wohlstetter. In essence, RAND was maturing, losing some of the youthful élan that had characterized it during its glory days in the 1950s when it was at the heart of nuclear strategic policy. As Wohlstetter later said, analysts had to leave RAND "so that you could do things with the people who had the power to exercise on the decisions you wanted to make."[46] Some observers said it was all due to the predictable passage of time, that RAND in the early days brimmed with energy and vigor because the average age of the staffer back in 1950 was under thirty; if there was a growing organizational inertia, it was as much a result of the expanding waistlines and receding hairlines of its personnel as of the normal growth of a maturing organization.

To compound the problem, the secretary of the Air Force had once again begun to crack down on RAND's independence—this time, with the support of Collbohm. Eugene M. Zuckert,[47] described as perhaps the most qualified person ever to head the Air Force, was certainly one of its most stubborn. Defeated earlier by RAND's all-or-nothing obstinacy in the fight for control over RAND's non–Air Force work, in 1965 Zuckert found new allies in the powerful chairman of the House Armed Services Committee, Carl Vinson, and his protégé, Virginia congressman Porter Hardy. Under Vinson's tutelage, Hardy initiated a series of subcommittee hearings on abuses in the government contracting field, hoping to politically embarrass McNamara and thereby increase the leverage of the branches of the military still struggling with the secretary of defense over control of the Pentagon budget.[48]

The Hardy hearings disclosed a number of abuses, particularly by the Aerospace Corporation, the prominent Air Force contractor and would-be RAND clone. Among other things, Aerospace had billed the Air Force for the shipment of the company president's yacht from New York to California. The lax oversight of Aerospace only confirmed the Air Force's desire to control RAND so as to avoid any possible further scandals—and to settle old quarrels. Zuckert announced to RAND board chairman Frank Stanton that he was ready to abandon Project RAND if the corporation did not comply with his directive to limit the size and scope of outside work. The board, in turn, defiantly reaffirmed its commitment to preserving RAND's independence.[49]

This struggle for control of RAND's future occurred at the same time that there was an even greater demand within the organization to expand into the increasingly profitable field of social research at home. By the mid-1960s, President Johnson's Great Society had begun to allocate tens of billions of dollars for investment in social causes in the United States. RAND administrators, wanting to distance themselves from the intractable Vietnam quagmire, were willing to be seduced by the sheer volume of the potential work. For instance, in May 1965, Henry Loomis, the deputy commissioner on education, approached RAND to conduct research on ways to improve the teaching techniques of the nation's schools. He indicated that his office's budget was $1 billion, with a planned increase to $3 billion by 1966, and that his research budget would likewise grow—by several hundred million dollars over the next few years.[50]

Collbohm personally turned down the proposal, as it offended his sense of the historic mission of the corporation. Although earlier he had proudly defended RAND's independence from the Air Force, in his heart he was still an airman; anything that drew RAND away from its original vision was anathema. As he told a congressional subcommittee in government operations in 1962, "I think the Air Force . . . started right out with a philosophy and a policy as to how to handle the type of organization that RAND is, that is practically perfect, I would say. And it would be very, very undesirable for the country as a whole, if this relationship should be changed."[51]

RAND's board of trustees disapproved of those sentiments, noble as they might have been, and similarly criticized previous decisions by Collbohm blocking expansion into nonmilitary work. The board was also mindful of Collbohm's tense relations with McNamara and his crew. Collbohm would relate, "Every time I was at a cocktail party in Washington where McNamara was there, I kept track of where he was and always stayed on the opposite side of the room . . . I didn't want to talk to him or be seen talking to him."[52]

When, unexpectedly, Zuckert resigned due to pressure from McNamara, who then named one of his own protégés, Harold Brown, to head the Air Force, the RAND board read the writing on the Pentagon wall and asked for Collbohm's resignation. It was a moment that Collbohm had never really expected. To the end of his life, he would harbor barely veiled contempt for the people who had ousted him and the way RAND had turned out. This is not to say that he found himself in any financial straits. After the board forced him out, Collbohm joined a financial outfit, Southwestern Research and Investment Company, as chairman. When, in 1985, he was asked how he was doing in retirement, he answered in his typical caustic fashion, "I do nothing I don't want to do and I do everything I want to do. Nothing could be nicer."[53]

After (considered) deliberation, the board of trustees chose as Collbohm's replacement Wohlstetter's favorite and Ellsberg's best friend at RAND, Harry Rowen. The former Whiz Kid would lead the think tank into new fields of research, fame, and national scandal. All the while, the war that he and the other Whiz Kids at first had encouraged, then questioned, and finally disowned kept spinning on its own accord. It would take one of RAND's own illuminati to put on the brakes.

PART 4

13

A Night in Rach Kien

DANIEL ELLSBERG was convinced the South Vietnamese major was coming to kill him. As he lay in his bed, half drunk on cheap beer and cognac, Ellsberg listened hard to the sounds in the hamlet controlled by the Army of the Republic of Vietnam. It had been a while since he'd heard the ARVN major firing his gun, but Ellsberg wasn't taking any chances. He took out his pistol and tried to put it at arm's length, but his cot was too narrow, so instead he balanced the gun on his chest in case the major succeeded in slipping past the guards outside.

It was around midnight, Christmas Eve, 1966. Ellsberg was sweating it out in the vicinity of a village called Rach Kien, in Long An Province, south of Saigon in the Mekong Delta. The only other American at the base, an Army captain serving as an adviser to the South Vietnamese troops, slept peacefully on the cot next to Ellsberg's, as oblivious to the danger as if he were spending the holiday back home in Wichita or Muskogee or wherever it was he hailed from.

Ellsberg rested on his back with his hands under his head, watching the flickering candle cast shadows on the walls of the hut. He had promised the captain he'd stand watch for the first four hours, but even without the promise, he would not have been able to close his eyes. The nighttime sounds of the delta—the constant cry of crickets, the occasional squawk of a passing bird, the almost human breathing of the trees and rice—intermingled with the snoring of the captain. The darkness smelled of loam, flowers, sweat, and dung; it pressed down on him as he lay on the cot fully clothed, ready to defend himself.

"He is drunk," the South Vietnamese lieutenant had offered as apology for his superior. He said the ARVN battalion commander and his officers were very sorry that the major had insulted Americans in front of Ellsberg. "They did not agree with that. They are angry at him. But he is a major."

"But do they disagree with what he said?" Ellsberg had asked.

"Well, they might agree with some things that he said, but not so strongly."

So maybe they were right, maybe it was all because of the Chivas and the Rémy Martin and the wine and the Vietnamese "33" beer that they'd all downed during that special dinner that the commander, a French-speaking Catholic, staged in honor of his American advisers. Ellsberg had even brought fruitcake that Deputy Ambassador William Porter had passed on for him to give to some nostalgic grunt in the field. Fish sauce, noodles, fruitcake, French cognac. The victuals of happy warriors.

There was no particular reason why the Vietnamese major had gone off on his rant. Ellsberg had sung Christmas carols at the table with him, later smiling and nodding at the officers' lachrymose Vietnamese songs. Besides, Ellsberg was only there to observe the pacification campaign, to give a warning word to Ambassador Lodge on whether too much American firepower in the province would be counterproductive and drive peasants into the arms of the Vietcong. His sympathies were still with the Vietnamese government, although he was beginning to harbor the thought that the Vietcong might have a solid argument.

Back home, in the cosseted confines of the RAND Corporation, he had insisted that the United States had no choice, that anything less than victory would subject all of Southeast Asia to Communist servitude, the worst kind of tyranny and enslavement. He briefly remembered the draft of a speech he had written for McNamara a year ago—"we are acting in Vietnam to keep a promise, to help preserve South Vietnam's independence, to do what was needed. How long before the U.S. tires of its wearisome task? Till hell freezes over."

Those were grand words, even if McNamara never did use the speech. Then Ellsberg had come in-country, running away from a failed love affair like an old-fashioned romantic. He had seen with his own eyes the mishandling of the war effort, the taking and retaking of territory to no purpose, the corruption, the murders. And now at times he felt like a redcoat, part of a foreign army that didn't know the lay of the land, overheated and oversupplied, fighting an enemy that would not surrender because there was nowhere else for the enemy to go. They were home already.

"Why are you Americans here?" the drunken major had demanded. "What do you think you have to teach the Vietnamese in Vietnam? Do you think we are not brave enough to fight the Communists?"

He had ranted on in Vietnamese to the other officers at the table and none of them dared to contradict him. Then he had gone to his hut and gotten his pistol, shouting that he would kill the Americans. He had fired at Ellsberg and the American captain, even as the young Vietnamese lieutenant was apologizing for the major's behavior.

"It's nothing, don't worry," the lieutenant insisted. "But you should stay inside here tonight. You will be safe. The commander ordered soldiers to watch him, and they won't let him come near this house."

A fifty-caliber gun rattled in the distance as the Vietcong announced their presence to the night: this is our land, our paddies, our cattle, and our people, and you will never win. A short while later the American forces responded with their own artillery fire. Then silence, and the crickets resumed their mournful song, and the wind stirred lazily, and the captain snored some more, and Ellsberg thought of his children, Mary and Robert, back home. He wondered if Christmas would come with a cool snap in Santa Monica or if the California sun would warm the yellow sands by his house in Malibu as usual. A chill went through him, even though sweat poured from his body.

This is a shitty way to spend Christmas Eve, he decided, as the call and response of more mortars echoed in the sultry night.[1]

14

The Price of Success

Every day in the fall of 1965, when Albert Wohlstetter left his apartment near Chicago's Lakeshore Drive, he counted his blessings—or he would have, had he believed in a divinity that takes part in human affairs. Wohlstetter, ever the rationalist, subscribed more to the Enlightenment view of the Creator as clockmaker and humans as his benighted watchworks.

All the same, Wohlstetter knew he had been lucky. He had tenure at the University of Chicago; a wonderful family; and a ravishing apartment with a view of the lake, plus legions of friends to look after him and for him to look after. Fame and fortune (excessive fortune, at least) were not for him. He left the pursuit of Mammon to his brother Charles, now busy stringing together a telephone empire across the country. Albert was content with being at the heart of things. Policy and influence, that should be every thinking man's Balaam. Not power per se, but access to power. To leave one's mark on history and know that one had left this a better world. A legacy of change for good. What else could a man possibly want?

There were bound to be disappointments along the way. Such as the time he was so ignominiously cashiered from RAND by Frank Collbohm, in a fit of pique and resentment orchestrated by Bernard Brodie in 1963. To think that such great men could have stooped so low! Well, at least Brodie was great once. Collbohm always had the scent of mediocrity about him—the believer who mistakes conviction for intellect and doggedness for courage.

The snap in the air felt invigorating as Wohlstetter walked out of his building. He congratulated himself on the foresight of teaching only in the fall and spring quarters, leaving the rest of the year for his consulting work back in Los Angeles. Who would ever endure the frigid Chicago winters if they could do otherwise? Greeting the doorman he remembered his own old joke, that at RAND he had spoken to so many people in blue uniforms he once started debriefing the doorman at Washington's Shoreham Hotel. He hailed a cab and sank into the backseat.

Twelve years—1951 to 1963—in the middle of his life spent at RAND. The best years? No, not quite. The best was still to come. Yet . . . to be shown the door so unceremoniously. Of course, the document Brodie saw that he had given to Harry Rowen *had* been classified, but really, that was a rule observed more in the breach than in the keeping. He wondered for a moment how he would write it in his memoirs, if he ever got around to them. Irate zealot expels skeptical realist? Blackguard stabs man of principle in the back?

Collbohm had demanded his resignation. When Wohlstetter refused, Collbohm fired him. Like that. His years of service, his reputation, his friends, none of that mattered. It was Collbohm's ultimate revenge for Wohlstetter going against the Air Force, for backing Kennedy and McNamara, for daring to speak the truth about the stultifying environment RAND had become. The shock had been so great that Wohlstetter had practically burst into tears when talking about it to Daniel Ellsberg. This was the one eventuality he had never prepared for, and with his lifestyle . . . well, somehow he had convinced Collbohm to give him time to find another job. Fortunately, he'd landed one teaching at the University of California, Los Angeles, and then an even better position with tenure had come through in Chicago.

The taxi arrived at the campus and Wohlstetter stepped out, stretching. He headed for his political science class, taking in the bright faces of the students all around him, mingling in the quad dressed in their peacoats, boots, and collegiate sweaters. Perhaps Collbohm had, in the trite expression, done him a favor, forcing him to diversify, to explore other avenues. Besides, it was poetic justice— Collbohm himself was out of the picture. Brodie was gone, too, stewing at UCLA over the injustices done by NATO to the French armed forces and their nuclear arsenal, their much-vaunted (and, like all things French, much overrated) *force de frappe*. In the end, Brodie had become a Gallic lapdog. Poetic justice, indeed.

That afternoon, at a reception on campus, Wohlstetter was introduced to the new graduate students. He was drawn to one in particular, who had a familiar look—pasty complexion, dark hair, thick lips.

"Did you say your name is Wolfowitz?" asked Wohlstetter.

"Yes. I'm Paul Wolfowitz."

"By any chance are you related to Jack Wolfowitz, the mathematician? I studied with him and Abraham Wald back at Columbia."

"As a matter of fact, he's my father."

Wohlstetter smiled broadly. "Well, young man, I think you're going to like it here in Chicago."[1]

1965 WAS an auspicious year for Wohlstetter. Safely ensconced at the University of Chicago, he could freely indulge in the didactic streak that had made him so influential and controversial while at RAND. As a political science professor he could, like a new Cato, advance the cause of military preparedness and lambaste the current administration for its obsession with Vietnam at the expense of the extant Soviet threat—while still keeping a profitable side business as a consultant.

More than anything else, the University of Chicago provided him with an opportunity to recruit more acolytes. Perhaps the most influential of these would prove to be the young mathematician Paul Wolfowitz, who would reach the apogee of his political career as assistant secretary of defense for President George W. Bush—and orchestrate the war on Iraq.

Born in Brooklyn, Wolfowitz was reared in Manhattan's Morningside Heights, near Columbia University, where his father taught mathematical statistics. Like his famous father, Wolfowitz early in life showed a proclivity for numbers and theoretical physics. A math major at Cornell University, he realized he didn't have quite the same drive of his colleagues when, during his time off, he would be reading history books while they were working on yet another math problem. Wolfowitz found pure math, with its abstract nature and separation from real life, sterile; he decided that if he could use his mathematical gifts to find a cure for cancer he would be more satisfied. He applied and was accepted at Massachusetts Institute of Technology for a Ph.D. in biophysical chemistry, yet, still unsure over his future career, he postponed that to pursue a degree in political science at the University of Chicago.[2]

Although at first Wolfowitz fell into the intellectual orbit of controversial philosopher Leo Strauss,[3] once he met Wohlstetter at the University of Chicago, Wolfowitz sought him out as his mentor.* Both Wolfowitz and Wohlstetter were secular Jews who were fierce

---

* At Chicago, Wolfowitz also became a student of Allan Bloom, the notorious philosophy teacher who influenced a generation of neoconservatives. His relationship with Bloom was fictionalized in Saul Bellow's final novel, *Ravelstein*.

advocates of Israel's interests—with an abiding interest in Middle East politics. Wohlstetter's approach to issues was numbers oriented, which fit easily with Wolfowitz's own proclivities; moreover, they shared the same policy perspective: that accommodation with the Soviet Union bordered on the obscene. All the different skeins that would eventually weave through Wolfowitz's career (the fact-based approach to problem solving; the belief in America's messianic role in the world; the sub-rosa Zionism that predicates the survival of Israel as essential to the survival of mankind—all joined to a bedrock conviction that democracy can grow vigorous roots anywhere in the world) were beliefs that were encouraged by Wohlstetter.

In Chicago, Wohlstetter would also encourage the career of another soon-to-be famous (and infamous) policy maven, Richard Perle. The man who would be called the "Prince of Darkness" by his adversaries and the "Pentagon's Brains" by his admirers, Perle had remained in touch with the strategist through college after attending Hollywood High School with Wohlstetter's daughter, Joan. In 1969, while Perle was doing graduate work at Princeton, Wohlstetter called on him to carry out some field research. Perle's job was to interview Senator Henry "Scoop" Jackson—then a prominent member of the Senate Armed Services Committee as well as chairman of the Committee on Interior Affairs[4]—along with other influential politicians in Washington for a report on the debate in the Senate on an antiballistic missile defense system.[5] A Democrat from Washington State, Jackson was known as the "Senator from Boeing" for his hawkish, prodefense views. Jackson, like Wohlstetter, was a believer in what they called moral foreign policy, morality meaning anti-Soviet, anti-Communist policy. Although a Lutheran of Norwegian origins, Jackson was a committed supporter of Israel and had sponsored legislation that linked nuclear disarmament talks to the freedom of Jews to emigrate from the Soviet Union.[6]

As Perle recounted,

[Wohlstetter] said, I've asked somebody else to do this too, and maybe the two of you could work together. The someone else was Paul Wolfowitz. So Paul and I came to Washington as volunteers for a few days, to interview people, and one of the people we interviewed was Scoop Jackson and it was love at first sight. I will never forget that first encounter with Scoop. Here we were, a couple of graduate students, sitting on the floor in Scoop's office in the Senate, reviewing charts and analyses of the ballistic missile defense and getting his views on the subject.[7]

That fateful interview would lead to Jackson offering Perle a job as an assistant at his office and, ultimately, in Ronald Reagan's first term, to Perle's appointment as assistant secretary of defense for international security policy—the first rung in Perle's ascent of the Washington bureaucracy.[8]

IN THE MID to late 1960s, while Wohlstetter was busy preparing himself and his wards for the future after the country's obsession with Vietnam ran its course, the RAND Corporation was breaking new ground in the field of social research. Once Rowen took over from Collbohm as head of RAND on January 1, 1967, any remaining taboos about straying from military work were disregarded. RAND's tools of case modeling, quantitative bases, and hierarchical chains of command, which worked for the Air Force and the Defense Department, were perfectly attuned to the Johnson-era zeitgeist. In addition, Rowen seemed the perfect man for the job of expanding RAND's methodology into social research. He told the RAND board, even before taking over, "I have been greatly impressed while in the Executive Office of the President by the need for research and analysis on domestic problems comparable to that done on defense. The

range of important and interesting problems here is enormous: education, health, crime, urban problems, poverty."[9] None of these fields
had been subjected to the kind of strenuous, logical, numerical case
testing that was RAND's forte. Rowen's plan was simple enough: he
intended to make RAND the brains of the Johnson administration.

A Boston-born industrial engineer, Rowen was a RAND veteran, having started in the think tank's Economics Department
under Charles Hitch in 1950. Rowen's first major assignment was
assisting with Wohlstetter's basing study. Rowen worked in close
collaboration with Wohlstetter until 1953, when Rowen told Hitch
that he wanted to get a Ph.D. in economics. "And I went to him and
he said, 'Study at Oxford.' 'How do I do that?' He said, 'I'll write
a letter to the Provost of Queens College' and that was the admis-
sions process."[10]

Rowen spent two years at Oxford. On his return to RAND, he
collaborated with Wohlstetter on "Selection and Use of Strategic
Air Bases," the follow-up to the original basing study. After John
Kennedy's election in 1960, Rowen went to work for Paul Nitze as
deputy assistant secretary of defense for international affairs. Rowen
held the job until 1965, when President Johnson ordered that the Department of Defense's budgeting methods be adopted throughout
the federal government; Rowen was appointed assistant director of
the Bureau of the Budget to shepherd the project. Two years later,
having completed his assignment, he had left government for a
teaching post at MIT when RAND offered him its top job. "I accepted the position of professor of political science at MIT and sold
the house in Los Angeles, bought a house in the Boston area. Then
the RAND board came to me and asked me to be president of
RAND. I said okay. Sold the house we'd never moved into in Boston,
had already sold the house in Los Angeles, had to buy a new house
in Los Angeles. And we had to sell the house in Washington. That
was five houses [sold and bought] in about six months, which was
painful."[11]

Three months after taking over RAND, Rowen restructured the think tank's internal divisions, making the organization better able to diversify. With his deep Rolodex of contacts in Washington, as well as his keen analysis of the needs of the corporation and of the government, Rowen quickly came up with the notion of establishing a center called the Social Urban Institute. The new institute would amount to a clone of the original Project RAND, only this time devoted to social policy studies. The center would utilize the think tank's researchers and recruit outside experts to focus on the domestic problems that many believed were sapping American strength abroad by undermining domestic social stability.

Riots in the Los Angeles ghetto of Watts in 1965, followed by equally violent racial disorders in Newark, New Jersey, and Detroit, Michigan, two years later, shook to the core the national complacency about domestic conditions. Problems of police brutality, poverty, and discrimination undermined the image of an equitable America bringing the fruits of democracy to Vietnam and other countries. How could the United States claim the high ground in foreign affairs—and proclaim the superiority of democracy to communism—if people were rioting for lack of jobs, shelter, and justice? The Johnson administration needed help to solve these problems and Rowen was certain that RAND's systems analysis would win the day.

As if to replicate not only the spirit but also the structure of RAND's early years, Rowen organized a conference in May 1967 to gather advice and support for his urban studies institute—much like the New York City conference John Williams had set up in 1947. Among the attendees at the Rowen meeting were Wohlstetter; Kenneth Arrow; former RAND analyst and assistant director of the Bureau of the Budget Charles Zwick; former special assistant to Secretary of Defense McNamara Adam Yarmolinsky; and political scientist and historian Richard E. Neustadt.

The conferees quickly realized that things would be more difficult for the new RAND center, which would not enjoy the disen-
gaged sponsorship of the Air Force: "It was generally agreed that
RAND had benefited from having a rich, 'stupid client' who was not
interested in meddling in the affairs of RAND or in receiving answers during the early years. The present environment for an urban
research group is entirely different."[12]

Participants recommended that RAND initially secure funding
for at least five years to avoid economic instability. They also suggested that the center be set up under a separate board of trustees
and housed in a location close to yet separate from RAND, since
they believed it would be able to recruit more young scientists than
could be accommodated by RAND's Social Science Department. It
was estimated that the proposed institute would employ about
twenty full-time senior staff, with an annual budget of approximately $2.5 million.

Although the institute would be bereft of Air Force sponsorship,
its birth seemed exquisitely well-timed otherwise. A bevy of government agencies, previously unable to get RAND expertise, were
eager to hire the think tank to find new solutions to national problems. The commissioner of education wanted RAND to conduct
studies on educational television and the uses of technology in teaching. The Health, Education, and Welfare Department was mulling
over a Rowen proposal for a program to study improvements in the
nation's health system, while the Department of Transportation was
interested in having RAND conduct studies on the use of sensors for
measuring traffic-flow rates.[13] Moreover, in March, President Johnson had asked Congress for an increase in funding for social research projects, establishing an Office of Urban Technology and
Research with a $20 million budget. Nevertheless, Rowen, in spite
of all his inside-the-Beltway contacts, had not anticipated that his aggressive campaign to establish RAND as the nexus of government

social policy research would be the catalyst for a competitor with even closer ties to the administration.

Joseph Califano was President Johnson's special assistant for domestic affairs, with supervision of the newly created Housing and Urban Development Department (HUD). The thirty-four-year-old Harvard graduate, originally recruited by McNamara to work in the Pentagon, was the Brooklyn-born-and-bred product of a working-class Italian Irish family. Califano was proud of his professional achievements, but he was especially proud of his political service to the administration. As LBJ told him shortly after bringing him to the White House, "They tell me you're pretty smart, way up in your class at Harvard. Well, let me tell you something. What you learned on the streets of Brooklyn will be a damn sight more helpful to your president than anything you learned at Harvard."[14]

Califano saw in Rowen's proposed Social Urban Institute a means for the administration to gain very favorable publicity, but he was not about to relinquish the limelight or the influence to RAND. On hearing of Rowen's conference, he realized that unless he acted quickly there would be little talent available for HUD to hire, so he organized his own meeting in June to consider establishing an institute for urban development. Out of that meeting and others that followed over the next few months, Califano decided that the proposed HUD urban research institute should be in the RAND style, in that it would "put some bright people to work thinking 'deep, broad thoughts' about the problems of cities in general." There would be one glaring exception: although ostensibly independent, the institute would be closely guided by HUD on day-to-day operations, funding, and administrative functions.[15] In other words, it would be an appendage of the Great Society, President Johnson's notion of America as a place where there was abundance and liberty for all with "an end to poverty and racial injustice"[16]—the vision that produced Medicare, Medicaid, and the Civil Rights Act of 1964.

In December of 1967, with President Johnson's blessings, Califano announced the creation of a "privately chartered, non-profit corporation" that would be called the Urban Institute.* Its first president would be former RAND analyst William Gorham, who had served as deputy secretary of defense under McNamara.

Califano used the Urban Institute to block RAND's access to social policy work. He leaned heavily on all federal agencies to channel a portion of their research funds to the institute. He also touted the work of the institute to policy makers around the country, sending letters to the governors of all fifty states and the mayors of the country's largest cities underlining President Johnson's commitment to the institute and encouraging them to establish a working relationship with it.[17]

A frustrated Rowen was left with no choice but to lead RAND into securing greater funding from nongovernmental sources, including private industry and large private foundations. Given its position at the apex of the military-industrial complex, RAND was certainly well placed to leverage its connections with the private sector. Two of its trustees were vice presidents of Standard Oil; in 1968, its board chairman would be Standard Oil vice president David A. Shepard. Paul Nitze suggested RAND do research on the connection between American foreign policy and oil interests in the Middle East. However, RAND was unable to carry out the work since oil companies wanted to keep the results of the studies to themselves, while RAND's charter explicitly prohibited it from contracting for proprietary research. Instead RAND turned to the Ford Foundation, just as in previous occasions, for a major portion of its social research

---

* To this day the Urban Institute, which advertises itself as a nonpartisan economic and social policy research organization headquartered in Washington, follows closely the RAND methodology: that is, picking the "right" issues; assembling the "right" teams; following the facts wherever they lead; subjecting the findings to peer review; and putting the results in the hands of the appropriate stakeholders.

funding. Perhaps most significant of all, RAND entered into a marriage of convenience with the one major figure in the national political landscape who seemed capable of standing up to the Johnson administration: New York City mayor John V. Lindsay.

The photogenic forty-three-year-old Lindsay was often dubbed the "Republican Kennedy." A decorated Navy lieutenant and Yale-educated lawyer, Lindsay was descended from old New England stock. Seven times elected congressman from New York's Silk Stocking district (the GOP strongholds of Park Avenue and Manhattan's Upper East Side), in 1965 he had won the mayoral race as the voice of reform. "He's fresh and everybody else is tired," was his slogan, cribbed from journalist Murray Kempton.[18] Journalists, liberals, and minorities gave him their votes and their hearts in what would amount to the last swoon of American big-city liberalism.

Lindsay was cut from the same cloth as then New York governor Nelson Rockefeller: Republicans who aimed to be both pro-business and pro–civil rights, in the process sometimes proving themselves more liberal than Democrats. As Lindsay said after first being elected to the House of Representatives, "I expect to lay out proof that the Republican Party . . . will stand for progressive measures designed to further the freedom and security of the individual."[19]

True to his word, in 1963 Congressman Lindsay fought to block attempts by Attorney General Robert F. Kennedy to expand the 1918 Sedition Act to curb criticism of U.S. policies by Americans abroad.[20] Years later, after his mayoral triumph, Lindsay pledged that he would bring to heel the powerful vested interests of unions and bureaucracies that controlled New York City. He therefore refused to meet behind closed doors with the transit workers union, which was threatening a subway strike, calling such backroom deals undemocratic.[21] Instead of being cowed, the union staged its strike the moment Lindsay became mayor on January 1, 1966. The walkout paralyzed the city for thirteen days, and in the end forced Lindsay to give in to the union's demands. Like President Kennedy in

Vienna, Lindsay began his term giving the impression of political weakness; throughout his administration, he would be forced to confront a series of political challenges arising from that perceived weakness.

Part of Lindsay's problems stemmed from his being a Republican in a city, and a country, controlled by the Democratic Party. The New York City Board of Estimate and the city council were under the heel of the last vestiges of Tammany Hall, the Democratic machine that had controlled New York politics since the late nineteenth century.[22] At the national level, President Johnson was no fan of Lindsay's either, and at times tried to undercut him by postponing or delaying federal housing grants.[23] In addition, Lindsay inherited a city rife with racial divisions and political tensions. That New York did not go up in flames during the riots of the summer of 1968—like Detroit, Washington, and Philadelphia—was due to the efforts of Lindsay, who personally visited the black and Hispanic ghettos without bodyguards, jacket slung over his shoulder, urging residents to keep calm.[24]

Lindsay and his band of idealists believed they could bring efficiency to government, reforming New York City much like McNamara had reshaped the Pentagon, squeezing politics out of government policy by examining it under the cool, considered gaze of objective, numerical rationality. It was only natural that they would welcome an alliance with RAND, the standard-bearer of Reason.

Lindsay's budget director, Frederick O'Reilly Hayes, had worked with Rowen at the Bureau of the Budget, and was familiar with the program budgeting and program analysis methods propagated by RAND throughout the federal system.[25] Hayes asked the Ford Foundation for a five-year, $4.5 million grant to set up a "RAND type corporation" that would study urban problems and suggest solutions. The Ford Foundation declined, seeing this as a way for the Lindsay administration to create policy without the input of the elected—even if Democratic and union-controlled—Board of Estimate and city council. Jilted, the Lindsay administration turned to RAND. On January 8, 1968, Lindsay and Rowen unveiled four contracts with RAND to conduct six-month studies of the city's fire department, police department, health services administration, and housing and development administration. As Lindsay said, "I regard this as the most important development in the search for effectiveness in city government in many, many years."[26]

In theory, the alliance was an ideal match of aspirations. New York would be a laboratory for RAND to perfect its application of systems analysis and research methodology to urban problems. The Lindsay administration in turn would receive nonpartisan, objective reports on the city's problems and how to solve them—while scoring points against the obstructionist, inefficient Democrats. By 1969, the partnership was formalized through the creation of the New York City–RAND Institute, an independent, nonprofit research organization supported by RAND and New York City. This time, with the RAND aegis guaranteeing a minimum of partisanship, the Ford Foundation signed on, becoming a main benefactor to the new entity. By 1971, the work of the New York City–RAND Institute would comprise close to half of RAND's urban studies.[27]

RAND's alliance with New York City lent the final air of legitimacy to the military think tank's expansion into social research. By the end of 1968, RAND had secured contracts—from the Office of Economic Opportunity, the Department of Transportation, the Department of Housing and Urban Development, the Ford Foundation, and other foundations—worth more than $2 million. Essentially, RAND shut its major competition in the field, the Urban Institute, out of New York City affairs. However, there was a price to be paid. RAND found itself in the middle of bitter, no-holds-barred battles over the future of New York, next to which the bureaucratic infighting of the Pentagon seemed like choosing cakes over scones at a college faculty tea.

The police department fell off the RAND bandwagon first.[28] Although the contract to examine and propose improvements to New York City's finest was the largest, worth close to a $1 million, the police department terminated it within a year of signing. The NYPD was in the grip of forces that thrived on massive corruption and inefficiency; hundreds of officers were implicated in narcotics scams, while police abuse of minorities and generally brutal conduct was the order of the day.* There was little desire for change, much less reform, and the department did its best to ignore directives from a liberal mayor widely despised by the rank and file. RAND was also perceived as insensitive to the problems of the force. Critics pointed to the refusal of its researchers to be inconvenienced by being stationed at police headquarters or precinct houses, even though such a move would have gained the confidence of many officers.[29]

RAND research did little to lessen the NYPD's distrust: New York City–RAND attempted to dissect the department's recruitment, selection, and training practices, putting together a database of information about the nearly 2,000 officers who had joined since the late 1950s. This included highly confidential material such as criminal records, employment histories, education, criminal charges, and civilian complaints—a laundry list of possible transgressions that could terminate an officer's career if leaked to the press.[30]

Such a possibility was not remote. New York City–RAND drafted an ostensibly confidential report on police misconduct that used the information in the database to support charges of police abuse, which landed on the front page of the *New York Times* in November of 1970.[31] It charged police with a consistent pattern of brutality and disregard for public opinion, pointing out that only in 5 percent of cases involving accusations of criminal activity or abuse of citizens did an officer ever receive anything more severe than a reprimand.

---

* This state of affairs was popularized years later in movies such as *Serpico* and *The French Connection*.

The report furthered the impression among police that New York City–RAND was the mayor's plaything, since the information was being used to advocate wholesale changes in the department.

The New York City–RAND studies on housing policy proved equally explosive, leaving in tatters the organization's reputation as a nonpartisan research group. The institute tackled the issue of rent control reform, a highly charged subject in a city with a growing population of low-income, white, elderly residents and equally impoverished minorities. The Lindsay administration wanted to modify rent control laws to encourage landlords to improve their properties and remedy the blight of the inner city. However, critics—including many minority leaders—saw this as an attempt to raise rents and drive poor tenants out of their housing. This in spite of the fact that by 1968 close to 100,000 vacant units—enough to house the population of Jersey City—had been abandoned by their owners in New York because of a lack of financial incentives to keep them viable.

In a series of reports, New York City–RAND drew up proposals that would allow the free market to determine the price of rentals, with some limitations.

> Non-welfare families would be issued rent certificates for the difference between what they could afford and the pre-established schedule of minimum rents . . . Landlords would cash these certificates—similar to food stamps for grocers— with the city, which would redeem them only if the building were free of code violations.[32]

Community activists got wind of the supposedly confidential rent control reports by the end of 1969, even while housing officials denied the existence of them. In February of 1970, the mayor's office finally acknowledged the existence of the studies but claimed that they had not been completed. Less than ten days later, the *New*

York Times ran a front-page article describing the full set of RAND recommendations.[33] Again, critics—among them future New York City mayor Abraham Beame—charged New York City–RAND with being the intellectual minion of city hall, instead of being an independent analysis group.

The health division of the New York City–RAND Institute conducted well-received research in areas like lead poisoning, venereal disease, and nurse training, but a lack of stable leadership in the group impeded it from implementing many of its recommendations.[34] By contrast, RAND's alliance with the fire department was an unqualified success, attributable in part to the fact that the fire department was the most centralized, hierarchical, and disciplined organization that RAND dealt with in New York City—that is, it offered the closest equivalent to the environment of the Pentagon, where efficiency could be pursued without the messy problems of partisan politics, social value judgments, and personal ethical considerations.

RAND's success at the FDNY was also a matter of coordination and, especially, luck. RAND actively sought to become part of the FDNY team, placing researchers at station houses, developing results desired by the department and relevant to their mission, such as reducing the total number of false alarm responses and streamlining procedures for answered calls. In addition, the fire department was profoundly grateful to RAND for bringing them "slippery water."

New York City–RAND's top fire researcher, Edward Blum, was a chemical engineer who had consulted for Union Carbide years earlier. He was aware of a polymer product developed by Union Carbide that, when added to water, increased dramatically its flow rate through hoses. He convinced the department to try the additive in 1968, which gave spectacular results—by reducing the friction in hoses, the product increased the amount of water discharged by up to 80 percent without any corresponding increase in pumping pressure. Slippery water became a fixture of the department, and other firefighting organizations across the nation soon adopted the innovation.[35]

These varied studies, useful to New York as they might have been, were not enough by themselves to prolong the life of the New York City–RAND Institute, nor could they sustain the Lindsay administration through its many political crises. By 1973, Lindsay had switched to the Democratic Party and run unsuccessfully for president. Faced with a disillusioned electorate, and as tired as his opponents had been in 1965, he opted not to run for a third term as mayor of what he had once optimistically dubbed "Fun City."[36]

While city comptroller in 1970, the new mayor, Abraham Beame, had blasted the Lindsay administration's expenditure of $75 million on outside consultants and refused to honor $2 million worth of RAND contracts. Now, having replaced Lindsay, he moved to terminate all RAND research, following recommendations by the city council that New York use its own experts at City University for any consulting work. When its last contracts with the city expired, the institute was dissolved and its remaining personnel transferred to Santa Monica headquarters.[37] Years later, another New York City RAND subsidiary would open its doors from 1996 to 2005 but this time its work would be limited to comparative educational research.[38]

One of the main lessons RAND learned from its experience with the New York City–RAND Institute was the need to avoid the impression of partisanship. From the 1970s on RAND deliberately tried to cultivate parties on both sides of the political fence, favoring neither Democrats nor Republicans in their analyses. Under Rowen's direction, RAND began a series of programs of research in environmental policy, communications, broadcasting, and education that are still being pursued today. Above all, New York City–RAND paved the way for the day its livelihood would be equally supported by the civilian and military sectors. That state of readiness proved useful when one of RAND's brightest stars plunged the organization into the greatest—and most dangerous—controversy in its history: the Pentagon Papers.

RAND founder and president Frank Collbohm (right) meeting in his office with General Maxwell Taylor (left), army chief of staff, in 1958. *Photo by Leonard McCombe/Time Life Pictures/ Getty Images*

RAND mathematician and founding father John Williams in 1959. *Photo by Leonard McCombe/Time Life Pictures/Getty Images*

Futurologist and controversial RAND author Herman Kahn waiting to speak in 1968. *Photo by John Loengard/Time Life Pictures/ Getty Images*

Mathematician Albert Wohlstetter at his stylish Hollywood Hills home discussing national defense with his closest RAND colleagues in 1958. From left: unidentified man, Henry Rowen, Andrew Marshall, and Alain Enthoven. Wohlstetter has his back to the camera. *Photo by Leonard McCombe/ Time Life Pictures/Getty Images*

Albert Wohlstetter, his daughter, Joan, and Roberta Wohlstetter in 1955. *Photo by Julius Shulman*

RAND analysts at a war game in 1958, conducting mock strategy in an air and missile battle. The man in the middle is Daniel Ellsberg, who had just joined RAND. He was so pessimistic about the possibility of a nuclear war he declined to enroll in RAND's pension plan.
Photo by Leonard McCombe/ Time Life Pictures/Getty Images

The RAND building in Santa Monica in the 1950s. Located just a few blocks from the beach, it was open day and night for the benefit of RAND analysts who kept unusual working hours.
Photo by Julius Shulman

RAND's godfather, U.S. Air Force Chief of Staff General Curtis LeMay (right), sitting next to President John F. Kennedy in January 1962. The two were constantly at odds, with LeMay comparing Kennedy's defense policies to those of the Soviet Union. *Hulton Archive/Getty Images*

General LeMay at home playing with his dogs in August 1961, during the height of the Berlin Crisis. *Photo by Ed Clark/Time Life Pictures/Getty Images*

Wohlstetter collaborator Alain Enthoven giving a lecture on budgeting for the Strategic Air Command at RAND in 1958. Shortly after this Enthoven would quit RAND out of frustration with management. Hired by Secretary of Defense Robert McNamara, he became one of the Whiz Kids that reshaped the Pentagon. *Photo by Leonard McCombe/Time Life Pictures/Getty Image*s

U.S. Air Force Chief of Staff General Thomas D. White conferring in his office at the Pentagon with RAND executives in 1958. By this time RAND analysts had become the brains guiding the brawn of Strategic Air Command and the Air Force. *Photo by Hank Walker/Time Life Pictures/Getty Images*

RAND employees enjoying a joke made by Socialist presidential candidate Norman Thomas during a lecture in 1965. By the mid-1960s many at RAND had begun to pull away from the think tank's conservative ideological leanings. *Photo by Leonard McCombe/Time Life Pictures/ Getty Images*

Two RAND engineers inspecting an oil drilling platform for possible use as a missile launching pad for the Corona Project, a top-secret reconnaissance satellite program. *Photo by Leonard McCombe/Time Life Pictures/ Getty Images*

Paul Nitze, one of the seminal figures of the Cold War and a longtime RAND associate, speaking at an economic summit in 1963. As President Kennedy's assistant secretary of defense he and Robert McNamara ushered in an era of widespread RAND participation in the federal government. *Photo by Ralph Morse/Time Life Pictures/Getty Images*

New York City Mayor John V. Lindsay (center) during a walking tour of Harlem in 1968. Lindsay, a liberal Republican, hired RAND to conduct a series of studies aimed at reforming city government—and undermining the power of the local Democratic Party machinery. It was RAND's most ambitious and ultimately most unsuccessful foray into urban policy making. *Photo by John Dominis/Time Life Pictures/Getty Images*

Albert Wohlstetter (left), Roberta Wohlstetter (center), and Paul Nitze (right) were awarded the Medal of Freedom on November 1, 1985, by President Ronald Reagan at the White House. Roberta was so moved she could say little more than "I'm dazzled and very deeply honored." *Photo by Diana Walker/Time Life Pictures/Getty Images*

RAND alumnus and Albert Wohlstetter protégé Zalmay Khalilzad, U.S. ambassador to the United Nations, is to the right of President George W. Bush and next to Secretary of State Condoleezza Rice. Sitting behind them at the U.N. General Assembly in September 2007 is National Security Advisor Stephen Hadley. *Photo by Jim Watson/AFP/Getty Images*

15

Stealing Away

It is the evening of October 1, 1969.

Daniel Ellsberg stuffs the bound papers into his scuffed briefcase and walks nervously down the halls of RAND headquarters in Santa Monica. The documents he carries, all stamped TOP SECRET, are part of a Pentagon-commissioned forty-seven-volume series of studies on the Vietnam War dating back to 1945. Only two full sets of the documents exist. Ellsberg has one set; the other is secreted in the offices of Secretary of Defense Melvin Laird. The papers trace the history of American involvement in Southeast Asia, but to Ellsberg they also detail decades of murderous deceit. He is determined to tell the entire sorry tale, even if he spends the rest of his life behind bars as a convicted traitor.

Since 1967, he has attempted to stop the war from inside the government, pointing out the failure of a Vietnam policy that at best could only lead to a bloody stalemate. No one has listened—not Robert McNamara, not President Johnson, not Henry Kissinger, not even his own superiors at RAND. To American leaders, change means retreat, retreat means dishonor, and death is preferable to dishonor. No matter that President Nixon pledged to wind down the war, and that the United States is holding peace talks with North Vietnam; Ellsberg has seen secret cables indicating that Nixon will continue the war, expand it, through secrecy and covert action. Perhaps even drop a nuclear bomb on Hanoi. The only way to stop the madness is to bring the entire history before the American public. Ellsberg is sure the country will turn in revulsion against the people who have committed these war crimes in its name.

Ironically, Ellsberg can carry out this mission because he is the sole civilian keeper of the history project. In 1967, newly appointed RAND president Harry Rowen suggested to McNamara that a study be made of the "lessons" of Vietnam and how America had found itself involved in Southeast Asia.[1] McNamara enthusiastically agreed. Rowen put Ellsberg, his protégé, in charge. Now Ellsberg is turning his back on the man he calls his best friend, knowing it will probably cost Rowen his job and, worst of all for a federal bureaucrat, his security clearance.

Ellsberg has made arrangements to meet that night with Anthony Russo, his fellow RAND researcher whose experiences with the Vietcong motivation study soured him on the prospects of peace in Southeast Asia. Russo's girlfriend, Lynda Sinay, owns an ad agency with a late-issue Xerox machine, which Ellsberg and Russo intend to use to make copies of all the documents and turn them over to Congress and the press. However, getting the papers out of RAND may not prove easy.

Security at RAND is even tighter than at the Pentagon, where Ellsberg worked for several years. He often had taken top-secret cables with him as he traveled between the Office of the Secretary of Defense, the State Department, and the White House without even a sideways glance from security officers. But here at the think tank all classified material is kept in top-secret safes unless it is being used. Ellsberg has never been searched when leaving the building, but he has no reason to believe he won't be searched tonight either.

His heart racing, Ellsberg opens the twin security doors to the lobby. Two guards sit at the desk. On the wall behind them hang posters from World War II: WHAT YOU SEE HERE, WHAT YOU SAY HERE, LET IT BE HERE, LET IT STAY HERE. Another shows a hapless suspect questioned by guards, with the caption, WANT TO MEET NEW FRIENDS, VISIT INTERESTING PLACES? LEAVE YOUR SAFE UNLOCKED. He hesitates a moment at the glass doors then strides through with all the confidence he can muster. One of the guards looks up, gives him the once-over, then smiles.

"Good night, Dan," says the guard.

Ellsberg waves with his free hand, nods, and eases out of the midcentury modernist building down the succulent-lined walkway to the parking lot. The sky looms a Hessian blue above the Santa Monica police station across the street. Exhilarated, Ellsberg climbs into his Alfa Romeo and drives out to Russo's apartment in West Hollywood, making sure to observe the speed limit.

Sinay's ad agency is above a flower shop at the corner of Melrose and Crescent Heights, in a neighborhood popular with artistic types. Sinay leads them up an outside staircase with iron railings to her office door, inserting a key to switch off a burglar alarm. The Xerox machine by the door is large and fast—for its time—but still Ellsberg realizes he will be working all night to copy the cache of documents. The Moratorium, a national strike to protest the war, is scheduled for October 15, and he wants to have the papers out in time for the action. Ellsberg hopes his documents will be published in time to give extra weight to a letter he, Konrad Kellen, and several other RAND analysts are planning to send to the *New York Times* in the next few days publicly demanding the withdrawal of American troops from Vietnam within the year.

Ellsberg struggles with the large bound books of purloined papers. He tries pressing them down on the glass to copy two pages at a time, but the image at the center comes out faint and uneven. He takes the books apart and presses down the pages, the glass emitting an otherworldly green light as the roller underneath traverses the length of the page. He gives the first copies to Russo and Sinay to collate and returns to the machine.

Two sharp knocks on the glass door interrupt him: a couple of uniformed police officers stand at the top of the stairs. One of them gestures at Ellsberg to open up. *Jesus Christ!* thinks Ellsberg, amazed at the speed with which he has been found out. *These guys are fantastic! How did they do it?*

Ellsberg quickly places the lid of the copier back down on the document he's copying. As he advances to the door, wondering what will happen to his children, he covers a pile of documents marked TOP SECRET with a piece of plain paper.

"What's the problem, officers?" asks Ellsberg, opening up.

"Your alarm has gone off," says one.

With as much sangfroid as he can summon, Ellsberg turns to Russo and Sinay.

"Lynda, there are some people here to see you."

The police troop in.

"Hi, Lynda. You've done it again, huh?" says one of the officers.

"Oh, God, I'm so sorry," she replies, stepping out to greet them, as Russo covers up his pages. "I'm hopeless with that damned key."

"Oh, no problem," says the cop. "You've got to get a lesson on that thing."

"Oh, I will, I will!" promises Sinay.

The officers wave good-bye and walk out of the office. Ellsberg looks at Russo and Sinay in stunned silence for a moment, then they all return to work.[2]

16

Plus Ça Change

THE DISCLOSURE of the Pentagon Papers was a savage blow to
RAND. To think that someone like Daniel Ellsberg—the golden boy
of Harry Rowen and Albert Wohlstetter—had disclosed top-secret
information to the *New York Times* was as inconceivable as Saint
Paul deciding he'd throw in his lot with the Pharisees after all and
turn Saint Peter over to the Romans.

Yet to some in RAND the news about Ellsberg was not surprising. Albert and Roberta Wohlstetter were having lunch at Oxford with their daughter and the Sovietologist Nathan Leites on June
13, 1971, when they heard of the publication of the Pentagon Papers.
Silence fell; then they turned to one another and exclaimed at the
same time, "Dan!" They felt he was the only RANDite who would
take classified information to the public at large. Leites sniped, "After
all, he's approaching forty and he still hasn't written a book." Leites
thought Ellsberg should have put all his expertise on Vietnam into

a treatise that would synthesize his arguments, instead of feeding the raw data to the *New York Times*.[1]

It had taken Ellsberg three years to surreptitiously copy and finally publish the multivolume Pentagon Papers project; during that time the war in Vietnam had progressed from bad to atrocious. During his final months in office, President Johnson had started negotiating with the North Vietnamese in Paris and stopped bombing the North. And although President Nixon continued formal contacts with Hanoi and began a program of "Vietnamization" to scale down the participation of U.S. troops, 15,000 more American soldiers had died in battle. In addition, the conflict had expanded. In 1970, American planes had bombed neighboring Cambodia, whose Prince Norodom Sihanouk had been deposed by a U.S.-backed army general. The following year, South Vietnamese troops had invaded Laos in pursuit of North Vietnamese units. There had been more civilian casualties than ever before and the war still showed no sign of winding down.[2]

In the United States, widespread antiwar sentiment had cleaved the nation in two. Nixon, who had taken office in 1968 saying he had a plan to end the war, had become almost as unpopular as Johnson had been. Public confidence in Nixon had dropped to 50 percent and support for the war had slid to 34 percent. More than half of the country felt that the conflict was "morally wrong." Vietnam veterans, haunted by the destruction they had witnessed and created, now led the antiwar protests. In April 1971, 200,000 demonstrators staged a huge rally in Washington, practically shutting down the city for two days and prompting a confused Nixon to come out and talk to some in the crowd. One of the leading speakers was former naval officer John Kerry, who would become a senator from Massachusetts and the 2004 Democratic Party presidential candidate. Speaking eloquently on behalf of his fellow veterans, he pledged to "reach out and destroy the last vestige of this barbaric war."[3] The American public therefore eagerly lapped up Ellsberg's revelations about deception and government officials who willfully ignored warnings of a quagmire in Vietnam.

When it was confirmed that Ellsberg was indeed the apostate, Harry Rowen accepted responsibility for the breach in security and resigned. Economics Division head Charles Wolf, Jr., Ellsberg's immediate boss, still dripped venom when interviewed about the incident more than thirty years after the fact. For one thing, he concluded with disdain, Ellsberg's actions were not rational,[4] given that President Nixon had already committed to withdrawing American troops from Vietnam. In Wolf's opinion, all Ellsberg achieved was to besmirch the reputation of the place that had nurtured him and encouraged his talent. Donald B. Rice, who replaced Rowen, still believes Ellsberg committed a crime. "In the moral sense, absolutely. In the professional obligation sense, absolutely. Whether it's legally a crime or not, I don't know, that's for lawyers and courts to decide."[5]

Yet Ellsberg was not the only RAND analyst who had contemplated disclosing the secret report. At least two other researchers who worked on the Pentagon Papers told a former RAND staffer that even though they themselves would not have gone to the media with the material, they were happy that Ellsberg had done so.[6] Konrad Kellen framed it this way: "It was all madness and we had to stop it somehow."[7]

Interviewed at his spacious home in the San Francisco Bay Area, Ellsberg admitted that for years before his disclosure of the Pentagon Papers, he had been torn by the conflicting demands of his friends and family on one side, and his conscience on the other. Already in 1969, the publication of the letter signed by RAND analysts in opposition to the Vietnam War had shattered his relationship with Wohlstetter. The éminence grise of RAND might also have been opposed to the war in Vietnam, but the thought of stepping outside channels was anathema to him.

"My two best friends were Albert Wohlstetter and Harry Rowen, with Albert more like a father and Harry more like an older brother. Albert felt that [with the letter] I had betrayed Harry. He didn't know that Harry had approved it. When I told him he said, 'If Harry told you to take out your cock in the street at high noon, would you do it?' I told him, 'That's what this all means to you, doesn't it, Albert? Pure exhibitionism?' "

Ellsberg and Wohlstetter never spoke again after that incident. When the Pentagon Papers were published two years later, his relationship to Rowen also was destroyed.

The decision to go public with the secret study was a painful separation from RAND for Ellsberg, who had planned to stay at the think tank for the rest of his life. "I had no thought of going back to the academic world until the Pentagon Papers. RAND was perfect for an intellectual. The working conditions at RAND were ideal, you didn't have to teach classes. It was an idyllic existence."[8]

Ellsberg's Parnassus effectively ended the moment the FBI found out he had been handing out copies of the Pentagon Papers to Democratic congressmen. Ellsberg resigned from RAND almost at the same time as Nixon ordered the Justice Department to prosecute him for divulging state secrets. A series of injunctions against any newspaper that published the Pentagon Papers only succeeded in getting Ellsberg and his associates to distribute the documents to an ever-larger circle of news organizations until finally the U.S. Supreme Court ruled against the Justice Department and allowed their publication.

To countermand the drubbing his reputation had taken, Nixon ordered a special clandestine unit known as the "plumbers" to "plug the leaks." Nixon's special counsel Charles Colson, former CIA agent E. Howard Hunt, and retired FBI agent G. Gordon Liddy recruited a group of operatives that engaged in all kinds of illegal activities, among them drawing up an "enemies list" of prominent journalists and actors, as well as breaking into the office of Ellsberg's psychiatrist to get more information about Ellsberg's contacts.

Finally, they broke into the headquarters of the Democratic National Committee at the Watergate Building in Washington, D.C., provoking the constitutional crisis that would be known as the Watergate scandal.

Ultimately the government's charges against Ellsberg of illegally copying government information were dismissed when Watergate prosecutor Earl Silbert informed the judge that the Nixon administration had authorized the illegal break-in to the office of Ellsberg's psychiatrist. Even though publication of the Pentagon Papers did not directly bring an end to the Vietnam conflict, as Ellsberg had hoped, it did prepare the ground for the eventual impeachment proceedings of Nixon. Nixon aide H. R. Haldeman wrote that without Vietnam there would have been no Watergate, but neither would there have been a Watergate without Ellsberg.[9] After Watergate, an empowered Democratic-controlled Congress cut off funding for further expansion of the war. Less than two years later, Saigon fell to the North Vietnamese. Ho Chi Minh had finally won.

Over the following decades, Ellsberg became a well-known speaker, prominent writer, and public intellectual. In a recent interview, he confided that he occasionally has dreams that he's back working at RAND, dreams that contain elements of both normalcy and nightmare. However, to this day, Ellsberg is persona non grata at Santa Monica headquarters; the last time he entered the building for a chat with old friends he was asked by management to leave the premises immediately.[10]

DONALD RICE was a preppy-looking golfer in his early thirties who after working in RAND as an analyst had migrated to the U.S. Office of Management and Budget as assistant director. Much to his surprise, in the wake of Rowen's departure, representatives from the RAND board of trustees approached him to be their new president in 1972. To this day, Rice is still not quite sure why they picked him.

Rice saw his first responsibility when he took over as "cleaning up the mess" that Ellsberg had left behind. "I made sure that a nationally important organization didn't slide down the tubes. There was a lot of hand-wringing, a lot of concern of what was going to happen to the organization." At times Rice feared the White House would shut down RAND altogether. "[White House chief of staff] Bob Haldeman would have taken political retribution if they could. [Then Office of Management and Budget director and future secretary of state] George Schultz arranged for us to have a two-on-one meeting with the president, so Nixon would know somebody who had worked at a senior level in his administration was going out there to run the place."

One immediate effect of the disclosure of the Pentagon Papers was a reinforcement of security measures at RAND. For a while, everyone was subjected to searches when they left the Santa Monica headquarters; staffers were forbidden from doing their own photocopying. RANDites were instructed anew in the precept of, as one of them put it, "What you see, hear, write at RAND belongs to RAND for time immemorial."[11]

Another was that RAND as an institution lost some of the luster it had acquired during the 1960s. There was speculation that the think tank would soon evolve—or devolve, according to your point of view—into another house of brains for hire in the private sector away from policy making, that is, a consulting firm like Booz Allen Hamilton.[12] Rice was criticized as being a hands-off manager more interested in securing grant money to keep the machinery going than in advancing the cause of basic research that had been the hallmark of RAND.

In fact, under Rice's direction during the 1970s and 1980s, RAND plunged into research fields that would be crucial for its development in the late twentieth and early twenty-first centuries—housing assistance, educational reform, terrorism, family life in

developing countries, criminal justice system reform, drug preven-
tion, and immigration. RAND made political connections, sponsored pioneering studies, and cultivated the talent that would link it
once again to the highest echelons of power in Washington, bringing on what can properly be called the silver age of the organization.

As Rice knew, it helps to have friends in Washington. For a few
years, he had the good fortune of being assisted in the reconstruction of RAND's reputation by a very good friend, former RAND analyst James Schlesinger, who had been named secretary of defense
by President Nixon in 1973. A tweedy, pipe-smoking economist with
seven children and a deceptively soft speaking voice, the white-haired
Schlesinger had joined RAND in 1961. Although late to the party,
he soon became a convert to the house doctrine of counterforce,
writing in 1967 that one of the goals of arms control was "to keep
war at a low level and directed toward military rather than urban
targets."[13] By 1969, he was directing RAND's Strategic Studies Program and had written a book-length study on controlled nuclear
war inspired by the works of Thomas Schelling.

Like Rowen and Rice, Schlesinger spent a period of apprentice-
ship at the Office of Management and Budget before moving on to
other government posts, most notably a four-month period as director of the CIA in 1973 immediately preceding his ascension to the
Pentagon.[14] Only forty-three years old at the time of his appointment
as secretary of defense, he managed to have so many of his former
colleagues hired at different levels of the administration that one observer described them as "the cohort of RAND alumni."[15] That web
of consultants and friends proved useful to Rice in launching one of
RAND's most successful studies to date outside the national security
field, a wide-ranging, multiyear project entitled simply the Health Insurance Experiment.

In the early 1970s, with the process of implementation of Johnson's Great Society programs finally completed by President Nixon,

a great debate arose about the cost and effectiveness of medical insurance. Fundamental questions about the effects of cost sharing—for example, having co-payments and deductibles on health care—were examined in scientific journals, in newspapers, and by Congress as the administration sought to cope with the wave of people applying for services after Medicare was created in 1965. How much should a person pay—and how many medical services does a person use when he or she knows that there is a deductible to pay? Is there a corresponding relationship between services utilized and co-payment owed, and if so, what is the relationship to the health of the payer and the health of the nation at large?[16]

There was little hard scientific data on the effects of cost sharing in health care, with some critics opining that making people pay for their treatment was "penny wise and pound foolish," as patients would be reluctant to treat illnesses because of costs until they were seriously ill and hospitalized. It was also hard to know whether people with generous health insurance used more medical services because they had them, or whether they had procured the insurance because they were sicker than the general population to begin with.

In response, the Nixon administration contracted with RAND to carry out an experiment that would finally answer questions about the effect of cost sharing—as well as that of the newly invented health maintenance organizations on people's personal health and their use of medical services. RAND, through its Health Division, became the insurance company for more than 5,000 people in six sites around the country, enrolling them in plans with thirteen different cost-sharing variations. All the plans had a $1,000 limit on out-of-pocket spending for middle-class and rich families, and an income-related limit for poor families. Three of the plans had no deductible but instead charged a 25, 50, or 95 percent coinsurance rate on a range of medical services. To test whether people would choose free hospitalization over outpatient care, one plan had a $150 deductible in outpatient services but offered inpatient services for free. The study concluded its fieldwork in 1982, at a cost of almost a quarter of a billion dollars in today's money. Nothing on this scale had ever been conducted.

Certain conclusions of the study were expected, but more than a few were counterintuitive. Among adults, free care led to better health only for those with poor vision and for low-income people with high blood pressure. While cost sharing did reduce overall spending, it also cut dollars spent and quantity of use equally. Cost sharing worked to reduce the amount of services, not the number of patients searching for lower prices. While rich and poor people alike had similar reductions in their use of medical services after cost sharing, poor people were less likely to seek care in a year but were more likely to be hospitalized. Finally, the response was similar for dental and medical care, even though poor people initially took more advantage of the plan than the middle class and the rich—presumably because they had never had the money to have much dental work done. The study also found that mental care was strongly affected by insurance: people with no coverage would buy only 25 percent as much psychological and psychiatric services as those who had full coverage.

The most surprising conclusion of the study was that cost sharing did not contribute to significant differences in health among people on the different plans. "Regular medical screening (Pap smears, breast and rectal exams) was better with free care but other health habits (exercise, diet, smoking) except for flossing were worse."[17]

The message of the RAND study was not lost on the insurance industry and the federal government—it gave them a reason to discard cost-free medical care for patients, since payments did not diminish the quality of health services. When the study's preliminary results were announced in 1982, only 30 percent of plans had a deductible for hospital services. By 1984, 63 percent did and by 1987, more than 90 percent did. Today, deductibles are practically universal. Over the years, other RAND studies on health and health care would calculate that national health insurance would improve quality of life but not necessarily extend life expectancy, and that demand for outpatient care declines for those paying higher rates but that inpatient care use remains steady regardless of rates. RAND's Health Division eventually would become the largest private program in health policy research and analysis in the United States and one of the largest in the world.[18]

During Rice's tenure, RAND also began to look for projects to conduct in foreign countries, achieving its greatest success in the Netherlands. In the 1970s, the Dutch government contracted RAND to carry out what was envisaged as a simple research study to find ways of protecting an estuary, the Oosterschelde, from seasonal floods. By the time RAND researchers concluded the study, they had convinced the Netherlands government to embark on the creation of the largest man-made dam in the world, an engineering marvel designed to protect against storm surges that occur only once every 400 years. A corollary of that work in the early 1980s was a comprehensive policy analysis of water management in Holland, addressing problems of shortage, salinity, quality, and flooding.[19] Their pioneering work was due, in part, to the absence of competition in Europe.

"There just isn't a history of RAND-type organizations much anywhere else in the world," Rice said recently, "so we could provide broad systems analysis, which the Dutch government could use to explain to people why a permeable barrier was what they ought to do."[20] RAND's success in the Netherlands made it easier for the think tank to take on more work in other European countries. Currently among its many projects, RAND is advising United Kingdom officials on Internet video regulation, studying fertility rates for the European Society for Human Reproduction, and guiding the European Commission on the creation of a European Institute of Technology to rival Caltech and MIT.[21]

Still trim and fit, Rice is now chairman of Agensys, a Santa Monica–based medical research organization trying to find a cure for cancer. He is also a current member of the RAND board of trustees, as well as a member of the board of directors of Chevron, Amgen, and Wells Fargo.[22] Appointed secretary of the Air Force after his RAND tenure, Rice has in a frame on his office wall the lanyard of the first "smart bomb" that fell on Baghdad during the Persian Gulf War.

RAND's increasing volume of nonmilitary work during Rice's tenure, which ended in 1989, did not mean an end to national security research. In fact, the period would culminate with RAND not only completely reconciling with the Air Force but also bridging the traditional interservice rivalry by setting up a research organization to deal with land-based military issues, the Arroyo Center. Originally, the Army had sited the center at the California Institute of Technology in Pasadena, using that university's affiliation with the Jet Propulsion Laboratory to conduct its studies. However, in 1982, things blew up for the Army at Caltech when the faculty kept raising objections, saying they didn't want Caltech's name on policy recommendations unless they got a chance to review them.

"That was untenable, so the Army was in a quandary," remembers Rice. "I had developed a personal relationship with Frank Storman, the vice chief of staff of the Army, and I persuaded them to come to RAND. The Air Force, for the most part, was quite sanguine about it. We had already done work for the Office of the Secretary of Defense. They had seen evidence that we could work on their problems while working for other parts of the government without conflict."[23] In other words, the McNamara revolution brought about by the Whiz Kids was now institutionalized—the different branches of the armed forces had finally learned to share and get along.

Another of Rice's major achievements was his formal establishment of what would become the largest private-policy graduate school in the country, the Pardee RAND Graduate School, which the Carnegie Foundation has compared favorably with similar institutions at Harvard, Berkeley, and Carnegie Mellon. The Pardee RAND

Graduate School is unique in that it grants its students firsthand experience by having them work in conjunction with RAND analysts on real-world problems. At first, the graduate school organized its core curriculum around just four major required areas: quantitative methods, including statistic and data analysis; micro- and macroeconomics; social science; and technology. Soon after its foundation, a subspecialization became prominent: Soviet studies.[24]

Building on the early work of Leites and other RAND Sovietologists—but disregarding those analysts' dated apocalyptic views of the Soviet Union—RAND transformed itself into one of the world's leading private centers of research on the Soviet Union. Perhaps its most prominent graduate was future secretary of state Condoleezza Rice, who spent a summer as an intern in Santa Monica. Like most graduate students, she may have been angling for a research job with RAND afterward but, as one current RAND member stated, "She was not staff material."[25] That is to say, she was too obviously ambitious to be a faceless researcher. Apparently so was future assistant secretary of defense Paul Wolfowitz, who also spent a summer at RAND without a job offer. However, once Rice ascended into the upper echelons of policy making, she was invited to join the RAND board of trustees, where she served from 1991 to 1997.

As Daniel Ellsberg has observed, RAND's influence is more evident in the people who passed through its portals than in any one single policy paper it has issued, for from the 1970s on a gallery of future foreign policy leaders spent time in Santa Monica almost as a sort of postgraduate-school requirement. Among those who studied at RAND—and landed jobs—were Francis Fukuyama, the influential historian and author of *The End of History and the Last Man;* Bruce Hoffman, the renowned terrorism expert who would eventually become a RAND vice president; and Zalmay Khalilzad, a Wohlstetter protégé who would rise to be director of the Pardee RAND Graduate School, ambassador to Afghanistan and Iraq, and current ambassador to the United Nations.

And then there was Donald Rumsfeld, who formally affiliated with RAND during Rice's tenure. Perhaps the most controversial U.S. secretary of defense, Rumsfeld associated with RAND analysts practically from the time he was named director of President Nixon's Office of Economic Opportunity.[26] Rumsfeld was a RAND trustee board member from 1977 to 2001—and served twice as its chairman—leaving it only to join the cabinet of President George W. Bush.[27]

All in all, when Donald Rice left RAND in 1989 to become secretary of the Air Force, he could look back at an era of skillful political consolidation. He not only helped RAND to survive the Ellsberg scandal but he also implemented many of the ideas in foreign policy and military research that would make possible the Reagan era—and the demise of the Soviet Union.[28]

17

Team B Strikes

ALBERT WOHLSTETTER would not give up the floor. Standing at the podium in the ballroom of the Beverly Wilshire Hotel, backed by his charts and his indignation, Wohlstetter denounced détente. The world was in peril, the United States was in supreme danger, and Wohlstetter was not going down without a fight.

Outside the Spanish baroque hotel on Wilshire Boulevard, another sunny morning unfurled in balmy Beverly Hills that summer of 1974. Rodeo Drive was open for business: limos and Mercedes drove stars to their brunches at Le Dome and La Scala, while agents from William Morris planned the next assault of young Hollywood lions on the out-of-touch movie studios. A new mayor, the first black man to hold the seat, made promises that Los Angeles would become a true world-class city. The Watergate scandal, at that moment rocking the East Coast establishment, barely registered on the local political landscape. Inured to seismic drama, Californians paid little attention to the slow-motion collapse of the Nixon administration.

Yet it was here, at the edge of the American Arcadia, that Wohlstetter was choosing to make his stand. That morning he had read about the resignation of his friend Paul Nitze from the second Strategic Arms Limitation Talks (SALT II) with the Soviets. Watergate had poisoned the atmosphere, accused Nitze. Secretary of State Henry Kissinger and President Nixon just wanted an agreement with the Soviets—any agreement would do—in order to divert attention from the metastasizing Watergate crisis. Nitze, a grizzled veteran of foreign policy, stated that in such an atmosphere, there was little prospect negotiations would enhance national security, so he was getting out.[1]

As at other times when he had sounded the alarm, Wohlstetter was making his presentation to a select audience, the illuminati of the foreign policy establishment. He had tested the waters the night before, at a dinner in the home of his former RAND colleague James Digby. Over a dinner of spanakopita, poached salmon, poulet au riz basquaise, and zabaglione, accompanied by a 1971 Steinberger Spätlese and a superb 1964 Clos Vougeot, Wohlstetter had preached his usual gospel of preparedness to a choir appreciative of both the food and the arguments. The syndicated columnist Joseph Kraft had been there, as had the editorial editor of the *Wall Street Journal*, Robert L. Bartley, and *Time* magazine's senior editor, Jason McManus.

The dinner and Wohlstetter's speech would prove but a warm-up for the prolonged campaign he would wage tirelessly in public forums throughout the country during the next six years. What he called the legacy of the missile gap, the common belief among policy intellectuals that the United States habitually overestimated Soviet forces, was a myth, he declared that morning in the hotel ballroom. In fact, warned Wohlstetter, there was a consistent *under*estimation of the Soviet arsenal in terms of size, cost, and deadliness. He cited declassified figures, illustrated his points with graphs and charts, and talked on and on without stopping. He would not sit or yield the floor in spite of winks, nods, and interruptions. It was a performance meant to wake up his colleagues, to galvanize into action—or at least further reflection—the forty-some scholars and bureaucrats who had assembled for what they thought would be a sedate talk on one of the many topics chosen by the California Arms Control Seminar: "Alternatives to MADness";* "The U.S. Strategic Defense Posture in an Arms Limitation Environment"; "Once More About What We Should Not Do Even in the Worst Case: The Assured Destruction Attack."

True, Wohlstetter was not at RAND anymore, nor was he even in government, but his word carried immense weight with this audience. They all knew him as the most prominent nuclear analyst in the country, the one college professor whose calls were returned not just by his former students at the Pentagon but by the secretary of defense, the secretary of state, and the president's national security adviser, when not by the president himself. Wohlstetter was a man with clout, a master who pulled strings behind the scenes, and they all knew it. What he said was important and had to be paid attention to.

Wohlstetter had cautioned against wearing rose-colored glasses when viewing the Soviet Union's growing military threat back in 1969, when he had testified before Congress on the Anti-Ballistic Missile Treaty—ultimately approved by Congress in 1972 in spite of his jeremiads.[2] He had warned then that the United States would be duped by Russian promises while Moscow deployed more missiles, warheads, and bombers under SALT I. The country's leaders

---

* A pun on mutual assured destruction, or MAD, the official targeting policy of the United States in the event of a nuclear war.

were turning a blind eye to American vulnerability, which, if not repaired, could lead to a nuclear holocaust.

Several hours later, Wohlstetter finally surrendered the podium and sat down to booming applause. Not everyone was convinced of his figures, for he had based his estimates of missile strength on two-year-old data, neglecting the many more U.S. warheads that would be operational that year, a fact known to many in his audience. However, that was not the point. Wohlstetter had organized this exercise to rouse the people who counted from complacency; by the looks of it, he had succeeded. A few weeks later, he renewed his challenge in an article in *Foreign Policy*[3] whose repercussions would approximate those of his 1959 *Foreign Affairs* piece, "The Delicate Balance of Terror." It was a preamble to a long, hard campaign to alter what he saw as dangerously misguided government policy, a campaign that might not conclude until the country's leadership was removed from power.

CIA director William Colby was among the first to take up Wohlstetter's challenge, sending copies of the *Foreign Policy* article to his staff for their comments. Years later Colby stated that he found Wohlstetter's views "pretty compelling" and was disappointed with the "defensive stuff" offered as a response by CIA analysts.[4] Yet, in a letter to the Chicago Council on Foreign Relations on July 25, 1974, Colby claimed Wohlstetter had oversimplified the record:

The broader context includes projections of weapons technology, i.e., qualitative factors as well as numbers of launchers deployed, and defensive systems, such as ABMs, as well as offensive weapons. Viewed in this broader context, the record of intelligence projections is considerably more mixed than Professor Wohlstetter's article suggests. There are about as many examples of overestimation as there are of underestimation.[5]

⌢ Colby failed to realize that Wohlstetter's salvo was a declaration of deep philosophical differences over détente, a call to war over the direction and character of the country. Wohlstetter had stated in public what a number of conservative voices in and out of RAND and government had complained about in private for years—that the CIA and the National Intelligence Estimates it prepared were far too forgiving of the Soviet Union. It was an expression of a broader distrust of the way the Nixon administration had cozied up to the Soviet Union for domestic political purposes, neglecting the lacerating impact of this rapprochement on national security. The country was on the wrong course, and this time it would prove necessary to go outside the usual RAND channels of influence to change a misguided public opinion.

By the end of his first term in 1972, President Nixon had inaugurated a new era of cooperation with the Soviet Union. He traveled to Moscow and signed SALT I, as well as the ABM Treaty, with Soviet premier Leonid Brezhnev. Nixon's moves, although prompted by domestic political concerns, were part of a changing reality in the country. After the Vietnam debacle, Americans were tired of war of all kinds—hot and cold. The peacenik movement had become the mainstream. By 1974, a wide majority of Americans believed that the United States should do more to reduce the number of nuclear armaments,[6] while nearly half of the population thought the country was spending too much on defense. In addition, a plurality had a favorable view of the Soviet Union, and few thought there was still much threat of a nuclear war.[7]

Memos of meetings between Secretary of State Kissinger and Premier Brezhnev reveal a cozy, almost fraternal relationship between the representatives of the two superpowers, with Brezhnev mussing the hair of young diplomats and indulging in heavy-handed pranks.[8] This feeling of trust and camaraderie was reflected in the assumption of the Nixon administration that it could reduce defense spending without endangering national security. Yet as a dedicated and very vocal minority were protesting—such as former California governor Ronald Reagan, Senator Henry "Scoop" Jackson, Secretary of Defense James Schlesinger, and, naturally, Wohlstetter—détente, for Moscow, did not preclude an end to competition on the fringes of the developed world. In Third World countries such as Angola, Namibia, and Nicaragua, the Soviet Union was utilizing Cuban troops as surrogates to prop up Communist and Communist-leaning regimes.[9] Angola was the prime example, where 50,000 Cuban soldiers aided the Socialist MPLA party candidate, Agostinho Neto, who prevailed in a civil war against the South African–backed party of Jonah Savimbi, UNITA.*

Administration critics also pointed out that while the United States had dominated the arms race under presidents Kennedy and Johnson, in the 1970s the Soviet Union was hustling to surpass American power. Nitze and others feared that Nixon, wanting to distract the country from his possible impeachment, was about to institutionalize a permanent American inferiority in strategic armaments. This was a dangerous state of affairs in a world where the only competing superpower was still sworn to destroy America.[10]

Pro-détente forces inside and outside the administration argued that Soviet nuclear armaments, though more numerous, were not as deadly as the American ones, while the anti-détente crowd argued that the sheer number and physical size of Soviet missiles and armaments was plain evidence of Soviet superiority. Partisan diatribes on the efficacy of multiple independently targetable reentry vehicles (MIRVs) grew to be the strategic equivalent of the old medieval argument about the number of angels dancing on the head of a pin. An MIRV could carry several atomic warheads on its tip; each warhead in turn could be programmed to attack separate and distinct

---

* This Cuban intervention, according to Kissinger, came as a surprise and destroyed the growing rapprochement between the United States and the Cuban government headed by Fidel Castro, at odds since the failed Bay of Pigs invasion in 1961.

targets. MIRV missiles had been developed by the United States to penetrate a ring of antiballistic missiles (ABMs) that had been placed around Moscow in the late 1960s. The Americans and the Soviets had signed SALT I[11] to prevent just such an endless round of ABM and MIRV competition.

Foes of détente argued that the Soviets had been taking advantage of the United States by installing their own MIRVs to make possible a preemptive nuclear first strike of such magnitude that the United States would not have second-strike capability. They bewailed the enormous "throw weight" or lift capacity of Soviet missiles—that is to say, the sheer size and power of Soviet missiles that would allow them to hurl a considerable number of warheads at American targets. Pro-détente forces in the Nixon administration downplayed these warnings, pointing out that American missiles were more efficient and more miniaturized and therefore did not need the brawn or mass of the Soviet missiles to be even more deadly.[12]

To critics like Wohlstetter and Nitze, détente without restraints was also morally wrong. The Soviet Union should not be rewarded for enslaving its own people. Détente should be a quid pro quo, with the quo being greater political freedom in the Soviet Union. Senator Jackson in particular sought to link the commercial advantages of détente—lowered tariffs, increased trade, most-favored-nation status for the Soviet Union—to a relaxation of the oppression of Jews.[13] Encouraged by Soviet dissidents Natan Sharansky and Nobel Prize–winning writer Aleksandr Solzhenitsyn—who claimed the linkage was weakening the hold of the Communist Party—opponents of détente refused as a matter of principle to trust any Soviet promises. One of the foremost critics was Secretary of Defense Schlesinger, famously quoted at the time as saying, "Spengler was an optimist."*

---

* Oswald Spengler, of course, was the German author of the gloomy tome *The Decline of the West*, which influenced a number of conservative thinkers, including Nitze.

Schlesinger had been named to his office thanks to the strong support of Senator Jackson; like their friend Wohlstetter, he was equally worried about Soviet ascendancy. Schlesinger said a few weeks after his appointment in 1973, "The Soviets . . . have a mailed fist. It is now encased in a velvet glove . . . The détente is the velvet glove."[14]

Notwithstanding the borderline paranoia of extreme right-wingers, it is an incontrovertible fact that soon after signing SALT I the Soviets had begun increasing their strategic offensive nuclear forces in ways that pushed at the limits of the accord. Schlesinger was among the first to sound the alarm, demanding a hard line on the SALT II negotiations. (Ultimately, the clamor against ratification would grow so raucous that the Senate would vote not to ratify the SALT II agreement.)

When Nixon resigned and Gerald R. Ford became president in August 1974, Schlesinger found himself at odds with the new commander in chief, who considered the secretary of defense much too right-wing for his taste.[15] Seeing a growing slump in his poll numbers, and concerned that voters saw him as ineffectual, unable to mediate between a hawkish Schlesinger and a détente-minded Kissinger, in 1975 Ford fired Schlesinger and instituted a wholesale makeover of his foreign policy echelon. In the process, Ford introduced a number of players who would crop up in high office under both Democratic and Republican administrations for the next thirty years.

To replace Schlesinger at the Pentagon, Ford picked the politically astute Donald Rumsfeld, making the forty-three-year-old former congressman from Illinois the youngest secretary of defense in the nation's history.[16] Ford retained Kissinger as secretary of state, but named General Brent Scowcroft as his national security adviser. He chose a Rumsfeld ally, Richard Cheney, as his chief of staff, and in what he would call the biggest act of political cowardice of his life, Ford pressured Vice President Nelson Rockefeller into not running for reelection with him in 1976, picking Senator Robert Dole of Kansas instead. Finally, Ford recalled from China the U.S. envoy to

Beijing (there still had not been any exchange of ambassadors between the two countries) and named the Connecticut-born, Yale-educated, former Republican congressman and Texas oil tycoon George H. W. Bush as the new director of the CIA.[17] As Lyndon Johnson might have said, Ford needed some fresh meat.

California governor Ronald Reagan, who announced he would run against Ford for the Republican nomination in 1976, took advantage of the fracas by charging that Schlesinger had been let go for daring to point out that the United States was growing weak while its enemies were getting stronger. In Reagan's words, Ford was "afraid to tell the American people the truth about our military status."[18]

The political broadsides of the anti-détente crowd in his own party prompted Ford to allow one of the most unusual exercises of political power in modern American history: a group of outsiders was appointed to review classified information and present an alternative to the official opinion of the CIA. The group, called Team B, proudly traced its origin to a couple of Bloody Marys that an out-of-work government official, Eugene V. Rostow, knocked back on Thanksgiving in 1975.

Rostow was, like Nitze, a friend of Wohlstetter. Unlike Wohlstetter, though, Rostow delighted in being a bureaucrat. As undersecretary of state for political affairs in the Johnson administration, he had been a fervent advocate of the Vietnam War. He and his brother Walt Rostow, President Johnson's national security adviser, asserted that the United States had a moral obligation to prevent Communists from taking over South Vietnam. Morality had always been one of Eugene Rostow's highest concerns; as dean of the Yale Law School, he had written articles decrying the internment of Japanese Americans during World War II, saying they were being placed in camps "on a record which wouldn't support a conviction for stealing a dog."[19]

An admirer of Senator Jackson, Rostow had supported the conservative Democrat in his failed 1972 run for the presidency. Just a few months before Wohlstetter's critical 1974 Beverly Hills speech, Rostow wrote, "We confront two implacable facts: the Soviet military build up is continuing building up at an ominous rate and Soviet political policy is more and more obviously fixed in a mood of muscular imperialism."[20] Two years later Rostow chaired the Foreign Policy Task Force of the Coalition for a Democratic Majority, which charged the Nixon administration with propagating the "myth of détente," a phrase that would become a battering ram for conservative attacks.[21]

That Thanksgiving Day in 1975, inspired by vodka and bile, Rostow penned a letter to Nitze suggesting they reestablish the old Committee on the Present Danger to alert Americans about the growing Soviet menace.* The group's first meeting was a lunch at downtown Washington's Metropolitan Club. From the start, the circle thronged with enemies of détente of both the Democratic and the Republican persuasion. Among them were AFL-CIO leader Lane Kirkland; former secretary of defense Schlesinger; former deputy secretary of defense and cofounder of the computer company Hewlett-Packard, David Packard; former chief of naval operations, Admiral Elmo Zumwalt; and Max Kampelman, a close aide to the 1968 Democratic presidential candidate, the "Happy Warrior," Minnesota senator Hubert H. Humphrey. Not present, but committed to the committee's goals, were Reagan; former secretary of state Dean Rusk; future secretary of state George Schultz; Harvard professor and Sovietologist Richard Pipes; and economist Herbert Stein.[22] They all pledged to a campaign that would alter the foundation of American foreign policy.

Possessed by a sense of urgency, the group unleashed a relentless wave of propaganda against détente. Rostow and Nitze wrote

---

* The original Committee on the Present Danger had been established in 1940 to warn about the dangers of American neutrality in the face of the growing Nazi menace in Europe.

articles, and Wohlstetter sailed into the fray with pieces in *Foreign Policy* and *Strategic Review.*[23]

The committee obtained crucial support in its quest from a new group of political pundits in Washington, popularly called neoconservatives. Led at first by mostly Jewish intellectuals with a strong interest in Israel's survival, neoconservatives were largely former Socialists and liberals who, as Irving Kristol memorably put it, had been "mugged by reality."[24] Neoconservative commentators such as Jeane Kirkpatrick, Norman Podhoretz, and Kristol were disheartened by what they perceived as the "amorality" of détente, and proclaimed human rights to be as important as free trade in the nation's foreign policy, especially toward the Soviet Union. Their goal was to disrupt the camaraderie between Washington and Moscow, and break the chains of treaties between East and West; they targeted the CIA as the weakest link.

In the 1970s the Central Intelligence Agency was convulsed by a series of explosive revelations about its undercover operations. Ever since the failure of the CIA-sponsored Bay of Pigs invasion in Cuba, and especially since disclosures about the involvement of CIA operatives in the Watergate scandal and in domestic spying on anti–Vietnam War groups, the CIA had been blasted, in U.S. senator Frank Church's words, as "a rogue elephant."[25] The scandal reached its apogee on February 28, 1975, when CBS News revealed what everyone at the agency referred to as the "family jewels": CIA involvement in various plots to assassinate foreign leaders.[26]

Subsequent investigations, such as that of Senator Church's committee and that of the Presidential Commission on CIA Activities Within the United States,[27] confirmed that the CIA indeed had engaged in illegal activities and other violations of its charter. These included domestic spying and intercepting mail—not to mention such peccadilloes as trying to murder Fidel Castro, toppling governments in Guatemala and Iran, and fomenting military coups in Chile, El Salvador, and a host of other Third World countries.[28]

Since anything the CIA did was now ipso facto suspect, it became the prime target of the anti-détente crowd. In his articles Wohlstetter had been careful not to impugn or even mention the CIA, but everyone in the national security establishment knew his figures had been lifted from the National Intelligence Estimates prepared by the agency. To be sure, Wohlstetter had all but admitted that NIEs were just formal estimates, a sort of bet on what the world was going to look like in the next twelve months. Moreover, they were "intrinsically uncertain, reversible by the adversary himself between the time of prediction and the actual deployment."[29] Still, they were wrong and had to be changed.

The vehicle for transformation was an obscure government panel set up in 1956, the President's Foreign Policy Advisory Board. Eisenhower had created it to monitor intelligence programs; Kennedy subsequently had changed its name to the President's Foreign Intelligence Advisory Board (PFIAB). Nixon had then commissioned it "to supplement the analysis in the National Intelligence Estimates."[30] In its latest configuration, under Ford, it was packed with a conservative-leaning group with roots in RAND. Members included such prominent RAND associates as former director of the Office of Management and Budget and future secretary of state Schultz; former RAND engineer John Foster, who had been director of the Lawrence Livermore National Laboratory; and longtime RAND confrere Edward Teller, the father of the H-bomb.[31] The chairman was Admiral George W. Anderson Jr.; the vice chair, Leo Cherne, was chairman of right-wing Freedom House. All of them would become the intellectual authors of Team B.

After Wohlstetter's first critiques of détente appeared, PFIAB chairman Anderson sent a letter to President Ford charging that the NIE for 1974 was seriously misleading. Anderson then authorized Foster to meet with board members Teller and Robert Galvin, chairman of Motorola, to create a subcommittee to evaluate the NIEs. This group included Richard Latter, who had left RAND to become the head of the Theoretical Division of the Lawrence Livermore National Laboratory. Latter suggested creating a second CIA, but Teller—afraid of overreach—proposed instead that a group of outside experts dispute the official figures. The group, called Team B, would use all the highly classified information available to the intelligence community to make its own independent assessment.[32]

When the PFIAB made its formal proposal of a Team B in 1975, CIA director Colby rejected it out of hand, perceiving it as a hijacking of government policy under the guise of objective analysis by outsiders intent on basing policy on ideological considerations.

> Our annual estimates on Soviet strategic abilities . . . utilize all the information known by and the best analysis available to the U.S. Government . . . It is hard for me to envisage how an ad hoc "independent" group of government and non-government analysts could prepare a more thorough, comprehensive assessment of Soviet strategic capabilities [underscored in the original].[33]

Colby's indignant denial of the need for Team B was unavailing. For one thing, he was a lame duck. The month before he drafted his reply, Colby had tendered his resignation at the request of President Ford. Given that the attempt to block Team B had come from a director with one foot out the door, Foster and Teller acted as though they had never received a response and pressed CIA officials to authorize a new assessment of intelligence regarding the accuracy of Soviet ICBMs, air defense, and counters to U.S. submarines.

Foster and Teller formally renewed their request shortly after George H. W. Bush's swearing in as new CIA director. Bush was hesitant, not seeing the need to second-guess the agency. Some of his subalterns were in favor of the proposal, however, particularly since Colby—in the wake of Wohlstetter's charges—had already ordered a backtrack study of the last ten years of NIE predictions. Bush finally authorized the creation of two teams: Team A for the ordinary NIE, and Team B to go through the same facts and arrive at their own conclusions.[34] Afterward the president's national security adviser "would review the experiment and critique its results."[35]

The teams originally were divided into the three areas of interest corresponding to the national defense triad: missiles, bombers, and submarines. But when the head of naval intelligence, Admiral Bobby Inman, became aware of the study, he raised a mighty outcry. Properly evaluating the vulnerability of submarines would have entailed disclosing the exact number and location of their fleet. Operational information on the nuclear submarine force was the most closely guarded secret in Washington and the Navy refused to share it with anyone, including the CIA. Inman succeeded in blocking that phase of the exercise and instead the third group was ordered to study Soviet strategic objectives.

The competing panels on air defense and missile accuracy, although ostensibly friendly, in the end were unable to reconcile their philosophical differences on the significance of the figures on the Soviet forces. Since the panels were charged with examining mostly technical details, and their interpretations did not amount to rewriting accepted fact, there was little controversy over their disagreements. The clamor would be over the third and most well-known group, the Strategic Objectives Panel. Given that the panel's work involved deciphering the enemy's intentions, a host of subjective considerations came into play, with the results being predictably skewed. After all, spring showers mean flowers to some and lightning to others.[36]

The chairman of the Team B Strategic Objectives Panel was Richard Pipes, a founding member of the 1970s incarnation of the Committee on the Present Danger. Pipes was a Polish-born Sovietologist teaching at Harvard University;[37] like Leites, he was convinced the Soviets were intent on achieving world conquest.[38] He had been a protégé of Richard Perle, who in turn claimed Wohlstetter as a mentor. Therefore, it was no surprise when Wohlstetter was nominated for the panel. Perle recommended the appointment of Paul Wolfowitz, who at the time was special assistant for SALT II. Pipes also brought in Nitze and a number of RAND people, including retired Air Force colonel Thomas Wolf. It was a cozy, almost incestuous circle of panel members, many of them having worked at RAND, with RAND people, or with Wohlstetter. In the end, Wohlstetter did not serve on the panel, although his articles were used as a resource and his influence was great, particularly after his close friend and former RAND colleague Andrew Marshall, who had just been installed in the Pentagon's Office of Net Assessment, was hired as a consultant.

At the first general meeting of the competing groups, Team A members, mostly midlevel analysts, naïvely thought they were convening to exchange views on classified information. According to one of the Team A participants, "We were overmatched. People like Nitze ate us for lunch." At one point, in response to a sharp attack by Nitze, the leader of the group sat speechless, his mouth open, unable to reply. Another used a sports analogy: "It was like putting Walt Whitman High against the Redskins." Quickly it became obvious to the CIA panel that Team B was out to destroy the very validity of Team A's working assumptions in order to impose a different frame of reference on the data. As a Team A member remarked, "If I had appreciated the adversarial nature, I would have wheeled up different guns. I thought it was not intended to be a zero-sum discussion."[39] From that point on, cooperation between the two groups practically vanished. Three days after that meeting, Jimmy Carter was elected the thirty-ninth president of the United States in a landslide victory over Gerald Ford.

Final reports by both teams were presented to the PFIAB and Bush in early December, with Pipes immodestly recounting that the

PFIAB members were "thunderstruck" by the accuracy of Team B's interpretation.[40] The teams met again, almost as in a college debate, in the main auditorium in CIA headquarters on December 21. The corresponding analyses were as expected. Team A admitted that the Soviets were building up their nuclear and warfare capability, but was nebulous as to when they might reach parity with or overtake the United States. Team B emphasized the insatiable lust for power of the Soviet Union and asserted the accuracy of Soviet missiles, a point quickly dismissed by the Air Force chief of intelligence.

Afterward, as is often the practice inside the Beltway, there was a luncheon. Bush made a point of sitting with the Team A members, a slight that even twenty years later still rankled Pipes. According to one of the people sitting with Bush, he was asked, "What happens next?" Bush's answer: "Nothing. I have to go along with my own guys."[41] In the end, Bush had turned out to be another East Coast Republican moderate, not a true believer in American supremacy like Reagan—or Bush's son during his tenure in the White House decades later.

Even if Bush had wanted to put into effect Team B's recommendation to alter the NIE to denote a much graver threat from the Soviet Union, it would have proven moot, since Bush's days as CIA director—as Colby's before him—were numbered. President Carter refused to allow him to remain and replaced him with Admiral Stanfield Turner. Only one of the policy recommendations of Team B was adopted by the new administration: President Carter used Team B's opinion that the Soviet air defense missile shield was impenetrable as an excuse to cancel a planned bomber since it would have proved useless in an attack.

Team B members would claim partial victory in their defeat, arguing that they managed to change the tone of the NIEs to highlight the intrinsically nefarious character of the Soviet system. While there is still some debate on the total effect of the Team B report, there is no doubt that the NIEs did become more ominous. As the *New York*

Times reported, the NIE for 1976 "was more somber than any in more than a decade . . . it flatly states that the Soviet Union is seeking superiority over United States forces."[42]

In the end, Team B and the Committee on the Present Danger decisively won the war. When Reagan took office in 1980, fifty-one members of his administration were members of the committee— including President Reagan, CIA director William Casey, National Security Adviser Richard V. Allen, UN Ambassador Kirkpatrick, Navy Secretary of State John Lehman, and Assistant Secretary of Defense Perle.[43] Within weeks, the Reagan administration evinced a new combative attitude toward the Soviet Union, increasing by severalfold the national defense budget—just like Team B and its RAND-affiliated members had demanded.[44] The Leites/RAND weltanschauung had triumphed again. As one observer said, "I know of no private public affairs organization that has had a greater influence in such a short period of time on U.S. foreign policy issues."[45] It was an exercise later duplicated in the administrations of George H. W. Bush and George W. Bush by some of the very same players, with graver consequences.

PART 5

18

Witnessing End Times

THE MORNING OF November 7, 1985, found Albert Wohlstetter in the East Room of the White House waiting to receive the Presidential Medal of Freedom from Ronald Reagan. Also being awarded a medal in the same ceremony was Paul Nitze, who preceded Wohlstetter at the microphone.

As Nitze praised the president's choices in foreign affairs, Wohlstetter confidently scanned the room, then turned to his wife, Roberta, his faithful companion since that day at Columbia Law when he sat next to her and told her they should be together because the initials of their last names—W for him, M for her maiden name, Morgan—were the same, only inverted. She smiled back, holding up in the bright lights better than he, as always.

Finally it was Reagan's turn. How pleasant, no, how pleasing his words, as he reminded everyone why the Wohlstetters had been chosen for the highest honor a civilian could receive from the government of this country.

"Roberta and Albert Wohlstetter—one citation, but two medals," intoned the president.

> Participants in the nuclear era's most momentous events, Roberta and Albert Wohlstetter have shaped the ideas and deeds of statesmen, and have helped create a safer world. Over four decades, they have marshaled logic, science, and history and enlarged our democracy's capacity to learn and to act. Through their work, we have seen that mankind's safety need not rest on threats to the innocent, and that nuclear weapons need not spread inexorably. Their powers of thought and exposition are, in themselves, among the Free World's best defenses.

He passed the microphone to Roberta, who was parsimonious in her response: "I'm dazzled and very deeply honored. Thank you very much."

Now it was Albert's turn to receive the heavy enameled cross. He moved to the microphone, bringing it closer so everyone could hear him. His daughter, Joan; Richard Perle; Paul Wolfowitz; Harry Rowen—all those whose careers he had sponsored and guided. He hesitated a moment then plunged right in.

> Mr. President, I receive this great honor not only for myself but for the brilliant and devoted research men and students with whom I've been lucky enough to work for nearly 35 years. I take particular pride in being given this Medal of Freedom from a President who's stressed that it's freedom that we're defending, that we have to defend it without bringing on a holocaust that would end both free and un-

free societies. I'm most grateful and honored, Mr. President. Thank you very much.[1]

And that was that. The audience waited a moment for more elucidation, and then everyone burst into loud applause. The Wohlstetters didn't need to say anything else. If not for them and their friends, none of this would have happened. Jimmy Carter would still be president, and the nation would still be wearing the sackcloth of diminished expectations instead of basking in the warm sunshine of a Reaganesque morning in America with a rising economy, a Soviet empire in retreat, and the best government money could buy.

IN 1985, the future was now for Wohlstetter and the other RANDites who had reshaped the world under presidents Kennedy, Johnson, and Nixon, only to find their advances checked by Ford and Carter. Under Reagan, their old dream of whittling the Soviets down to size—plans gestated long ago when they used to meet regularly at the Wohlstetters' Hollywood Hills home—was all coming true.

For decades, RAND analysts and Sovietologists had been predicting the death of the Soviet Union through economic exhaustion and ethnic dissension. Economics Department head Charles Wolf, Jr., had advocated spending the Soviet Union to death through an arms race, assured that the Soviet economy was too feeble to withstand the shock.[2] Nevertheless, it took the blind faith of a true believer like Ronald Reagan to put it all together.

Taking office after a landslide vote, the seventy-one-year-old former California governor carried out a revolution that transformed American society. The Reagan Revolution was built on two premises: thorough reform of taxation and government regulation, and a fierce anticommunism that justified sizable increases in defense spending coupled with a muscular foreign policy. Both of these postures were supported by RAND analyses—and the RAND-gestated theory of rational choice.

Alone among all the previous occupants of the White House, Ronald Reagan believed that the Soviet Union could be defeated, not just contained. In his view, communism would collapse of its own weight by its internal contradictions, and he was certain he had been elected to accelerate that demise. As Reagan declared in his inaugural address, quoting a fallen soldier from World War I, "America must win this war. Therefore I will work, I will save, I will sacrifice, I will endure, I will fight cheerfully and do my utmost, as if the issue of the whole struggle depended on me alone."[3] On another occasion, reverting Marx's famous phrase about capitalism, Reagan promised to "leave Marxism-Leninism on the ash-heap of history."[4]

One of the major tests of what came to be called the Reagan Doctrine took place in Afghanistan, which had been invaded by Soviet forces in late 1979. Wohlstetter had pressed the Carter administration to supply advanced weaponry to native Afghani mujahideen fighting the occupation.[5] Once Reagan took office, Wohlstetter lobbied successfully for continual and greater American support, which he said would checkmate any Soviet designs on the region. A defeat in Afghanistan—which he considered Moscow's Vietnam—would demoralize the Soviets with the subsequent hemorrhage of money, soldiers, and equipment.[6] When the Soviet forces finally withdrew, Wohlstetter's—and by extension RAND's—reputation as a sterling source of strategy was secured. Other attempts by Reagan to thwart Soviet influence—as in Nicaragua and El Salvador—would not meet with the same kind of apparent success, but RANDites would not be as intimately involved with those and their high regard in government circles would not decline.

It didn't hurt that many of the RAND brotherhood landed highly influential jobs within the Reagan administration. Wohlstetter's disciple, Richard Perle, had been hired as deputy secretary of defense and put in charge of the Soviet desk. RAND policy hawk

Fred Iklé, another Wohlstetter confrere who had headed the think tank's Social Sciences Department, helped with the Reagan transition team and wound up as undersecretary of defense for policy, while Paul Wolfowitz was placed at the State Department in charge of policy planning. Even Nitze—who had waged such an effective war against the SALT II accords that the Senate had refused to ratify the treaty—became Reagan's arms control negotiator.

Most important, RANDites picked up an influential ally in the editor of that most august of American financial publications, the *Wall Street Journal*. Robert L. Bartley had taken the helm of the financial news flagship in 1972, right around the same time as Reagan had begun to define a new kind of conservative politics. When Reagan assumed office, Bartley opened the editorial pages of the *Journal* to Wohlstetter and other intellectuals to spread the tenets of the Reagan Revolution of less government and more national defense.[7] Bartley would also publish the writings of a number of administration supply-side economists, such as Arthur Laffer and Jude Wanniski, who firmly believed that tax cuts created budget surpluses.

From the start, the RAND philosophy of counterforce was enshrined as the official defense policy of the Reagan administration. In 1982, Secretary of Defense Caspar Weinberger issued a "Defense Guidance" paper stating that the official strategy was for the United States to increase its nuclear arsenal of second-strike capabilities so that it could "prevail and be able to force the Soviet Union to seek earliest termination of hostilities on terms favorable to the United States."[8] That is, the administration was preparing to win a nuclear conflict by holding back a reserve force after striking to make the Soviets quit lest they be hit again——the same argument for winning nuclear wars that RAND's William Kaufmann made to Robert McNamara in 1961.

An emphasis on stronger defense ruled the day. Reagan's first defense budget was 13 percent higher than Carter's, an increase of close to $44 billion, with more money slated for nuclear weapons, airplanes, surface ships, submarines, cruise missiles. Even more money would come the following year and the next and the next. To top it off, Wohlstetter's old dream of an antiballistic missile defense system was revived by Reagan under the moniker Strategic Defense Initiative (SDI). A skeptical public dubbed the system, which aimed to knock down incoming Soviet ICBMs with American missiles that intercepted them in space, Star Wars.[9]

The change in attitude toward the Soviet Union expressed itself in words as well as actions. Secretary of State Alexander Haig, Vice President George H. W. Bush, and Reagan publicly speculated on fighting and winning a limited nuclear war with Russia. Even Reagan's asides drove the point of his blithe anticommunism—as the instance when he joked to what he thought was a dead microphone, "My fellow Americans, I am pleased to tell you today that I've signed legislation that will outlaw Russia forever. We begin bombing in five minutes."[10]

To Moscow, Reagan's words were no laughing matter. His administration's cavalier attitude toward nuclear war and its insistence on placing new midrange missiles in Europe provoked a crisis in the Soviet Union. According to CIA declassified reports, by the end of 1981 the KGB was convinced that the United States planned to launch a preemptive nuclear attack.

When Leonid Brezhnev died the following year, KGB head Yuri Andropov became Soviet general secretary. He then ordered an intelligence alert to monitor U.S. war preparations. By the fall of 1983, Moscow believed the United States was in the final stages of readiness for its surprise attack. Had the Soviets ordered a counter-alert and had American intelligence detected it without knowing the reasons for it, the world could have come quickly to the brink of nuclear holocaust. Fortunately, some Soviet agents informed the United States and Great Britain about the Soviet war scare. Both countries then took measures to reassure Moscow they were not planning a first strike. Still, the tension was such that French president François

Mitterrand compared the situation to the 1962 Cuban Missile Crisis. A few years later, newly appointed Soviet leader Mikhail Gorbachev commented, "Never, perhaps, in the postwar decades was the situation in the world as explosive and hence, more difficult and unfavorable, as in the first half of the 1980s."[11]

Just as Reagan's blustery insouciance about winning a nuclear war had raised hackles in Moscow, so did his comments revive something that had been absent from the American scene for years: a peace movement. Alarmed over the Reagan defense buildup and the new talk of nuclear war, activists in the United States and Europe staged massive marches demanding a nuclear freeze. Protests over the deployment of Pershing missiles in Europe were widespread and effective, to the point that RAND analysts, when describing the security situation in Western Europe, wrote there wasn't a single country whose citizens would willingly accept the deployment.[12] Moreover, scientists began to publish articles on a new and unforeseen consequence of any nuclear war, no matter how small: nuclear winter. Pollution and radiation from even a localized conflict would literally have a chilling effect on the planet, dooming it to death from the darkness that would ensue. To this, Wohlstetter responded with a highly polemic piece, charging the peace activists with using unverifiable figures and indulging in unscientific speculation.[13]

This time the counterattack from Wohlstetter missed its mark. Public opinion became so galvanized in opposition to a new nuclear race that the Reagan administration started disarmament talks in earnest—to such a degree that some conservatives felt Reagan was no longer one of them. John T. "Terry" Dolan, then chair of the National Conservative Political Action Committee, complained, "The administration hasn't co-opted the 'peace' movement. The 'peace' movement has co-opted the administration."[14]

Ironically, it took a Soviet leader to finally crown the efforts of the RAND strategists and destroy the Soviet Union. Gorbachev's accession to power in Moscow as secretary-general of the Communist

Party came in 1985 after the sudden death of three other premiers. He took the helm of a country that was economically stagnant, politically divided, and too educated to be amenable to Stalinist repression. From the start of his tenure, Gorbachev sought a complete rearrangement of internal Soviet politics in order to allow for more government flexibility and greater economic development. Newly declassified documents reveal that by the end of 1985 two of Gorbachev's most trusted assistants, Alexander Yakovlev and Eduard Shevardnadze, were proposing the democratization of the Communist Party, to the point of allowing multicandidate elections and perhaps even splitting the party into two parts to promote more political competition.[15]

Pressed by political forces in the United States, Reagan sent a letter to Gorbachev the same day of his accession, expressing his hope that negotiations between the two powers would lead "toward our common ultimate goal of eliminating nuclear weapons."[16] Gorbachev quickly replied in kind. That exchange led to a meeting in Geneva, Switzerland, at the end of 1985, and another summit conference at Reykjavik, Iceland, the following spring, where the two leaders tried but failed to come to an agreement to abolish all nuclear weapons and deployment of SDI. All the same, the degree of trust evidenced by Reagan did result in the Intermediate-Range Nuclear Forces Treaty, which eliminated INF missiles from Europe, and the Strategic Arms Reduction Treaty I, which scaled down U.S. and Soviet strategic nuclear arsenals. More important, it gave Gorbachev the confidence that the United States would not try to attack the Soviet Union while he proceeded with his reforms of glasnost and perestroika. Little did Gorbachev—or Reagan—envisage that those market-oriented, "rational" reforms would result in the end of the very system they were meant to reinforce. By 1989, the Berlin Wall had come crashing down; by 1991, the Soviet Union was no more, written out of existence by forces it could not control.

ALTHOUGH IT WAS by happenstance that Reagan got his wish to see the Soviet Union collapse years after his term ended, the economic reforms he instituted had an immediate result—the irrevocable alteration of the American economy. Declaring "Government is the problem, not the solution," and citing Calvin Coolidge as his inspiration, Reagan attempted to return the country to pre–New Deal policies. His counterpart in the United Kingdom, Margaret Thatcher, who likewise initiated the radical change in the British welfare state known as Thatcherism, echoed his sentiments: "There is no such thing as society. There are individual men and women, and there are families."

The contributions of RANDites to the Reaganesque privatization movement on both sides of the Atlantic during the 1970s and 1980s were profound. Their studies laid the intellectual foundation for the collection of economic reforms dubbed "Reaganomics" in the United States, revolving around the notion that fewer taxes, deregulation, and smaller government inevitably inured to the benefit of nations.

To a large degree, Kenneth Arrow had sown the first seeds of that devolution to smaller government during his time at RAND when he published his book, *Social Choice and Individual Values,* in 1952. Social responsibility did not exist, only individual choice. Notions of collective obligations were at best pipe dreams, at worst strictures concocted by dictators who aimed to enforce the will of one party. The implied solution was less government, less regulation, and, by extension, fewer taxes. From there, it was only a step to the famous line in the movie *Wall Street:* "Greed is good."

Other RANDites further developed the notion of rational or social choice, linking it to earlier theorists who had written about the useful role of selfishness in human affairs. Many of them received Nobel Prizes for work the committee considered had improved the lot of society. Among the winners was 1983 Nobel Prize laureate in economics, Gerard Debreu, who worked for RAND in the 1950s.

His *Theory of Value: An Axiomatic Analysis of Economic Equilibrium* provided the mathematical foundation for the "invisible hand" theory of Adam Smith in which self-seeking people, by pursuing only their own goals, actually improve the lot of all of society.

Soon rational choice theory expanded into other areas of American life. RAND economist Gary Stanley Becker applied its methods and assumptions to fields that previously had been thought to have no connection to economics, such as sociology, criminology, anthropology, and demography. His central premise was a perfect echo of Arrow's—that rational self-interest controls practically all aspects of human behavior. For his contributions he was awarded the Nobel Prize in Economics in 1992.

RAND consultant Tjalling Charles Koopmans, who worked at the think tank in 1948 and again from 1952 to 1966, developed a method called "activity analysis," which analyzed and allocated resources to obtain economic objectives at the lowest cost. Edmund S. Phelps, who received the Nobel Prize in Economics in 2006, and whose first job was at the RAND Corporation, introduced the theory of what has been termed the natural rate of unemployment—and how government should react (or not) to it. Another immensely influential RAND consultant from 1948 until 1990, Paul Anthony Samuelson argued in *Foundations of Economic Analysis* (1947) that the key to all economic theory is the rational nature of consumer behavior. A consultant for the President's Council of Economic Advisers and to the Federal Reserve Bank, he delved into the dynamics and stability of economic systems, international trade, welfare economics, and government expenditure. He received his Nobel Prize in Economics in 1970.

Perhaps the best-known member of RAND's gallery of Nobel laureates was Thomas Schelling, an original associate of Wohlstetter's band of nuclear analysts. Affiliated with RAND for nearly fifty years, he distilled his theories of conflict and cooperation into his seminal book *The Strategy of Conflict*.[17] He originated the concept of "focal points," boundaries of mutual expectations that allow opposing parties to reach compromises. He was corecipient of the Nobel Prize in Economics in 2005 "for having enhanced our understanding of conflict and cooperation through game-theory analysis"[18]—work carried out largely during his time at RAND in the late 1950s.

Schelling's colleague, Vernon L. Smith, a RAND consultant in 1959, laid the theoretical foundation for the deregulation of energy markets in the United States, Australia, and New Zealand; he was corecipient of the Nobel Prize in Economics in 2002. Finally, William Vickrey, a consultant at RAND during 1967 and 1968, who shared the 1996 Nobel Prize in Economics with British economist James A. Mirrlees, provided the rationale for the high fees charged by electric and telephone companies and airlines during peak periods of use.[19] He also originated the theory of road pricing, that is, that charging motorists tolls and assorted fees for the use of roads will show consumers what the true costs of road upkeep are, with the consequence of lessening traffic congestion—or providing a handy source of revenue for local governments. In fact, at times it seems that about the only aspect of American life that RAND's rational choice theories did not transform was sports (although the expansion of the free agent clause certainly follows from rational choice).*

Certainly starting with his 1980 campaign promise to abolish the Department of Education and the Department of Energy, Reagan propelled an ever-growing national tendency toward deregulation, following RAND-inspired reform policies to encourage the growth of free markets. One of his first acts in office in 1981 was to dismantle the remaining price controls on oil that had been allowed by

---

* Perhaps one reason why sports have largely avoided the structural reforms affecting all other aspects of American life is that sports teams, especially in baseball, are allowed by the government to function as monopolies.

presidents Nixon, Ford, and Carter. Deregulation in finance, trade, and transportation soon followed.

However, Reagan's most important free-market initiative was firing the striking air traffic controllers in August 1981 by invoking a rarely used law that declared that striking federal employees forfeited their jobs. His success at breaking the strike encouraged the right of private employers to hire and fire at will, a right that, in Federal Reserve chairman Alan Greenspan's words, "was not fully exercised before." This move resulted in waves of firings throughout the country, with unemployment spiking to 10 percent by 1982. Ultimately, Reagan's antiunion stance may have contributed to low unemployment and inflation over the course of his administration,* but it raised job insecurity to levels not seen since the Great Depression and made lifetime employment an obsolete notion.[20]

Reagan was a believer in economist Arthur Laffer's controversial curve, which purports to show that a reduction in income taxes has the counterintuitive consequence of raising federal tax revenues (a theory that was introduced into government by RAND board trustee and future Pentagon boss Donald Rumsfeld and future vice president Dick Cheney, after Laffer drew the curve for them on a cocktail napkin in 1974).[21]

Reagan slashed individual tax rates from 70 to 28 percent and corporate ones from 40 to 31 percent, with the largest reductions given to those with the highest incomes. He also eased or eliminated price controls on cable TV, long-distance phone service, interstate bank service, and ocean shipping. Banks were allowed to invest in a broader set of assets and enforcement of antitrust laws was sharply reduced. As an unexpected complication, thousands of savings and

---

* Inflation went from 10.4 percent in 1980 to 4.2 percent in 1988, while unemployment decreased from 7 percent in 1980 to 5.4 percent in 1988.

loans overextended themselves and had to be bailed out by the government to the tune of $125 billion.[22]

The spread of RAND's rational choice continues to this day. Even the only Democratic president to serve after Reagan—Bill Clinton—co-opted many of the same ideas, proclaiming in 1994, "The era of big government is dead." Today we all live with the consequences of the alliance of Reaganesque conviction and RAND intellectuality that radically altered the character not only of the United States but of the entire Western world. Likewise, we live under the shadow of the consequences of another RAND-inspired event: the defeat of the Soviet Union in Afghanistan, a debacle that pointed the way to the horror of September 11, 2001.

19

The Terror Network

In the year of the new century and nine months,
From the sky will come a great King of Terror . . .
The sky will burn at forty-five degrees.
Fire approaches the great new city . . .
In the City of York there will be a great collapse,
Two twin brothers torn apart by chaos
While the fortress falls the great leader will succumb
Third Big War will begin when the big city is burning.

—NOSTRADAMUS

THE MORNING of September 11, 2001, Michael Rich, the executive vice president of RAND, headed to the Pentagon for a meeting with General John W. Handy, the Air Force Vice Chief of Staff. A wiry, olive-skinned man partial to morning walks, Rich was pressed for time after going on a long jaunt. He skipped breakfast, and after rushing to check in with RAND's Washington office just across the way from the Pentagon, he hurried over to the massive federal building.

Based at corporate headquarters in Santa Monica, Rich had flown to Washington the day before to discuss current projects with key figures at the Defense Department. It was a visit he had made many times. His father, Ben Rich, had been an engineer at Lockheed Aircraft's Advanced Development Project, familiarly known as the Skunk Works. That outfit, under contract to the Air Force, had developed America's first jet fighter; launched the world's most successful spy plane, the U-2; and, most spectacularly of all, had created the F-117A Stealth Fighter.[1] Although trained as a lawyer, Rich had spent most of his working life at RAND, beginning as an analyst and slowly wending his way up to the number-two position.[2]

Rich had made plans to fly to Geneva that day to attend a meeting of the Council of the International Institute of Strategic Studies. In concert with RAND president James Thomson, Rich supervised the think tank's foreign offices, shepherding the decades-long expansion into Europe and especially the Middle East. Already a new RAND base in the Persian Gulf state of Qatar was in the planning stages. On his way to the Pentagon, Rich received ominous news: "BREAKING NEWS from CNN.com: World Trade Center damaged; unconfirmed reports say a plane has crashed into tower. Details to come."

Rich's appointment with General Handy was set for 9:45 A.M. Another RAND executive, Vice President Natalie Crawford, had been slotted for an earlier time. A vivacious woman who had joined RAND's Engineering Sciences and Aeronautics Department in 1964, Crawford was to go over RAND's research plan for the fiscal year 2002. General Handy had wanted to meet with her separately before bringing Rich into the discussion. When Crawford walked into the general's office for her 9:30 meeting, she found the staff gathered around TV sets, regular early morning talk shows preempted by the live coverage of the disaster in New York. Crawford was informed that General Handy was out of the room; the Air Force brass was discussing how to react to the event in New York, now being called a terrorist attack.[3]

Soon everyone was riveted to the TVs, as the flames spread throughout the north tower of the World Trade Center. There was heavy fire and smoke on the top floors, and there were gasps in the room as some stations showed people dropping from high on the east side, near the impact floors. Just as newscasters were announcing that authorities in the south tower declared the building secure and that workers did not have to evacuate, a second hijacked airliner, United Airlines flight 175 out of Boston, slammed into it. Billions of people witnessed the nightmare vision of the toylike 747 slicing into the east face of the tower, as unbelievable as a cheesy special effect out of a 1970s movie.[4]

General Handy entered the room a few minutes later, nodded stiffly at the staff, and then closed himself in his private office. By that time, Rich was walking down Corridor 1 on his way to the A ring of the oddly shaped structure, still trying to make it to his 9:45 meeting. Meanwhile, news kept coming: the Federal Aviation Administration had shut down all New York City–area airports and the Port Authority had ordered all the bridges and tunnels in and out of New York closed. At the White House, officials were trying desperately to activate combat air patrols over Washington, while First Lady Laura Bush, Vice President Cheney, and other top-ranking administration members were spirited away to safe locations out of the area.[5] The nation's top command was preparing for continuing attacks both in the United States and abroad.

Finally, at 9:30, President Bush spoke to reporters in Sarasota, Florida, confirming that the country had suffered an "apparent terrorist attack," before boarding Air Force One.[6] The Federal Aviation Administration, for the first time in history, halted all air traffic in the nation and ordered all flights to land immediately. At the White House, counterterrorism officials received notice that radar had picked up aircraft headed their way.[7]

At 9:40 A.M., Crawford and everyone in General Handy's office was knocked to the floor when the third terrorist-hijacked airliner crashed into the building. The impact, as Crawford would put it, felt "like some giant had picked up [the Pentagon] and slammed it down."[8] Everyone ran to the window. They could see people gathered in the parking lot, pointing at another part of the building. One of the Air Force officers who went across the hall to peek out another window saw black clouds of smoke spewing from the top of the building.

Alarms went off, sprinklers turned on, and even as the TV reports announced that the Pentagon had been struck, nervous security officers evacuated everyone from the building.[9] Rich, who was about to enter Corridor 9 to the general's office, retraced his steps and exited the way he had come in, out onto the Concourse and back out of the building via the Metro station. When he took the escalator to the ground level, he was assaulted by the smell of burning fuel as a cloud of black smoke billowed above his head. For her part, Crawford hustled out with Handy's staff, down the steps in front of Donald Rumsfeld's office and out the River entrance. The evacuation was swift but orderly, and as they came out, evacuees witnessed the fuming gap left by the Boeing 757 when it had smashed into the foremost symbol of American military might.

At RAND's Washington office in the glass-and-steel tower of the Pentagon Mall, across from the Pentagon, Bruce Hoffman had watched the events in New York incredulously. A native New Yorker, the dark, lean analyst was stunned by the tragedy unfolding before his eyes, a disaster he had many times foretold.

Hoffman was one of the world's leading terrorism experts, recognized for his contribution to the study of political violence. Two year earlier, in his book *Inside Terrorism,* he had argued that the rise of religious fanaticism, coupled with the increased availability of weapons of mass destruction, foretold an era of great bloodshed. Hoffman had testified before congressional committees numerous times, warning that although the incidence of terrorist attacks had gone down in the past few years, their ferocity had greatly increased. He had pointed to a new kind of terrorist, different from the Japanese Red Army, the Italian Red Brigades, the Basque ETA, and even the Irish Republican Army. Groups like al Qaeda, motivated by religious conviction rather than political ideology, saw themselves engaged in a life-and-death struggle with Western values; they bombed symbolic targets to attract attention to their causes.

Hoffman had stated before that he did not think the new terrorism could undermine national security.[10] The events of this day

were forcing him to revise his opinion. For if this was al Qaeda—
and the attack bore all the hallmarks of Osama bin Laden's group—
then their work was not done yet. Where would they strike next?

Hoffman had his answer at 9:40 A.M. The ground shook, a loud
boom shattering windows across the street, rattling the glass fig-
urines on Hoffman's desk, shaking his framed diploma from Oxford
off the wall. Hoffman hurried to his window and looked at the Pentagon's hulking mass a few blocks away.

A great plume of smoke, accompanied by massive tongues of
flames, rose from the far side of the Pentagon, as ambulances
screeched and an F-16 jet swung low over downtown Washington.
Hoffman could barely make out the tail end of the downed plane,
American Airlines flight 77. He deduced that the terrorists had probably wanted to hit the Potomac River entrance, where Secretary of
Defense Rumsfeld's office was located, but missed.

Never had the Pentagon building been attacked. In fact, the War
of 1812 was the last time an enemy had bridged the ocean and struck
in the nation's capital. This was not a tactical sneak attack like Pearl
Harbor; this was a military excursion of a higher order. In Hoffman's eyes, this was a clear attempt to strike a knockout blow to the
United States, a declaration of war by an enemy that would not rest
until America and its values were crushed, until the whole world
was ruled by a caliphate not seen since the glory days of the Arab
empires. Unlike the previous conflict between America and the Soviet Union, this would be a hot war of actual battles, bullets, and
blood rather than spies, missiles, and threats. But without a clearly
defined enemy or territory to conquer—nothing less than the whole
world itself—this conflict might go on forever.

To Hoffman, this was the beginning of World War Three.[11]

THE NOTION OF terrorism as a global conflict was not new. Notorious international terrorist Carlos the Jackal had said more or
less the same thing to the Organization of Petroleum States oil min-

isters he captured for ransom in Vienna in 1975: "The Third World War has started."[12] The difference was that in 2001 the concept of a worldwide war on terrorism would become American national policy—with the full weight of the U.S. government behind it. As Deputy Secretary of Defense Paul Wolfowitz phrased it, "Our struggle against these people will be a struggle perhaps even longer than the Cold War. It will test our resolve perhaps even more than the conflicts of World War II."[13] A clash of civilizations, a global war on terrorism, a holy jihad, all would spring from the fountainhead of September 11, 2001.

For the longest time RAND analysts had warned that the clouds of conflict were gathering; however, successive administrations had decided that the United States was immune. Terror networks were seen as intrinsically foreign and exotic; only occasionally did instances of homegrown extremism, such as Timothy McVeigh's bombing of the Alfred P. Murrah Federal Building in Oklahoma City in 1995, shatter that complacency. The threat was not seen as organized or imminent; therefore, little federal money was devoted to its study. Perhaps terror studies had needed a charismatic spokesman, like Albert Wohlstetter, to rouse the smug federal bureaucracy. Only now, when the carnage was inescapable, was Washington ready to listen to its Cassandra of perpetual war.

Indeed, as Hoffman reminded the members of the House Committee on Intelligence on September 26, he had appeared before them ten years earlier, urging centralization of all counterterrorism activities to avoid a tragedy like the one that had just occurred. He rebuked the intelligence agencies for still being configured to fight the Cold War, when the main enemy in that conflict had crumbled long ago.

> An estimated 60% of the intelligence community's efforts, for example, are still focused on military intelligence pertaining to the standing armed forces of established nation-states . . .

Given the emergence of formidable, transnational, non-state adversaries, and the lethally destructive threats that they clearly pose, this balance is no longer appropriate.[14]

He pointed out that although the U.S. intelligence budget was more than $30 billion, the last formal comprehensive foreign terrorist assessment had been done in 1991, during the Gulf War. He urged the redistribution of personnel, budget, and resources, as well as the creation of a new body similar to the Drug Enforcement Agency to oversee these efforts. In other words, he called for something akin to the Homeland Security Department, which President Bush did create a few weeks later.

Hoffman saw the conflict with al Qaeda as the natural evolution of decades of terrorist activities, dating back to the slaughter of Israeli athletes by a Palestine Liberation Organization offshoot named Black September during the Munich Olympic Games in 1972. It was then, when the Western world first contemplated the possibility that terrorism would be more than a passing phenomenon, that RAND analysts broke new ground in the field of intelligence by creating the discipline of terrorist studies.

One of Hoffman's colleagues at RAND, Brian Jenkins was the first analyst to establish a terrorism research program in the United States. A former Green Beret and occasional consultant for RAND, Jenkins sold the think tank on the concept in 1972 when he was introduced to newly installed president Donald Rice. Later that year, Jenkins sired the Chronology of International Terrorism (now known as the Terrorist Data Bank), the first systematic compilation of all known international terrorist actions. He and other RAND analysts issued dozens of reports on how the United States could and should combat terrorism long before anyone believed foreign terrorists would ever directly affect daily life in America.

At first, RAND supported the studies out of its own in-house funds, since it could not convince any government agency to sponsor a systematized study of terrorism. After all, for the entire period from 1968 to 1974, RAND recorded only 507 incidents of international terrorism, most of them of a minor nature.[15] It was several lean years before the federal government finally recognized the validity of the discipline.[16]

Terrorism, of course, is not a new phenomenon. Historians have pointed out that the practice of terrorism dates back to Roman times, with the first recorded use of the term during the Reign of Terror of the French Revolution in 1793–94.[17] Yet even centuries later, it remains difficult to define terrorism precisely since, like pornography, it can depend on your point of view: an act of politically inspired violence is an act of terrorism if I don't agree with it. As the cliché goes, one man's terrorist is another man's freedom fighter. RAND's Konrad Kellen observed, "The early American revolutionaries would have been regarded as terrorists by contemporary standards. Thomas Jefferson, who said, 'The tree of liberty must be fertilized from time to time with the blood of tyrants,' might qualify for the label."[18]

Wanting not to devote too much time to the ontological implications of terrorism, initially Jenkins defined it as "the use of criminal violence to force a government to change its course of action. The terrorist purpose . . . is to force a government to withdraw from or desist from undertaking something . . . Terrorism is a political crime."[19]

Jenkins's definition was valid only if one adopted the other old saw about everything in human affairs being political.* It could not encompass late-twentieth-century millenarian groups such as the

---

* A view, not coincidentally, propagated by extremists and terrorist groups of the time. George Habbash, the founder of the Popular Front for the Liberation of Palestine, perhaps put it best: "In today's world, no one is innocent, no one is neutral. A man is either with the oppressed or with the oppressors. He who takes no interest in politics gives his blessings to the prevailing order, that of the ruling classes and exploiting orders" (Jenkins, *International Terrorism*, p. 16).

Japanese religious group Aum Shinrikyo, which wants to destroy whole nations, if not the world, to bring about a new society.[20] Nor would it include Islamic jihadists, who seek religious transfiguration through suicide bombings and indiscriminate slaughter. Terrorism as a pathway to salvation is a far cry from the 1970s hijacker who demanded to be flown to Cuba, or the Symbionese Liberation Army gangster unleashing a hail of bullets in a suburban California bank.

Yet, except for occasional waves of political violence attributed to syndico-anarchists* at the close of the nineteenth century, terrorism was rare in the West for almost a hundred years. Not until the late 1960s, with the societal divisions caused by the Vietnam War and the youth revolution allied to the growth in anticolonial, radical revolutionary movements, did terrorism come again to the fore. Although employed mainly by Socialist and leftist groups inspired by Mao Tse-tung, Fidel Castro, and Che Guevara, terrorism also became the weapon of choice for groups of nationalistic character such as the Basque ETA separatists and the Irish Republican Army.

Since most terrorist acts before the 1990s were committed by groups with political ideations, Jenkins's delineation of terrorism as an intrinsically political act was a serviceable one. It allowed RAND to analyze the structure of the groups, their leadership, and their origins, with a view toward neutralizing them and ultimately eradicating them. Over the years, RAND refined its definition of terrorism, concluding finally that it is the nature of the act and not the political goals or identity of the group that is of importance. In its

---

* Some observers today claim there is little difference between jihadists and the equally suicidal anarchists who took the life of President William McKinley and Czar Alexander II. They argue that the Islamic fundamentalists will fade away, just like the Black Hand and others of their ilk, and that Western governments would be better served by paying closer attention to the real future enemy, China. See Mary Evans, "For Jihadist, Read Anarchist," the *Economist* (18 August 2005).

most simple form, terrorism is "violence or the threat of violence calculated to create an atmosphere of fear or alarm."[21]

From the inception of the Terrorist Data Bank, RAND analysts complained that the United States was not equipped to deal with terrorism. In 1982, in a paper for a RAND conference on terrorism, Jenkins wrote, "[Terrorism] is a conflict for which we are inadequately prepared . . . Our embassies have been destroyed, our citizens have been kidnapped and killed, our jet fighters have been blown up on the ground."[22] But then, with the exception of Israel, few countries back then were ready to impose the kind of strict security measures needed to thwart terrorists.

RAND's fundamental contribution to the field of terrorist studies sprang from the recognition that terrorism is a weapon of the weak. "Terrorism is theater,"[23] made for the benefit of the audience watching and not for its victims, nor for the people directly affected by the act. Writers such as Franz Fanon, who in the 1950s advocated acts of violent revolt against entrenched power structures to rectify wrongs against the dispossessed, had already recognized this fact.[24]

Jenkins, Hoffman, and others linked the theatricality of terrorism, its need to obtain popular support, to the main military strategy of Mao Tse-tung against the Nationalist Armies of Chiang Kai-shek in China. Mao, who waged a protracted guerrilla war to attain power, affirmed that gaining the trust of the people was the key to a successful campaign, since revolutionary forces can then recruit soldiers who otherwise would have been bystanders in a standard military conflict. "Political power grows from the barrel of a gun," wrote Mao, a saying that's particularly apt when the firing of that gun is a news event broadcast to all corners of the world. Terrorism is thus a perfect example of what Daniel Ellsberg termed "judo politics,"[25] or what military analysts now call a variant of an asymmetric strategy—the use of low-tech weapons to attack targets at specific times, which will render maximum publicity value against an enemy with superior weapons and greater manpower.[26]

Jenkins pointed out that terrorists have a limited number of modes of attack. Their repertoire consists of six basic tactics: bombings, assassinations, armed assaults, kidnappings, barricade and hostage situations, and hijackings.[27] More imitative than innovative, terrorists continue using a preferred mode until governments catch on and improve security measures. Thus, airplane hijackings and hostage taking were popular in the 1970s until hostage-rescue units were created and international treaties against hijackings were vigorously enforced. (Thus, New York's World Trade Center was attacked twice—in 1993 and 2001.)

By the mid-1980s, RAND analysts observed a very disturbing trend: terrorism was becoming bloodier. Whereas in 1968 the bombs of groups like the Croatian separatists were disarmed before they could injure anyone, by 1983 Hezbollah followers were ramming trucks full of explosives into U.S. Marine barracks in Lebanon, killing American servicemen by the score.[28] This last incident brought attention to what would become the most worrying trend of all, suicide attacks by extremists in and from the Middle East.

According to RAND analysts, the first record of a suicide attack since ancient times occurred in May of 1972, when Japanese terrorists acting on behalf of Palestinian causes tossed a hand grenade into a group of Christian pilgrims at the airport in Lod, Israel.[29] The attack claimed twenty-six victims but also exposed the terrorists to immediate retribution from security agents at the scene; two of the three terrorists were killed in what amounted to a suicide mission, similar to the "divine wind" or kamikaze immolations of World War II. RAND analysts believed this self-sacrifice shamed the Palestinians into similar action. If Japanese were willing to die for a foreign cause, Palestinians must demonstrate their readiness to sacrifice themselves for their own cause.[30] The inevitable next step was the glorification of death in battle as the bloody gate to paradise.

This transformation in tactics gave terrorists unexpected results. By most accounts, after the bombing of the Beirut barracks, Reagan administration officials decided Lebanon was not worth the American funeral candles; the marines packed up and went home. American withdrawal from Lebanon and the Soviet defeat in Afghanistan, when conjoined to the rise in Muslim fundamentalism fueled by the financial support of Saudi Arabia, created a belief among terrorist groups that they had finally found a way to change the policies of Western powers. Given that the West and Israel could not be defeated by conventional warfare, terrorism would become the tactic of necessity, as witnessed by the hundreds of suicide bombers who for years have turned Israel into a garrison state.[31]

RAND analysts in the 1990s pointed out that terrorists until then had come in five different categories—revolutionaries, dissatisfied individuals, ethnic minorities, economically disadvantaged groups, and anarchists. They warned that henceforth the greatest danger would come from another group, religious extremists. Their next targets would be Western financial institutions like the World Bank, American and Western corporations, and other religions and their leaders, as prefigured by Mehmet Ali Ağă's attempt on the life of Pope John Paul II. Above all, terrorists would concentrate on the symbolic value of their targets, for they would seek not military victory but the psychological defeat of their adversaries through fear. RAND warned that at some point in the future terrorists might resort to weapons of mass destruction, like nuclear, biological, or chemical weapons, especially state-sponsored terrorist groups such as Hezbollah, backed by Iran, and Hamas, sponsored by Syria.[32]

In response to this shift, in the 1990s RAND developed a new way of examining terrorist activities. John Arquilla and David Ronfeldt originated the concept of "netwar," which they defined as "small groups who communicate, coordinate, and conduct their campaigns in an Internetted manner, without a precise central command."[33] This new way of coordinating attacks made the fight against international terrorism maddeningly difficult, as, without a traditional power structure, groups would replicate like so many viruses in a

computer network. Arquilla and Ronfeldt assumed that the terrorist netwar would be conducted on the Internet, with technologically
savvy terrorist groups bringing down the electronic houses of the
West—banks, power supply, the defense establishment. Instead, as
Hoffman pointed out, al Qaeda and its many offshoots used the
concept to spread branches of the organization around the globe,
even as they carried on with the traditional methods of terrorism—
bombs, kidnappings, and assassinations.

RAND analysts believed that the ultimate solution to terrorism
was to change the conditions that gave rise to it; especially in the
Middle East, people had to be shown there were avenues more profitable and effective to achieve their goals than murder and mayhem.

By 2006, following the U.S.-led invasions of Afghanistan and
Iraq to smash al Qaeda and to remove terrorist-friendly regimes,
Jenkins added a cautionary note: American military responses to
terrorism might prove counterproductive.[34] If the United States attempts to eliminate all terrorist groups and attacks all nation-states
that host terrorists, the conflicts will only spread the terrorist seed
around the globe, much like the mujahideen morphed and scattered
after Afghanistan. Terrorism will be defeated by a combination of
tactics and weapons, but, above all, by ideas. Armed force alone
will not succeed; conviction and ideology will. Jenkins also urged
that the drive to eliminate terrorism not trigger a change in American values. Counterterrorism will triumph if America preserves its
traditional freedoms, abjuring torture, partisanship, and needless
bravado. Should American democracy and the American Constitution be among the victims of terrorism, America's most potent
weapons—its traditional freedoms—will be lost for the sake of a
Pyrrhic victory. As Jenkins concludes, "Whatever we do must be
consistent with our fundamental values. This is no mere matter of
morality, it is a strategic calculation, and here we have at times miscalculated."[35]

20

Yoda and the Knights of Counterforce

THE IMAGES of the American-led attack on Baghdad in April 2003 are indelible. Missiles launched from ships hundreds of miles away coursed the nighttime skies with eerie precision, bringing down selected targets with what seemed otherworldly ease. Unlike Operation Desert Storm in 1991, when Baghdad was blanketed with thousands of tons of bombs, Operation Iraqi Freedom seemed like something out of a science-fiction movie—military conflict as a surgical operation.

If the invasion of Iraq was *Star Wars* and the American forces were the Jedi Knights, then the Yoda of the operation was former RAND analyst Andrew Marshall. A wizened octagenarian, Marshall has been given the nickname of the diminutive sage for his soft voice and cryptic advice. Marshall's influence is vast, and although his writings are few, in them he set out the guidelines for what has been called the Revolution in Military Affairs (RMA) that guided Operation Iraqi Freedom and its earlier counterpart, Operation Desert Storm. In fact, one could argue that the wars in Iraq were gestated twenty years before Saddam Hussein finally heard the fearsome whistle of American missiles in Baghdad—and that the creators came from RAND. The scope of the plans was stupefyingly vast: to modernize the U.S Army so its forces could set in motion a series of political transformations that would redraw the map of the world, allowing America to never again face an armed adversary. The whole world is living with the painful consequences of that misguided dream.

For a period of a few months after the U.S.-led invasion—before the Iraqi insurgents and jihadists rose up in suicidal rage, before the Coalition Force occupiers got bogged down in an unhappy replay of America in Vietnam, the Soviets in Afghanistan, or the French in Algeria (take your pick)—all of Marshall's theories about modern war were proven right. Armed conflict in the twenty-first century could be waged like a George Lucas movie, with hardly any loss of American lives. Even the drones, the pilotless aircraft that sent deadly missiles to the obdurate enemy, could be manned from a cushy chair at an Air Force base in Nevada 5,000 miles away.[1] The RMA Marshall had advocated was an undeniable success. The subsequent occupation and the bloody failures of an inept counterinsurgency plan would be somebody else's department. (In fact, RAND published a number of studies warning against overconfidence and predicting that insufficient numbers of troops would cause the occupation to fail, as was acknowledged by Ambassador L. Paul Bremer.[2])

Since 1973, Marshall has headed the Office of Net Assessment, a secretive Pentagon department set up by his former RAND colleague, Secretary of Defense James Schlesinger. Marshall, who joined RAND's Economics Department in 1950, was a close friend of Albert and Roberta Wohlstetter. It was Marshall who encouraged the latter to undertake her groundbreaking study on the Japanese attack on Pearl Harbor. Marshall also advised the Gaither Committee in the late 1950s, and collaborated with Herman Kahn on civil defense, and with Thomas Schelling on game theory. He stayed through the massive defection of RANDites to the Pentagon in the 1960s, leaving only after the Pentagon Papers scandal.[3]

Seven successive presidents have supported Marshall's office at the Pentagon with hardly any changes in purview or personnel. Marshall, who has no apparent intention of retiring, is the only prominent nuclear strategist from RAND's golden age still in government service. One of his disciples, former secretary of the Navy James Horner, facetiously introduced him during a ceremony in 2003:

> Andy was the head of the Office of Net Assessment when Admiral Farragut was around and was appointed to the job by General George Washington just before he relinquished command of the Continental Army. He celebrated his 50th wedding anniversary last night. And ladies and gentlemen, tonight is his 82nd birthday. He is still working full time at our Pentagon. General John Jumper and I have often relied on one of his many sayings to help you cope with tough times. He once said to me, "There simply are limits to the stupidity any one may or can prevent." General Jumper and I call upon that time after time.[4]

During his first few years at the Office of Net Assessment, Marshall turned out a series of studies on the comparative strength of the American and Soviet armed forces. By the early 1980s, under the influence of Wohlstetter, he began to reexamine the foundational thinking of American military might, which held that supremacy in nuclear weaponry alone was enough to triumph in the battlefield. Ironically, he found inspiration in the writings of one of America's ideological enemies, Soviet field marshal Nikolai V. Ogarkov.

In the late 1970s, Ogarkov had come to an amazing conclusion: nuclear weaponry had become dated. In a pamphlet entitled *Vsegda v Gotovnosti k Zashchite Otechestva* (Always Ready to Defend the Fatherland) he argued that due to the universal reluctance to use nuclear weapons in war, the enormous changes brought about by developments in technology would give the nation that knew best how to harness those innovations an unsurpassable advantage on the battlefield.[5]

Marshall acknowledged this point of departure. As he put it, "At that time . . . it was the Soviet military theorists, rather than our own, that were intellectualizing about [the groundwork for the revolution in military affairs] and speculating on the longer-term consequences of the technical and other changes that the American military had initiated."[6]

The Pentagon received its first formal proposal of RMA guidelines in a report from the Commission on Integrated Long-Term Strategy, a panel Marshall and Wohlstetter put together in the early 1980s with the help of their former RAND colleague Fred Iklé— then under secretary of defense for policy in the Reagan administration. The study group contemplated the state of war making twenty years into the future with the goal of making policy recommendations that best served the national interest as the authors defined it.[7] (Among its predictions: by the year 2000, some forty countries would have the capability to make nuclear weapons, among them Saudi Arabia, Iraq, and Argentina.)

Theorists such as Andrew Krepinevich, a former student of Marshall's, define RMA as a "discontinuity in methods of fighting," or a series of transformations through the ages. In their view, these discontinuities are usually brought about by changes in technology that give an unforeseen advantage to a previously second-rate power. Beginning with the widespread use of chariots in the battlefield during the eighteenth century B.C.; to the ancient Greeks, whose phalanxes allowed them to defeat their traditional enemies, the Persians, and conquer half the known world; to the social and political evolutions that transformed tactics and logistics during the Napoleonic era, these historians have identified at least a dozen cases of revolutions in military affairs. Of those, six have occurred in the last 200 years, and three since 1939 alone.

It was no coincidence that the American march on Baghdad in 2003 bore more than a passing resemblance to the German offensive on Belgium and France during World War II; in the world of RMA advocates, the Nazi blitzkrieg stands out as one of the most significant recent revolutions in warfare. No longer would having the greatest number of soldiers in the field be the sole measure of the strongest power; instead, innovative uses of new technology—tanks and tank radios along with developments in organizational and operational concepts and tactics—would be the key to victory.* A parallel revolution occurred in naval power during World War II. With the building of large aircraft carriers that could act as bases for armed excursions, the United States did away with the ancient concept of naval warfare, which called for large battleships to blast away at each other at relatively close range.

Finally, there came the most radical of all the RMAs, the development of nuclear weaponry. The blasts over Hiroshima and Nagasaki immediately changed the entire nature of warfare, particularly as the further invention of the hydrogen and neutron bombs and the successful deployment of intercontinental missiles made real the possibility of the end of entire civilizations. As Krepinevich states, echoing Bernard Brodie, "In the minds of most strategists, however, the sole purpose of the new weapons had shifted from war fighting to deterrence."[8]

Marshall and Wohlstetter were the first Americans to formalize this new military thinking among Pentagon intellectuals. Much like the RAND eggheads who changed the nation's perspective on

---

* For instance, in 1940 French tanks were more technologically advanced than German tanks. However, by deploying an operational concept of deep penetration on a narrow front backed by air support, Germany overcame the initial French technological superiority.

strategic analyses with counterforce and fail-safe, so did Marshall, Wohlstetter, and their acolytes transform theories of war with their emphasis on Star Wars technology, such as the antiballistic missile system favored by the Reagan administration. Over the next few years the RMA, with its insistence on smarter weaponry, would become the gold standard of the military—transfiguring the traditional Pentagon lust for more, bigger, and deadlier weapons.

The most important innovation was the wide use of microchips, which transformed warfare much like tanks, aircraft carriers, and nuclear bombs had done in previous decades. Digital communication was the not-so-secret ingredient that allowed the United States to de-emphasize its rapidly aging nuclear strategic force and develop the lean and highly mobile enlisted fighting force that crushed Saddam Hussein. As Richard Perle stated, the 2003 invasion of Iraq was "the first war that's been fought in a way that would recognize Albert [Wohlstetter]'s vision of future wars. That it was won so quickly and decisively, with so few casualties and so little damage, was in fact an implementation of his strategy and his vision."[9]

Former assistant secretary of defense Paul Wolfowitz credits Wohlstetter with being the first to realize that precision guided munitions could be even more useful than nuclear weapons in a battlefield. During the long drawn-out debate of the SALT II negotiations, the Soviets were only willing to reach an agreement if the United States banned all cruise missiles with a range greater than 600 kilometers, such as Tomahawks. Carried by attack submarines, these nonnuclear missiles had been built at Henry Kissinger's request as a sort of bargaining chip for the Strategic Arms Limitation Talks. The Navy was not too keen on them, as they took up valuable torpedo space that could be used by nuclear weapons.

According to Wolfowitz,

it was Albert and his group who said wait a minute, if you can have a conventional delivery system it's worth the torpedo space . . . The Secretary of Defense at the time, who was somebody named Rumsfeld, by whatever means he came to it, concluded it was not something he wanted to give up even if the Navy brass were prepared to . . . So it was a matter of considerable personal satisfaction to watch those missiles turning right angle corners in the Gulf War in 1991 and demonstrating that this stuff really could do what Albert Wohlstetter had envisioned 15 years before it might be able to do.[10]

One important factor in the ultimate triumph of RMA theory at the Pentagon was the lingering effect of the Vietnam War on national policy. As Wohlstetter wrote, "Of all the disasters of Vietnam, the worst may be the 'lessons' that we'll draw from it."[11] By that, Wohlstetter meant the conjunction of forces in the United States that would make the country wary of all foreign interventions—the leftist groups that violently protested the conflict and the right-wing isolationist believers of Fortress America. (Wohlstetter called this the SAC-SDS position, the philosophical alliance of the hawks of Strategic Air Command and the revolutionaries of the Students for a Democratic Society.) He warned that public sentiment might be such that voters would emerge from their narcissistic shell only when confronted with danger of direct physical attacks on the continental United States.

Worse, Wohlstetter feared that there would be no change in America's nuclear policy of mutual assured destruction, "which tended to make every confrontation a choice between nuclear war or doing nothing . . . not so bad after all . . . (because we would always do nothing rather than something in between—according to the hopeful left; according to the hopeful right . . . because our adversaries would always do nothing, in order to avoid our massive retaliation, and if not they would be overwhelmed by it)."[12] Wohlstetter, always the advocate of preserving America's right to intervene anywhere to protect its interests, was horrified by both tendencies. A pragmatist by nature, he saw a way out of the Vietnam syndrome in the development of nonnuclear weapons.

Though Wohlstetter and Marshall did not elaborate on this, the underlying principle of RMA is an assumption of America's benevolent intentions as the justification for its intercession in world events. Not coincidentally, this point of view informed all of their decisions—not to mention the plethora of analyses carried out by their RAND colleagues.[13] Studies by RAND's John Arquilla and by United States UN ambassador and former envoy to Iraq Zalmay Khalilzad are of particular interest in this regard—especially those of Khalilzad, since he was a student of Wohlstetter's at the University of Chicago. Like Plato parsing Socrates, Khalilzad attempts to codify the lessons of the master for a complex and conflicted world.

Born in Afghanistan and educated at the American University in Beirut, Khalilzad was one of Wohlstetter's favorites at the University of Chicago. Although fellow students in Beirut described him as a radical Afghani who attended pro-Palestinian meetings and hung a poster of Egyptian president Nasser on his dorm-room wall,[14] Khalilzad was transformed shortly after he arrived in Chicago in the mid-1970s for his Ph.D. in political science.

"I ran into some friends of mine," he stated in a phone interview from the ambassador's palace in Baghdad. "They asked me to sit in on this class taught by a Professor Wohlstetter, called Nuclear and Classical Wars. He is quite a professor, they told me, teaches it with anecdotes and real-life examples as well as theories how things are done in the real world, in the Kennedy administration. I said okay. I went in, I sat at the back of the class. Albert came in and started talking about the probability of war, about how the fixed probability of nuclear war made it, in the opinion of some people, inevitable, the perpetual probability of nuclear war. I raised my hand and I asked him what about the perpetual probability of peace? He asked me what my name was and then he asked me to stay behind after class. He wanted me to take his seminar. I told him I wasn't registered for his course, that I was just auditing. But he persisted, and I became his student, and by the end of the semester I was a consultant working for him."[15]

Wohlstetter's cosmopolitan lifestyle made a deep impression on the young doctoral student. A colleague recalls Khalilzad being enthralled by one of Wohlstetter's fabled soirees. Riding up to the professor's posh lakefront apartment, he was wide-eyed in wonder at the luxe that surrounded him, goggling on Wohlstetter's evident wealth. He borrowed his colleague's copy of French Marxist philosopher Alexandre Kojève's *Lectures on Hegel* and returned it to her with one sentence underlined, "The bourgeois intellectual neither fights nor works." The following summer, Khalilzad had secured a job at RAND through the good offices of Professor Wohlstetter.[16]

According to Khalilzad, Wohlstetter's designs for Afghanistan were part of the reason for the Soviet failure in that country. "In discussions with Albert, one of the things we talked about was how to challenge the assumptions of the Carter administration . . . that Afghanistan would be consumed by the Soviets. He disagreed and he pressed very hard . . . to get people to agree that with enough assistance the Afghanis might win."

Khalilzad joined Wohlstetter in his advocacy of American aid to the rebels. By then a professor at Columbia University, Khalilzad wrote a study dovetailing with Wohlstetter's thesis that the Soviets could be defeated militarily in Afghanistan. The two scholars pressed their point of view inside the Carter administration, which eventually relented and supplied shoulder-held Stinger missiles to the rebels. This momentous decision gave the mujahideen the means of negating the main Soviet advantage, which was the use of helicopter gunships to attack rebel positions.

"The message here [was] there was more we could do. Not just the Stingers but a whole range of things, intelligence, tons of other equipment," Khalilzad said. "Once America provided American know-how, the Soviets would either have to escalate or back down. Ultimately, they backed down."[17]

With Ronald Reagan's inauguration, Marshall and Wohlstetter found themselves in an ideal position to put into practice their theories about future wars. Their desire to reshape America's worldview had already surfaced in the late 1970s during their opposition to SALT and the Anti-Ballistic Missile Treaty, as well as their support for the Committee on the Present Danger and the Team B exercise. The RMA was the next logical step. In their new world order, presided over by America and guided by American principles, the United States would act preemptively and unilaterally, if need be, to protect its interests and promote American values abroad. Their prescription of "peace through strength" was nothing less than the old Pax Romana used by Caesar Augustus to expand the power of Rome—a precept that Wolfowitz seemed to endorse when he advocated a "Pax Americana."[18]

The neoconservatives who came of intellectual age in the early 1980s held it as almost a sacred principle that America should control the destinies of the world. (By 2001, influential neoconservatives like Max Boot would openly advocate that the United States declare itself an empire and start acting accordingly.[19]) Many of the midlevel and top-echelon leaders in the military-industrial complex during the 1980s became followers of Wohlstetter and Marshall. As Richard Perle stated, even Rumsfeld considered himself a Wohlstetter disciple, while the followers of Marshall grew to be so numerous they called themselves "the St. Andrews prep" boys.[20]

From his niche in the Office of Net Assessment, Marshall continued to press for the development of new weapons systems while Wohlstetter lobbied legislators for their approval. They argued for air-delivered, precision-guided, antiarmor submunitions that could stop the advance of an enemy armored force division in its tracks without the need for U.S. Army mechanized forces. They advocated cyberspace techniques that could disable the computer networks of the enemy and render it effectively blind during combat; they explored the possibility of mind-altering substances that could disorient soldiers in the field; they even foresaw a body armor for soldiers that could serve as an exoskeleton, complete with up-to-date communications equipment; they planned for smart missiles fired from submarines 100 miles away that could halt an Iraqi army advance by homing in on the sound of its tank engine.[21]

Beyond the daily chore of envisioning new technologically advanced ways to defend American interests worldwide, Marshall also conducted a series of seminars concentrating on possible responses to unanticipated adversaries, as befitting a man who reputedly goes to sleep every night worrying about the next war. In the early 1980s, Marshall was pointing at China as the next prospective enemy on the horizon. He was supported by studies out of RAND, edited by Khalilzad, which considered the rise of China one of the most pressing security concerns of the twenty-first century.[22]

Nowadays, Khalilzad feels that concern was premature: "A lot of people after the Cold War thought that China would be the most pressing problem. After 9/11, terrorism has become the prime issue of our time. Over time, China will become more important. I like to joke with people that China may have been indirectly involved in 9/11 just to get our minds off them and onto other problems."[23]

The dazzling unipolarity of power after the fall of the Soviet Union during the George H. W. Bush administration was confusing at first to Marshall and Wohlstetter. Oddly enough, neither one had foreseen how perestroika might trigger the collapse of the Soviet Union, leaving the Pentagon without a clearly defined adversary.[24] However, neoconservatives seized on the occasion as the most opportune moment in history to implement their credo of American supremacy.[25] Not only would the United States make sure no power could ever again rise to the position held by the Soviets but, as befitted a great imperium, the United States would secure the sources of energy necessary for its wherewithal. The Middle East, with its vast deposits of oil, became the focus of a well-coordinated campaign to extend American power and reshape the oppressive, anti-Semitic, reactionary states in the region—by means of politics and force.[26]

This policy fit in nicely with the pro-Israel views of Wohlstetter. A secular humanist, who once answered the question if he was Jewish with a typical witty reply, "Heavens no! But my parents were,"[27] Wohlstetter was a fierce advocate of Israel as the only working democracy in the Middle East. When the Soviet Union dissolved and the war between Iraq and Iran came to an inconclusive truce, he and Marshall realized that the United States would soon need to put American boots on the ground in the Middle East. Iraq's invasion of Kuwait in 1991 was the tipping point that lumped all the different neoconservative strains of imperialism, Zionism, militarism, and benighted idealism into a single policy: Saddam Hussein must go. It would also prove a real-life test for all the RMA theories about new weapons and military concepts.

"Saddam Hussein, who needs to be thrown out of Iraq as well as from Kuwait, illustrates what should have been obvious all along: that even as communist empires break up and many of their parts move toward democracy and free markets, the world will continue to present military dangers to critical interests of the U.S. and its allies. We need a strategy and forces shaped to meet these very real dangers," wrote Wohlstetter.[28]

Operation Desert Storm confirmed the RMA theories—but left a great deal undone on the political side. When President George H. W. Bush refused to topple Saddam after pushing the Iraqi army out of Kuwait, regime change in Baghdad and Washington became the holy grail of Marshall, Wohlstetter, and their allies at the Pentagon and at RAND. Their most potent weapon was a portly, cultured, and very rational Iraqi exile wanted for bank fraud in Jordan— Ahmed Chalabi.

21

Back to Iraq

AHMED CHALABI'S RISE to prominence in Washington circles came
at the instigation of Albert Wohlstetter, who met Chalabi in Paul
Wolfowitz's office.[1] Middle East scholar Bernard Lewis, a friend of
Wolfowitz and Wohlstetter, had already talked up the exile to both
men, knowing they would see the value of Chalabi's acquaintance.
Wolfowitz, Wohlstetter, and Lewis shared similar values and background; each of them secular Jews, defenders of Israel, devoted to
reason and to the spread of American values. Wohlstetter and Lewis
also shared a common fascination with how Kemal Atatürk created
the modern, secular Turkish state—seeing it as a model for the new
Iraq Chalabi would lead.*

---

* Lewis is such a Turkophile that he has refused to acknowledge Atatürk's attempted annihilation of the Armenian people. In 1993, a French court found Lewis guilty of denying that
the 1919 Armenian genocide had occurred—that is, it convicted him of repeating the official
line of the Turkish government. He was fined one franc.

Wohlstetter and Lewis expected that after the depredations of Saddam Hussein, Chalabi and his exile organization, the Iraqi National Congress (INC), could restore the cradle of civilization to her proper place in the world, with a secular government that would make peace with Israel, serve as an example to the Arab "street"— and never wage war on the United States. As Lewis would write,

> The nucleus of such a government is already available, in the Iraqi National Congress, headed by Ahmed Chalabi. In the northern free zone during the '90s they played a constructive role, and might at that time even have achieved the liberation of Iraq had we not failed at crucial moments to support them. Despite a continuing lack of support amounting at times to sabotage, they continue to acquit themselves well in Iraq, and there can be no reasonable doubt that of all the possible Iraqi candidates they are the best in terms alike of experience, reliability, and good will.[2]

That Chalabi was a charmer, nobody could deny. With his expensive suits, exotic accent, and soothing manners, he easily filled the role of the Oriental princeling. Yet few expected at the onset of his quixotic quest that he and his cadre of RAND-originated backers would succeed in convincing the American government to go back to Iraq to finally unseat Hussein. That they managed to do so is a fascinating story about the use and abuse of power, influence, and innuendo.

The scion of an ancient Iraqi family, Chalabi was a precocious child, regularly skipping grades in the Jesuit school he attended in central Baghdad.[3] After King Faisal II was assassinated and his government deposed in 1958, Chalabi's family fled Iraq, losing most of its fortune. Chalabi, then twelve years old, went to boarding school in England. He finished his studies in America, earning undergrad-

uate and master's degrees in mathematics from the Massachusetts Institute of Technology. He also earned a Ph.D. in mathematics at the
University of Chicago at the same time Wohlstetter was teaching
there, although according to Chalabi they did not meet then.[4]

In 1977, at the invitation of Crown Prince Hassan of Jordan,
Chalabi moved to Amman; there he founded the Petra Bank, which
soon became the country's second-largest financial institution. He
befriended the royal family of the small Hashemite kingdom; he lived
in an opulent villa filled with modern art, and his children rode
horses with the king's family. The pain of exile was mitigated by his
growing wealth, yet by 1989 Chalabi was fleeing Jordan to London
with his wife and four children, accused of causing the collapse of
his own bank. In 1992 a Jordanian court found him guilty in ab-
sentia of thirty-one charges, including embezzlement, forgery, and
theft; it sentenced him to twenty-two years of hard labor and ordered
restitution of $70 million.[5]

Chalabi had even weightier matters to deal with in the years
after his escape. In May of 1992, he cofounded in Vienna the INC,
a politically and religiously diverse group of Iraqis pledged to establish a representative government in Iraq.[6] Chalabi set up headquarters in the Kurdish region of northern Iraq. In the wake of the
cease-fire after the Gulf War, and under the subsequent no-fly zone
established by American and British planes over northern Iraq, the
mountainous region enjoyed something close to autonomy.

In July of 1992, Chalabi put in motion the first of several plots
to overthrow Hussein: a mechanized brigade of about 3,000 soldiers
and dozens of armored vehicles set off for Baghdad to overthrow the
tyrant. Republican Guard troops loyal to Hussein ambushed them,
however, and the attempted putsch was snuffed out. More than
eighty army officers were captured, tortured, and killed by Hussein's
forces.[7] Three years later, Chalabi tried again, but Hussein infiltrated
an INC conspiracy and arrested more than 100 officers before the

plot could unfold. Then, with the bribed cooperation of a Kurdish leader, Iraqi troops raided and destroyed INC headquarters in the Kurdish region.[8]

Having learned from those and other attempts that he could not defeat Hussein by force of arms, Chalabi turned to Americans to do it for him—a job that fit in nicely with the aims of Wohlstetter, Wolfowitz, Lewis, and their RAND brethren.[9] Zalmay Khalilzad would call Chalabi "one of the key figures in the fight against Saddam Hussein, organizing to generate support in Europe, the U.S., and Iraq."[10]

Through the good offices of Wohlstetter and Richard Perle, Chalabi soon had the ear of Republican Senate leader Trent Lott and House Speaker Newt Gingrich, as well as that of two powerful former secretaries of defense, Halliburton president Dick Cheney and RAND board of trustees chairman Donald Rumsfeld. He also worked closely with former CIA director James D. Woolsey and with General Wayne Downing (who would serve in the National Security Council under President George H. W. Bush) formulating plans to overthrow Hussein militarily.[11] Their vehicle for convincing the public that regime change in Iraq was in America's best interests was an organization founded in 1997 and similar in scope to the Reagan-era Committee on the Present Danger: the Project for the New American Century (PNAC), similarly boasting of several RAND luminaries as founding members.

From the start, PNAC expressly saw Iraq as the pivot for a new politics for the Middle East. In an open letter to President Clinton in 1998, the group urged him "to enunciate a new strategy that would secure the interests of the United States and our friends and allies around the world. That strategy should aim, above all, at the removal of Saddam Hussein's regime from power . . . This will require a full complement of diplomatic, political and military efforts."[12] The letter was signed by Wolfowitz, Perle, Dan Quayle,

Cheney, former RAND president Henry Rowen, Rumsfeld, and RAND Pardee School of Policy director Khalilzad.

Months later, the same signatories would go a step further and ask that the administration deal directly with Chalabi's INC as the sole representative of the Iraqi people. That year, President Clinton signed the Iraq Liberation Act, which declared, "It should be the policy of the United States to support efforts to remove the [Hussein] regime from power."[13] There were no teeth in that promise, as the law did not specify how the liberation would take place—at least not overtly. Covertly, the INC had been burning through a $100 million CIA war chest authorized by President Bush after the Gulf War to fund enemies of Hussein. After the Iraq Liberation Act, the State Department funded the INC with an additional $33 million. When that money was cut off in 2000, the Pentagon's Defense Intelligence Agency took up the slack, subsidizing the INC to the tune of $335,000 a month.[14]

In exchange for American support, Chalabi not only lent legitimacy to neoconservatives advocating regime change in Iraq but also provided them with information on purported Iraqi weapons of mass destruction. A panoply of informers, many of them recruited by a wide-ranging network of INC collaborators inside and outside Iraq, delivered ever-more ominous reports, most of which proved false—Saddam has laboratories making biochemical weapons; Saddam is collaborating with al Qaeda; Saddam is buying materials needed to make nuclear bombs—a constant chorus of impending doom from the INC in Washington and from neoconservative think tanks and advocacy groups.[15]

After the razor-thin victory of George W. Bush over Al Gore in 2000, PNAC packed the new Bush administration with its members, just as the Committee for the Present Danger had packed the Reagan administration with its own. Rumsfeld became secretary of defense; Wolfowitz was named deputy secretary of defense; Perle was appointed chairman of the Defense Planning Board; Richard L. Armitage became deputy secretary of state; Khalilzad was named U.S. ambassador to the Iraqis in exile, then ambassador to Afghanistan, then to Iraq, and finally to the United Nations; and, of course, Cheney became the most powerful vice president in American history.

In the weeks following the calamity of September 11, 2001, the neoconservative lobby was perfectly placed to advocate Chalabi's cause. Within days, Wolfowitz was telling the president that there was from 10 to 50 percent probability that Iraq had been involved in the attack. Soon the president was leaning on his intelligence people to find evidence that would link Hussein to 9/11.[16] Secretary of Defense Rumsfeld and Vice President Cheney, borrowing a page from the Team B playbook of the 1970s, established the Office of Special Plans to produce intelligence analyses that would override the CIA and prepare a justification for the upcoming war in Iraq—relying on information provided by Chalabi's INC.[17] In the media, neoconservatives continually whipped up the cries for war against Iraq, going so far as to affirm that deposing Hussein would be "a cakewalk."[18]

When President Bush thundered against Hussein during the 2003 State of the Union address, all but promising the invasion that would come a few weeks later, Chalabi famously sat close to First Lady Laura Bush, figuratively if not literally holding the hand of the administration.[19] Finally, when Secretary of State Colin Powell gave a speech at the United Nations justifying the American invasion, his reasons were founded on the allegations of an out-of-work engineer supplied by Chalabi's INC, who claimed Hussein hid mobile biochemical weapons labs in trailers.[20]

The launching of the U.S.-led invasion on March 20, 2003, was Chalabi's high noon of political influence. If he had expected to be installed as head of the new Iraqi government once Hussein was defeated, his hopes were promptly dashed by the Bush administration, which obtained authorization from the United Nations to go into

Iraq as an *occupying* power—meaning it would set up its own interim government first before turning the country over to Iraqis. The dream of former RANDites for an American empire in the Middle East did not include turning over power before U.S. troops controlled the ground.

The United States appointed Ambassador L. Paul Bremer III as its viceroy, who, as a consolation prize, included Chalabi in the government in a purely advisory role. All the same, Chalabi scrambled to near the top of the political pile, securing the job of oil minister. He also managed to install a number of relatives in key government jobs, not least of which was his nephew Salem Chalabi, the head of the Iraqi Special Tribunal charged with trying Hussein.

But Ahmed Chalabi's standing with the United States quickly deteriorated as rumors began to circulate that he was a currency counterfeiter, that he had stolen millions from the Iraqi Oil Ministry, and that he was in the pocket of the great Shiite power in the region—Iraq's neighbor, Iran.[21] Just as Chalabi had once openly praised America as the hope of Iraq, he now began loudly criticizing it for mismanaging Iraq. In this, he echoed his mentors from RAND, who had begun to discreetly distance themselves from the growing Iraq quagmire. A group of RAND legal experts, who had been sent to rewrite Iraq's constitution, were unable to make much progress in the Byzantine political arena under Bremer. Likewise, RAND-affiliated security experts were pessimistic about being able to defeat an anti-American insurgency with religious overtones that had grown to vast proportions.

Right after the invasion, RAND had published a report on nation building that warned that military occupations, to be successful, require more troops than the Bush administration was willing or able to procure. *America's Role in Nation Building: From Germany to Iraq* proved prescient about the difficulties that the Coalition Forces would encounter from Iraqi insurgents and warned, "There is no quick route to nation-building. Five years seems to be

the minimum required to enforce an enduring transition to democracy."[22] Shortly thereafter its lead author, James Dobbins—a former
U.S. ambassador to Afghanistan, and U.S. special envoy to Kosovo,
Bosnia, Haiti, and Somalia—declared the war in Iraq lost, and advised the Bush administration to train Iraqis to handle their own
defense and eliminate the American military presence altogether in
that troubled country.

Chalabi's critique of the American presence served him well in
the new Iraqi political landscape for a while. An apparent turn to
Islam, as well as his persecution by the occupation forces, made
Chalabi more appealing to Iraqi voters—not just to Americans with
dreams of Middle Eastern empires. The ever-rational Chalabi led
his INC into an alliance with the United Iraqi Alliance, the party of
the radical Shiite Muslim cleric Moqtada al-Sadr. A polarizing, controversial populist leader, al-Sadr at one point had been charged
with murder by the occupation government; his militia, the Mahdi
Army, had even fought with the occupation forces for control of
several Iraqi cities. He was everything Chalabi was not: religious,
provincial, rabidly anti-American, and most important, the proud
owner of a political power base independent of American forces—
with hundreds of thousands of armed followers ready to die for him.
In the January 2005 election, Chalabi's coalition with al-Sadr's
United Iraqi Alliance won a sizable bloc of seats in Parliament,
securing Chalabi the post of deputy prime minister.

By the end of 2005, the charges against Chalabi of counterfeit-
ing were dismissed for lack of evidence and all the nettlesome accusations were conveniently forgotten. He was again the Bush
administration's man from Iraq, touted as a possible prime minister. Visiting Washington, Chalabi was welcomed by Secretary of
State Condoleezza Rice at Foggy Bottom, and met in private with
Vice President Cheney.[23] Honored at the American Enterprise Institute with a standing-room-only press conference in the appropriately named Wohlstetter Conference Center, Chalabi dismissed

charges that he had misled the U.S. government into invading Iraq as mere "urban myths" to laughter and applause.[24]

Wohlstetter, another master manipulator of facts and fiction, would have admired Chalabi's bravura performance, but perhaps it was all too late. A few months later, Chalabi broke with the United Iraqi Alliance, and in January 2006, he ran on his own party label in yet another national election. His secularist Nationalist Congress Party garnered only .25 percent of 12 million votes—not enough to carry a single seat in the new Iraqi parliament.[25] Chastened by his defeat, he made peace with al-Sadr's party and in 2007 accepted a post with the al-Sadr-backed Shiite Iraqi government: head of the "popular committee for mobilizing the people" in the shadow of the surge of American troops into Baghdad.[26]

Faced with an Iraq fractured further every day along religious and ethnic fault lines—with, for instance, al-Sadr claiming that 60 percent of his militia had infiltrated government programs and installations[27]—Chalabi's and Wohlstetter's and all the other neoconservatives' grand dream of a secular Iraq that would be a reliable U.S. ally seemed out of reach. Chalabi ruefully admitted the failure, conceding that his major mistake was not seeing how the forces of irrationality, religion, and blind nationalism would rule Iraq. As he put it in an interview with Al Arabiya TV network: "Even the Iraqi Communist Party has almost changed its motto from: Workers of the World, Unite, into Workers of the World, Praise the Prophet."[28]

Dreams of empire die hard.

PART 6

22

Death of a Strategist

The evil that men do lives after them;
the good is oft interred with their bones.

—*Julius Caesar*, Act III, Scene 2

As I sat in a luminous living room in Manhattan one winter day interviewing Joan Wohlstetter, it occurred to me that the halcyon days of RAND had ended somewhere around the turn of the twenty-first century. By then most of its stalwart protagonists—except for the eternal Andrew Marshall—had turned their backs on RAND work, retired, or, like Albert Wohlstetter, were dead.

Now Joan, the only flesh-and-blood child of the extraordinary analyst who defined RAND for so long, looked grief stricken for a moment. She gestured at the tape recorder on the glass table, asking me to turn it off. We were nearing the end of several hours of interviews and had begun to discuss the last days of her father. Even though seven years had passed since his death, tears still welled up in her eyes.

"It really was a nightmare," she said, softly. "It didn't have to be that way, but it was."[1]

The New York skyline shimmered brightly through the picture window behind her. Former employees of Wohlstetter's consulting firm, now working at RAND, had put me in touch with Joan. She and I agreed to meet for the interview at the Upper East Side apartment of a friend, who, by coincidence, lives in the same East Sixties building as Joan.

I had seen her only in the photographs taken in her home by Julius Shulman, when she was the apple of her parents' eye, dressed in the bouffant skirts and ponytail of a 1950s adolescent. The middle-aged woman with the shock of white hair and the vaguely bohemian air who came to the door did not much resemble the girl, except for the glint of intelligence that seemed to have transmigrated from her father's eyes to her own, showing the same impish delight in pricking the balloons of folly of this world.

She came prepared, with folders full of drawings her father had sent her when he was visiting the power centers of the Western world in the 1950s. She showed me photographs of her parents at the pyramids of Mexico on their honeymoon; of her father driving Le Corbusier around New York; of two-year-old Joan and her father in bathing suits on a hot rooftop. All so idyllic, picture postcards from a place washed away by history.

Friends told me that Joan had rebelled against her parents' fame and power in typical 1950s fashion by choosing an intellectual path completely opposite to theirs—she had been a hippie, majored in Chinese studies, worked as a belly dancer. When asked, Joan would not confirm or deny, saying only, "This story is not about me." I could not help but think that, in spite of her youthful rebellion, Joan had become the dutiful daughter, the keeper of the flame. She was devoted to her ailing mother, who would pass away in 2006. Upon learning of my Cuban origins, Joan had asked me for a picture of the wide, sandy beach of Varadero, which Roberta requested when told I would be conducting the interviews.

Joan recalled how her father suffered a major heart attack on his birthday, December 16, 1996. She was in New York, her parents at their second, smaller home in the Hollywood Hills, having sold the large estate built by Josef van der Car years earlier. Roberta called her, worried because Albert had been ill since going out on his birthday. Thinking he had asthma, they had been consulting an allergy doctor.

"My mother said, 'I wanted to call when Albert was feeling better but he's awful, he's got some orthopedic thing, he can't move his arm, he's feeling terrible.'" Her mother added that she had not called an ambulance because she did not want to upset Albert.

Joan had recently taken a Red Cross CPR course; her mother's description worried her, as her father had had a bypass operation years before. Joan went down the symptoms of a heart attack. Her father had them all. "So I told her, 'I think you should call 9-1-1 but don't tell him.' So of course, she says, 'Joanie says I should call 9-1-1.'"

For twenty minutes, Joan and her husband kept insisting that an ambulance be called. When the fire department paramedics finally arrived, Albert told his daughter, indignantly, "This is ridiculous. Saturday night is a terrible night to go to an emergency room!"

At the hospital, doctors at first thought Albert had not suffered a heart attack, then they decided he had. While in intensive care, he phoned Al Williams, a top medical researcher at RAND, before deciding to have an angiogram.

"I told him, 'Daddy, when you're in ICU, you might have to let them make some decisions,'" Joan said.

Discharged from the hospital, Albert was sent home with round-the-clock nursing care. He moved his bed to the wide living room; the sliding glass door faced the pool and a grove of rare black bamboo he had planted years before. Unable to move his left side but, as always, congenitally unable to accept any situation without trying to modify it, he fashioned a chair to be placed in the bed that allowed him to half recline, half sit up and do some work. Joan said he seemed to be recovering, but no one knew that half of his heart was not working. Thirty days after his birthday, Albert Wohlstetter passed away, surrounded by his books, his artworks, and his filing cabinets full of classified research work. He was eighty-six years old.

RAND, which had both nurtured and exiled him, held a memorial service in his honor in the inner courtyard of the John Williams–inspired building. It was a fitting place for the laying down of old quarrels with the many ghostly personages from the creation of the postwar era who must have been in shadowy attendance— Frank Collbohm, Herman Kahn, J. Robert Oppenheimer. Musicians played Bach's Brandenburg Concerto No. 3 in G major and an aria from Mozart's *Le Nozze di Figaro* between remembrances from Harry Rowen, Fred Hoffman, Alain Enthoven, RAND president James Thomson, and members of Wohlstetter's defunct firm, Pan Heuristics. After jazz performers sparked to the rhythms of "Take the 'A' Train," the masterpiece composed by Wohlstetter's friend Billy Strayhorn, Charles Wolf, Jr., read the closing words, his goodbyes echoing down the winding halls and secret alcoves in the palace of reason of the military-industrial complex.[2]

It was a moving end to a momentous life—and an uplifting career. Uplifting, that is, to those who feel that peace means being eternally prepared for war, that national security is an ever-receding goal requiring incessant technological improvement, that American culture is the universal template for all cultures and all time. Some historians have argued that Wohlstetter's neoconservative movement, propelled by figures like Henry Jackson and Ronald Reagan, rid the world of the bloodiest empire in modern history, the Union of Soviet Socialist Republics.[3] Others have argued that the Soviet Union would have imploded anyhow, and that in reality, it was Wohlstetter and his colleagues at RAND who stopped the decay by concocting an unnecessary Cold War that gave the dying empire an

extra thirty years of life.[4] One thing is certain, Wohlstetter was the
supreme example of the technocrat, of the self-appointed expert who
decides, by ostensibly objective, impartial measures, how the world
is to be handled.

Wohlstetter must have died satisfied that his work had, in his
mind, toppled the Russian empire, kept America safe, and expanded
prosperity around the world. Certainly there was still more work to
be done—the incipient genocide in the Balkans had to be stopped,
and nuclear proliferation and the rise of obscurantism among Mus-
lims in the Middle East had to be addressed. But all in all, he had
accomplished a great deal to make the country safer and wealthier.
Did he ever, in moments of sharp-eyed reverie, intuit that the Soviet
monster he had fought for so long was actually a creaking corpse
propped up only by slogans and American trade agreements? Perhaps he did, and that was why he so blithely embarked on his last
campaign to halt détente. For the hollow monster still had nuclear
teeth, and as a former follower of Trotsky, Wohlstetter never put any
possible atrocity past the frigid-hearted leaders of the Kremlin. Stalin
allowed 20 million of his own people to perish in war, why shouldn't
a new Marxist czar condone the slaughter of 100 million foreigners
to win the world? After all, it would be the rational thing to do.

That years later Wohlstetter's neoconservative followers would
twist his message of analysis and sufficiency, failing to infuse foreign
policy with realism so it would not turn into naïveté, was certainly
not Wohlstetter's responsibility. In the words of Augustus Richard
Norton, a former Wohlstetter student and current Middle East
scholar at Boston University, "Many of the people who populate
[the Bush administration] are Albert's intellectual children, but I'm
not sure the father would approve of the great risk they're taking.
There's a lot of very flaky thinking out there."[5]

23

Whither RAND?

BACK IN THE freewheeling 1960s, RAND researchers often indulged in long bouts of painful self-analysis. In memos, essays, and articles, RANDites, trying to make a new world, agonized over which direction to take, particularly when relations with the Air Force grew strained following the migration of the Whiz Kids into the Kennedy administration. RAND had grown too flabby and too sleek, there was no longer any originality in RAND's work, too many competitors had stolen RAND's thunder. How could RAND possibly distinguish itself in a crowded field? Today that question is again particularly pressing for RAND, since so many other think tanks have sprung up in its wake. To make itself more distinctive in the crowded marketplace, RAND has embarked on overseas expansion, especially in the Middle East.

In 2003, RAND opened an office in Qatar, a small oil-rich kingdom hard by Saudi Arabia. Invited by His Majesty Shaikh Hamad bin Khalifa Al-Thani, emir of Qatar, RAND has begun to rewrite the textbooks of the country's educational system, aiming to institute a moderate brand of Islamic education.[1] In Iraq, RAND advisers to the Coalition Provisional Authority labored from 2003 to 2005 to reform the legal system of the country, with mixed results.[2] Finally, with an ambition not seen since its quest for a unified theory of war, in 2005 RAND sought to bring peace to the Middle East. Relying on the largesse of an individual donor who gave $2 million for the project, RAND analysts developed what they hoped would be a transformative map for the Palestinian-Israeli conflict.

Called the Arc, RAND's proposal outlines a comprehensive rail, highway, and infrastructure link between the West Bank and the Gaza Strip that would bring jobs, water, food, education, housing, and services to the Palestinian people of the region.[3] Nonrational forces of religion and nativism, however, have risen to cripple the Arc, which is fiercely opposed by both Israelis and Palestinian extremists. RAND is also dusting off some of the studies on counterinsurgency it commissioned back in the 1960s, hoping that lessons drawn from fighting rebels in Algeria will prove useful when dealing with the current insurgency in Iraq.[4]

Today there seem to be no skeptics left at RAND, no culture of self-analysis or reflection. The critics are outside the organization, like Richard Perle, who calls RAND "just another outfit running after contracts,"[5] or like Middle East expert Larry Diamond, who doubts the RAND analysts had much influence over events inside Iraq.[6] There is a more corporate feel to the outfit, a reluctance to admit dissent; like any successful organization, RAND is under pressure to impose a collective mind-set. This trait is self-contradictory, not to mention countervailing, in an organization that idolizes reason and independent thinking. When dealing with RAND, as with certain branches of the federal government, one has the feeling everyone has been warned to stay "on message." No RAND staffer will publicly criticize the corporation—there are no more Albert

Wohlstetters or Herman Kahns, the irritants in the smooth lining of the intellectual oyster that can, with luck, produce great pearls.

Then again, current RAND president James Thomson does not seem to rue their absence. Like a seasoned team manager, he concentrates on the ground strokes, the singles and line drives, instead of the out-of-the-park home runs a star can provide. "The strategists—Wohlstetter, Kahn, Brodie, those characters—caught everybody's attention, but the real grinding away at making progress and improving the Air Force was happening in spite of them."[7]

A former physicist, Thomson chanced into the military-industrial world when, without the requisite insider connections, he was hired as a researcher for the Europe Division of the Pentagon's System Analysis Office, the one founded by RAND's Alain Enthoven under Robert McNamara. Thomson rose to become assistant to National Security Adviser Zbigniew Brzezinski in the Carter administration before leaving the world of policy making for that of policy advice. Thomson has been RAND president and chief executive officer since 1989, keeping the rough parity of work between military and civilian contracting brought about by former RAND president Donald Rice.

In a speech to the Colorado chapter of the American Civil Liberties Union in late 2005, Thomson decried what he saw as a current lurch to obscurantism in the nation.

> It's worth finding out what we can about the likely effectiveness of a given policy proposal before we drift off into battles guided only by our personal opinions and biases, expressing our opinions about other opinions. Opinion-based battles rather than fact-based ones: That's the direction in which I fear this country is headed.[8]

During an interview in his corner office in the new RAND building, with a view of the Pacific Ocean and the Hollywood Hills, the lanky scientist discussed his apprehension about this new penchant for irrationality in American culture. "Growing partisanship has squeezed professionalism down in scope for influence, because people have strong views for one side or another and they want to win. I think that in the period after World War II, maybe because of World War II, and how important science and analysis were to winning that war, we went through a long period where government had a greater component of scientific thought and analysis. I've sort of seen a steady decline of this in my career. Analytical offices that existed in domestic agencies in Washington have largely disappeared."

Thomson added that nowadays RAND tries not to inject emotion into its analyses by avoiding charged descriptions, using what he calls "flat" language in reports. "Adjectives. I'm always beating adjectives out of things. People will say, 'The number came out six, a large number.' I say, 'Why don't we just say six. I mean, six is six. Why do we have to say it's a large number?'"

When asked whether the decline in appreciation for RAND's type of analytical work can be linked to the disastrous policies of the McNamara era, the "best and the brightest" who brought the country the carnage of Vietnam, Thomson countered, "I think the decline really started going with Reagan, checking, you had to be a Republican professional or you ain't working in this administration." He does not think a mere change of the parties in control of the White House or Congress will make any difference.

"It's part of the zeitgeist. It's not specific to the parties. People out there still care; it's Washington that's poisoned, it's not the country. Inside the Beltway is a whole other world. You make your appeals to the public and try to get your message out into the public domain. You just keep plugging along. If you give up, then you're just surrendering. We should be a bulwark against irrationality."[9]

REASON AS ultimate panacea was the credo of RAND and of the scientists and engineers who created postwar America—and the postwar Western world, for that matter. It should not be surprising that of the twenty-seven Nobel Prizes received by RAND researchers and advisers, all except for one have been for physics, economics, or chemistry. The exception is former secretary of state Henry Kissinger, who received the Nobel Peace Prize in 1973 (Kissinger was a RAND consultant from 1961 to 1969).

Our nation's Founding Fathers were of a different cast. As men of the Enlightenment, they were advocates of moderation in all things, even in the pursuit of reason. Many of the signatories to the Constitution had directly witnessed the extreme fervor of the Great Awakening, the religious revival of mid-eighteenth-century America, and were appropriately skeptical of the all-pervasive reach of rational discourse.[10] They recognized the dark powers that often take hold of men's souls: thus the separation of church and state; thus our government's checks and balances; thus the admonition of George Washington in his final address to avoid foreign entanglements.[11]

History teaches that some Gordian knots cannot be cut, they can only be unraveled by the passage of time and, with luck, a gradual change in the conditions that led to the knot. However, this is anathema to the Babbitts of this republic-cum-empire, who believe that a problem that can be imagined is a problem that can be solved. To which one can reply: Vietnam. Or Iraq. Or the mujahideen. As a spokesman for Iraq's radical Muslim cleric Moqtada al-Sadr said, "Americans should look at the Iraqis as Iraqis, not as Americans in training."[12]

RAND's rational choice is an argument that denies the obvious—cooperation, self-sacrifice, and abnegation do exist, people do love each other and don't always think of themselves first, elections are won fairly and agreed to by all contestants, elected officials do act on the public interest, marriages and institutions do last. Rational choice has given birth to a world shaped by decisions made in the dark, outside the realm of public debate—justified by false objectivity (change the parameters if you don't like the results) and biased scientific bases that denigrate collective responsibility (much like the corporate battle cry of "it's all for the shareholders," discarding as démodé previous social commitments of companies to employees, government, and community).*

Let us grant that the people of RAND—Kenneth Arrow, Thomas Schelling, Albert Wohlstetter, Herman Kahn—acted in good faith, wanting only to shed the light of reason on a dangerously irrational world. Their choice of instrument has unleashed world-changing responses driven precisely by the forces their instrument cannot handle—religion, nationalism, patriotism. Moreover, deliberately or not, rational choice theory has become a handy rhetorical weapon for groups whose political and financial aims are to reconstruct the social system of the United States—returning the country to pre–New Deal days, while making billions in the process. These changes have resulted in a society where, for instance, the top 5 percent of the population controls 60 percent of the wealth and where corporate executive pay is 400 times greater than that of the average worker.[13]

The final irony of rational choice theory is that it is not rational. It fails to comprehend the world as it is (in academic terms, it is normative but not empirical), positing a make-believe structure where only one kind of rationality is extant. This would be fine if the world was docile enough to bend to our desires, but reality has a way of turning around and biting those who fail to see it bare its fangs.

Beyond the economic inequities brought about by rational choice, RAND must also grapple with the dilemma of its original sin: subordinating morality to the advancement of U.S. government policy. This is the millstone borne by all the major participants in the RAND story. I once posed the following to a friend who is highly placed within the RAND structure: Suppose nation X comes to

---

* Among other things, that is why we have a volunteer army—a concept espoused and driven by laissez-faire economist Milton Friedman, a firm believer in the trade-offs of rational choice theory.

RAND and says it wants to hire it as an adviser on a specific project of national security. The objective of the study is to determine how much pain a person can be subjected to under torture and still not reveal secret information—that is, to determine a person's breaking point. Would RAND take on such a project? My friend paled at the thought and implied, in so many words, that RAND would most likely not accept such a project from a foreign government. He said they would try to divert the focus and (in another instance of the RAND approach of knowing the right question to ask) would try to get the project changed to asking whether torture is effective at all in obtaining useful and verifiable information. It wasn't until later that the thought occurred to me: Would RAND accept the job if it came from the American government? And where would the information obtained to determine the efficacy of torture come from?

RAND faces a Faustian predicament: knowledge of the world cannot save your soul—or spare you from charges of complicity in murder, mayhem, and torture, even when sanctioned by the government. Of course, those same charges can be laid at the doorstep of any other policy advisory group. They are aiders and abettors of their superiors' decisions and must be measured by the same yardstick as those who actually give the orders.

In the end, perhaps it is naïve to expect RAND or any other policy advisers to observe such high standards of moral purity. As Israeli prime minister Golda Meir observed when ordering hits on Palestinian terrorists: all nations at some point must make painful choices that conflict with their basic values.[14] Not to make them would endanger their security, but making them threatens the very essence of their character. Perhaps then, in RAND fashion, we should ask the right question: What do we Americans expect of our government and its advisers? Furthermore, how far should they go to make us safer, wealthier, happier? How much torture, if any, should we allow? How many millions—or thousands or just hundreds—of innocent deaths are we willing to accept to keep America prosperous? To keep America safe? How much slaughter and injustice are we willing to accept before we demand a change?

Herman Kahn hurled these very same questions back at his critics when they charged him with callousness, horrified by his Grand Guignol of nuclear war and survival. They had no answer, for we are all complicit in the unconscionable acts we allow others to perform so that we may preserve our way of life. I do not presume to have the answer to Kahn's woeful query. What I do know is that anyone who excoriates RAND is basically excoriating himself.

We, the American people, the voters and taxpayers, have created and allowed the continued existence of institutions that originate, explicate, and advocate morally dubious policies simply because they are perceived to be in America's best interest. The sin of RAND—the fate of RAND—is therefore that of America itself. For it is the American people who have bought into the myth of rational choice, it is the American public that wants to consume— politics, culture, technology—without paying the price of sacrifice and participation, it is the American voter who has closed his eyes and allowed morality to be divorced from government policy. We're okay as long as we get what we want, be it Arab oil, foreign markets for our products, or cheap T-shirts from China. The American empire is for the good of America, after all. Or so we're told.

If we look in the mirror, we will see that RAND is every one of us. The question is, what are we going to do about it?

Acknowledgments

STARTING AND FINISHING a book like this is impossible without a dedicated team. I feel lucky to be represented by such a good friend and astute reader as Joseph Regal. Likewise, my editor, Andrea Schulz, deserves enormous credit for buying into my vision of what the history of the most influential think tank in the world could be, for encouraging me to press on in spite of the mind-boggling scope of the work, and for demanding that my own voice be heard in these pages. Although I wrote all of the book—for better or for worse—I could not have finished it without the help of my assistant, Holly Painter, whose talent for finding obscure research material is surpassed only by her devotion to the job. Also, many thanks to Kate Segal for her advice and sharp sense of the mot juste.

Naturally, I owe a great debt to the leaders of RAND, who opened up their files and made themselves available for endless rounds of questioning, saying, go ahead, we are familiar with the shoe being on the other foot. My hat's off to Michael Rich, James Thomson, Iao Katagiri, Jack Riley, Rae Archibald, Brian Chow, Marcy Agmon, Charles Wolf, the incomparable Bruce Hoffman, Vivien Arterbery, Donald Rice, Richard Benjamin, Konrad Kellen, and so many others who showed patience beyond the call of duty.

I never had the chance to meet the remarkable Albert Wohlstetter, but I feel that talking to his daughter, Joan, was at times even more revelatory than conversing with the analyst would have been. I am very thankful indeed for her cooperation, guidance, and generosity. Fortunately, I was able to enlist the cooperation of Albert Wohlstetter's friend, and perhaps the most controversial RAND alumnus ever, Daniel Ellsberg. I am much obliged for his insights and information, which proved invaluable in navigating the stormy period of the 1960s and 1970s. Thank you as well to all those who graciously consented to sharing their remembrances of Wohlstetter—Zalmay Khalilzad, Nathan Glazer, Morton White, Henry Sokolski, Richard Perle, Julius Shulman, Harry Rowen, Peter van der Car, Chester Aaron. Likewise, a heartfelt thank-you to Larry Diamond and Ahmed Chalabi, whose lives are still writing the history of the Middle East.

Finally, many thanks to the American Enterprise Institute, the staff at the National Air and Space Museum of the Smithsonian Institution, and the National Security Archive at George Washington University. Let freedom ring.

Endnotes

FOREWORD

1. Articles of Incorporation and By-Laws (Santa Monica, CA: RAND Corporation, 14 May 1948), 1.

CHAPTER 1: A GREAT BEGINNING

1. See <http://www.arnold.af.mil/aedc/hap.htm>.
2. Winston Churchill, "Iron Curtain Speech," Westminster College Commencement, Fulton, Missouri, 5 March 1946, accessed 7 June 2004 at < http://www.nationalcenter.org/ChurchillIronCurtain.html>
3. Theodore von Kármán, "Toward New Horizons," *Air Force Magazine* 87, 1, accessed January 2004 at <http://www.afa.org/magazine/jan2004/0104vonkarman.asp>.
4. Bruce L. R. Smith, *The RAND Corporation: A Case Study of a Nonprofit Advisory Corporation* (Cambridge: Harvard University Press, 1966), 154–55. "The Fabulous 'Think' Companies." *Newsweek*. January 19, 1959, pp. 21–23.
5. "Franklin Rudolf Collbohm," RAND Corporation, 28 August 1986; Myrna Oliver, "Franklin Collbohm Dies; Founder of RAND Corp.," the

Los Angeles Times (14 February 1990): A3, A13; "Franklin R. Collbohm Dies, RAND Corporation Founding Leader, Aerospace Pioneer," news release, RAND Corporation, 13 February 1990.

6. Martin Collins and Joseph Tatarewicz, interview with Frank Collbohm, *RAND History Project,* 28 July 1987.

7. Ibid.

8. Edward L. Bowles, *RAND History Project,* 14 and 15 July 1987, 20 August 1987.

9. Fred Kaplan, *The Wizards of Armageddon* (New York: Simon and Schuster, 1983), 59; David Hounshell, *The Cold War, RAND, and the Generation of Knowledge, 1946–1962* (Santa Monica: RAND Reprints, 1998), 242–43.

10. Thomas M. Coffey, *Iron Eagle: The Turbulent Life of General Curtis LeMay* (New York: Avon Books, 1988), 225.

11. R. D. Specht, *RAND: A Personal View of Its History* (Santa Monica, CA: RAND P-1601, 23 October 1958), 2.

12. J. R. Goldstein, *RAND: The History,* paper P-2336-1 (Santa Monica, CA: RAND Corporation, 1960), 3.

13. Martin J. Collins, *Cold War Laboratory: RAND, the Air Force and the American State, 1945–1950* (Washington, DC: Smithsonian Institution Press, 2002), 43.

14. Hounshell, 242.

15. Bourgin, 6.

16. "RAND Corporation: Its Origin, Evolution and Plans for the Future" (Santa Monica, CA: RAND Corporation, February 1971), 4.

17. *Air & Space Power Chronicles,* Curtis LeMay biography at <http://www .airpower.maxwell.af.mil>.

18. Kaplan, 43.

19. Mary Jo Nye, "The Most Versatile Physicist of His Generation," *Science Magazine* (April 2002): 49–50, at <http://www.sciencemag.org/cgi/ content/full/296/5565/49>.

20. Kaplan, 53.

21. A. C. Grayling, *Among the Dead Cities: The History and Moral Legacy of the WWII Bombing of Civilians in Germany and Japan* (New York: Walker and Company, 2006), 72.

22. Thomas M. Coffey, *Iron Eagle: The Turbulent Life of General Curtis LeMay* (New York: Avon Books, 1988), quoted in Grayling, 171.

23. "Preliminary Design of an Experimental World-Circling Spaceship," Santa Monica Plant, Engineering Division, report number SM-11827, Contract W33-038 (Santa Monica, CA: Douglas Aircraft Company, Inc., 2 May 1946).

24. Benjamin S. Lambeth, *Mastering the Ultimate High Ground: Next Steps in the Military Uses of Space* (Santa Monica, CA: RAND Corporation, Project Air Force, 2003), 11.

25. "Preliminary Design."
26. Bruno Augenstein, "Evolution of the U.S. Military Space Program, 1949–1960; Some Key Events in Study, Planning, and Program Development," paper P-6814 (Santa Monica, CA: RAND Corporation, September 1982), 4; and Lambeth, 13.
27. Bernard Brodie, *Strategy in the Missile Age* (Princeton, NJ: Princeton University Press, 1959), 8.
28. Kaplan, 63.
29. John D. Williams, *The Compleat Strategyst* (New York: McGraw-Hill, 1954), 1.
30. William Poundstone, *Prisoner's Dilemma* (New York: Doubleday, 1992), 94.
31. Ibid., 95.
32. Ibid., 24.
33. David R. Jardini, *Out of the Blue Yonder: The RAND Corporation's Diversification into Social Welfare Research, 1946–1968,* doctoral dissertation (Carnegie Mellon University, May 1996), 37.
34. Ibid., 41.
35. Ibid., 29.

CHAPTER 2: THE HUMAN FACTOR

1. Leo Rosten, *Captain Newman, M.D.* (New York: Harper, 1962); and *The Education of H*Y*M*A*N K*A*P*L*A*N* (New York: Harvest, 1965).
2. Leo Rosten, interview by Brownlee Haydon, August 1969 (Santa Monica, CA: RAND, 1971), 4.
3. Ibid., 7.
4. RAND Corporation, *The RAND Corporation: The First Fifteen Years* (Santa Monica, CA: RAND, 1963), 11.
5. Kaplan, 72.
6. For more information about the history of the New School, see <http://www.newschool.edu/gf/about/history.htm>.
7. Franklin Collbohm, *RAND History Project,* op. cit.
8. University of California, "Charles Johnston Hitch, Economics: Berkeley," *1995, University of California: In Memoriam* (Berkeley: University of California, 1995); Alain C. Enthoven, "Tribute to Charles Hitch," *OR/MS Today* (1995), accessed 20 June 2007 <http://www.lionhrtpub.com/orms/orms-12-95/hitch-tribute.html>.
9. Kaplan, 71.
10. David R. Jardini, *Out of the Blue Yonder: The RAND Corporation's Diversification into Social Welfare Research, 1946–1968,* doctoral dissertation (Carnegie Mellon University, May 1996), 101.
11. R. D. Specht, "RAND: A Personal View of Its History" (Santa Monica, CA: RAND Corporation, 1958), 3.

12. Smith, 57.

13. Ibid.

14. Si Bourgin, Memorandum (Santa Monica, CA: RAND Corporation, 4 April 1962), 13.

15. H. Rowan Gaither, "Memorandum to Frank R. Collbohm. Subject: Formation of Non-Profit Corporation for RAND Project" (Santa Monica, CA: RAND Corp.), 18 December 1947.

16. Kaplan, 61–62.

17. Ibid.

18. Articles of Incorporation and By-Laws (Santa Monica, CA: RAND Corporation, 14 May 1948), 1.

19. For a history of the Ford Foundation, see <http://www.fordfound.org/about/history.cfm>.

20. Rosten interview.

21. President Dwight D. Eisenhower's farewell address, 17 January 1961, accessed 10 December 2006 at <http://www.eisenhower.archives.gov/speeches/farewell_address.html>.

22. S. M. Amadae, Rationalizing Capitalist Democracy: The Cold War Origins of Rational Choice Liberalism (Chicago: The University of Chicago Press, 2003), 36.

23. Joan Roelofs, Foundations and Public Policy: The Mask of Pluralism (Stony Brook, NY: State University of New York, 2003), 85.

24. See <http://www.liberty-tree.ca>.

25. Bourgin, 40.

26. Ibid.

27. Andrew David May, The RAND Corporation and the Dynamics of American Strategic Thought, doctoral dissertation (Dickinson College, October 1998), 47.

28. Ibid., 48.

29. Henry Rowen, personal interview, 27 April 2004.

30. Richard Bellman, I Am the Hurricane, manuscript, Brownlee Haydon Box, RAND Archives, 209.

31. Nathan Leites, The Operational Code of the Politburo (New York: McGraw-Hill, 1951).

32. Richard Holbrooke, "The Paradox of George F. Kennan," the Washington Post (21 March 2005): A19; and Tim Weiner and Barbara Crosette, "George F. Kennan, Leading U.S. Strategist of the Cold War, Dies at 101," the New York Times (19 March 2005): B11.

33. Paul H. Nitze, From Hiroshima to Glasnost: At the Center of Decision (New York: Grove Weidenfeld, 1989), 86.

34. Gregg Herken, Counsels of War (New York: Oxford University Press, 1987), 49.

35. "NSC-68: United States Objectives and Programs for National Security," part III (Washington, DC: National Security Council, 14 April 1950).

36. "The Evolution of U.S. Strategic Command and Control and Warning, 1945–1972," L. Wainstein, project leader, Department of Defense (Arlington, VA: Institute for Defense Analyses, June 1975), 34.

37. Dean Acheson, *Present at the Creation: My Years in the State Department* (New York: Norton, 1969), 303.

38. David Halberstam, *The Fifties* (New York: Fawcett Columbine, 1993), 348–52.

CHAPTER 3: THE WAGES OF SIN

1. Gregg Herken, *Counsels of War* (New York: Oxford University Press, 1987), 4.

2. James G. Hershberg, *James B. Conant: Harvard to Hiroshima and the Making of the Nuclear Age* (New York: Knopf, 1993), 466–67; and Sharon Ghamari-Tabrizi, *The Worlds of Herman Kahn: The Intuitive Science of Thermonuclear War* (Cambridge: Harvard University Press, 2005), 97.

3. *The Decision to Drop the Bomb,* prod. Fred Freed, *NBC White Papers,* NBC, 1965.

4. Kai Bird and Martin J. Sherwin, *American Prometheus: The Triumph and Tragedy of J. Robert Oppenheimer* (New York: Knopf, 2005), 465.

5. Bernard Brodie, "War in the Atomic Age," in *The Absolute Weapon: Atomic Power and World Order,* ed. Bernard Brodie (New York: Ayer Company, 1946), 52.

6. Kaplan, 18.

7. Ibid.

8. William Poundstone, *Prisoner's Dilemma* (New York: Doubleday, 1992), 71.

9. Bird and Sherwin, op. cit., 84.

10. Poundstone, 72–73.

11. Ibid., 145–147.

12. David McCullough, *Truman* (New York: Simon and Schuster, 1992), 608.

13. Kaplan, 25.

14. Ibid., 31.

15. John Lewis Gaddis, *The Cold War: A New History* (New York: The Penguin Press, 2005), 33–34.

16. John Lewis Gaddis, *The United States and the Origins of the Cold War, 1941–1947* (New York: Columbia University Press, 2000), 341.

17. Bernard Brodie, *Strategy in the Missile Age* (Princeton, NJ: Princeton University Press, 1959), 21.

18. Kaplan, 45.

19. Martin J. Collins, *Cold War Laboratory: RAND, the Air Force and the American State, 1945–1950* (Washington, DC: Smithsonian Institution Press, 2002), 184.

20. Ibid., 185.

21. Andrew David May, *The RAND Corporation and the Dynamics of American Strategic Thought,* doctoral dissertation (Dickinson College, October 1998), 125.

22. LeMay biography, *Air & Space Power Chronicles,* op. cit.

23. Kaplan, 47.

24. Joseph Schumpeter, *Capitalism, Socialism and Democracy* (London: Allen and Undwin, 1943), 59–200.

25. Kenneth Arrow, "Social Choice and Individual Values," in RAND RM-291 (Santa Monica, CA: RAND Corporation, 1949), 48–51.

26. Alan Bullock and Stephen Trombley, editors, *The Fontana Dictionary of Modern Thought* (London: HarperCollins, 1999), 669–737.

27. This section on Arrow's work is greatly indebted to the groundbreaking study by S. M. Amadae, *Rationalizing Capitalist Democracy: The Cold War Origins of Rational Choice Liberalism* (Chicago: The University of Chicago Press, 2003).

28. Poundstone, 22.

29. John von Neumann and Oskar Morgenstern, *Theory of Games and Economic Behavior,* 60th anniversary edition (Princeton, NJ: Princeton University Press, 2004).

30. For more on game theory, see Stanford Encyclopedia of Philosophy at <http://plato.stanford.edu/entries/game-theory>.

31. David McCullough, *Truman* (New York: Simon and Schuster, 1992), 758.

32. Poundstone, op. cit., 144.

33. David R. Jardini, *Out of the Blue Yonder: The RAND Corporation's Diversification into Social Welfare Research, 1946–1968,* doctoral dissertation (Carnegie Mellon University, May 1996), 51.

34. Kaplan, 86.

35. May, 70.

36. RAND Corporation, *The RAND Corporation: The First Fifteen Years,* op cit., 27.

37. Charles Hitch, "An Appreciation of Systems Analysis," P-699 (Santa Monica, CA: RAND, 18 August 1955), 22–25.

38. David Novick, "The Meaning of Cost Analysis" (Santa Monica, CA: RAND Corporation, 1983), 3.

39. Ed Paxson et al., *Comparison of Airplane Systems for Strategic Bombing,* Report R-208 (Santa Monica, CA: RAND Corporation, September 1950).

40. Kaplan, 63.

41. E. J. Barlow, "Preliminary Proposal for Air Defense Study," RAND Limited Document D(l)-816, 2 October 1950, RAND Classified Library, cited in Jardini, 67.

CHAPTER 4: A TALK BEFORE DINNER

1. This chapter was based on information gathered from a variety of sources: interviews, written material, newspaper accounts, books, and original documentary, all combined to create a vignette in the life of Albert Wohlstetter.

2. Annahrae White, "The House That Hangs in the Sky," *Los Angeles Examiner, Pictorial Living* (7 August 1955), 14–22; Martin Filler, "Landscape Visionary for a New American Dream," the *New York Times* (2 February 1997): Section H 32–33.

CHAPTER 5: THE SECRET KEEPERS

1. See Martin Bunzl, "Counterfactual History: A User's Guide," the *American Historical Review* 109.3 (June 2004), 6 November 2006 <http://www.historycooperative.org/journals/ahr/109.3/bunzl.html>; also, Niall Ferguson, "Introduction: Virtual History: Toward a 'Chaotic' Theory of the Past," *Virtual History: Alternatives and Counterfactuals,* ed. Niall Ferguson (London: Papermac/Trans-Atlantic, 1998), 8; and Bruce Bueno de Mesquita, "Insights from Game Theory," *Counterfactual Thought Experiments in World Politics: Logical, Methodological, and Psychological Perspectives,* eds. Philip E. Tetlock and Aaron Belkin (Princeton, NJ, 1996), 211–29; also, John Keegan, "How Hitler Could Have Won the War: The Drive for the Middle East, 1941," *What If? The World's Foremost Military Historians Imagine What Might Have Been; Essays,* ed. Robert Cowley (New York: Putnam, 1999), 297.

2. Joan Wohlstetter, personal interview, March 2004 and February 2006.

3. Richard Bellman, *I Am the Hurricane,* manuscript, Brownlee Haydon Box, RAND Archives.

4. Alan Wald, *The New York Intellectuals* (Chapel Hill, NC: University of North Carolina Press, 1987), 7.

5. Charles Wohlstetter, *The Right Place* (New York: Applause Books, 1997), 13–14.

6. Stephen Schwartz, "Trotskycons? Past and Present," *National Review Online* (11 June 2003).

7. Nathan Glazer, "Neoconservative from the Start," the *Public Interest* 159 (Spring 2005).

8. Wald, 107.

9. Charles Wohlstetter, 13.

10. "The Development of Strategic Thinking at RAND, 1948–1966: A Mathematical Logician's View," an interview with Albert Wohlstetter (5 July 1985). Interviewers: Jim Digby, Joan Goldhamer. Transcribed by Dana Bursk. (Santa Monica, CA: RAND, 1997), 15.

11. Wald, op. cit., 107.

12. Daniel Ellsberg, personal interview, January 2005.

13. Joan Wohlstetter, personal interview, February 2006.

14. Nathan Glazer, personal interview, October 2005.

15. Morton G. White, *A Philosopher's Story* (University Park, PA: Pennsylvania State University Press, 1999), 36–37.

16. Elaine Woo, "Roberta Wohlstetter, 94; wrote Pearl Harbor Study," *Los Angeles Times* (11 January 2007): B18. Family lore has it that Roberta Wohlstetter, née Morgan, was the model for one of the characters in McCarthy's noted novel *The Women*. Joan Wohlstetter, personal interview, March 2004.

17. See Leon Trotsky, *Revolution Betrayed* (New York: Dover Publications, 2004); and Irving Howe, *Leon Trotsky* (New York: The Viking Press, 1979).

18. John McDonald, "The War of Wits," *Fortune* (March 1951).

19. *Scientific American* (May 1957): 38.

20. Alain Enthoven, "Tribute to Charles J. Hitch," OR/MS Today, at <http://www.lionhrtpub.com/orms/orms-12-95/hitch-tribute.html>.

21. "The Development of Strategic Thinking."

22. Ibid.

23. Fred Kaplan, *The Wizards of Armageddon* (New York: Simon and Schuster, 1983), 98.

24. "The Development of Strategic Thinking."

25. Joan Wohlstetter, personal interview, March 2004.

26. Roberta Wohlstetter, *Pearl Harbor: Warning and Decision* (Stanford, CT: Stanford University Press, 1962).

27. Albert Wohlstetter, "Economic and Strategic Considerations in Air Base Location: A Preliminary Review," document (D-1114) (Santa Monica, CA: RAND Corporation, 29 December 1951).

28. Kaplan, 99.

29. Albert Wohlstetter, "The Development of Strategic Thinking."

30. Kaplan, 101.

31. Gregg Herken, *Counsels of War* (New York: Oxford University Press, 1987), 94.

32. Kaplan, 106.

33. Albert Wohlstetter et al., "Selection and Use of Strategic Air Bases," document (R-266) (Santa Monica, CA: RAND Corporation, April 1954).

34. Kaplan, 107.

35. Albert Wohlstetter, "The Delicate Balance of Terror," *Foreign Affairs* 37.2 (1959): 211–34.

36. Paul Bracken, "Instabilities in the Control of Nuclear Forces," in Martin Hellman, editor, *Breakthrough: Emerging New Thinking* (New York: Walker and Company, 1988), 48.

37. "The Development of Strategic Thinking."

38. Kaplan, 121.
39. Bernard Brodie et al. "Implications of Large Yield Weapons," Project RAND (Santa Monica, CA: RAND Corporation, 10 July 1952), 10.
40. Ibid., 23.
41. Kaplan, 141.
42. Tom Wells, *Wild Man: The Life and Times of Daniel Ellsberg* (New York: Palgrave, 2001), 297.
43. Kaplan, 223.
44. Herken, 78–85.
45. Andrew W. Marshall, J. J. Martin, and Henry S. Rowen, editors, *On Not Confusing Ourselves: Essays on National Security Strategy in Honor of Albert and Roberta Wohlstetter* (Boulder, CO: Westview Press, 1991), 158–59.
46. Martin Collins, interview with David Novick, *Rand History Project,* 24 February, 20 June 1988.
47. Kaplan, 123.

CHAPTER 6: THE JESTER OF DEATH

1. Herman Kahn, *On Thermonuclear War* (Princeton, NJ: Princeton University Press, 1960), 29.
2. Ghamari-Tabrizi, op. cit., 69.
3. Fred Kaplan, "Truth Stranger than 'Strangelove,'" the *New York Times,* 10 October 2004, accessed 10 March 2005 at <http://www.nytimes.com/2004/10/10/movies/10kapl.html>
4. Ghamari-Tabrizi, 62.
5. Ibid.
6. Richard Bellman, *I Am the Hurricane,* manuscript, Brownlee Haydon Box, RAND Archives, 262.
7. Ghamari-Tabrizi, 66–67.
8. Bellman, 263.
9. Ghamari-Tabrizi, 67.
10. Joan Wohlstetter interview, March 2004.
11. Herman Kahn and Andrew Marshall, *Methods of Reducing Sample Size in Monte Carlo Computations* (Santa Monica, CA: RAND Corporation, 18 August 1953).
12. Ghamari-Tabrizi, 11.
13. May, 448.
14. Ghamari-Tabrizi, 69.
15. Kahn, 86.
16. Ibid., 66–67.
17. James R. Newman, "Two Discussions of Thermonuclear War," review of *On Thermonuclear War,* by Herman Kahn, *Scientific American* 204 (March 1961): 197–204.

18. Paul Johnson, review of *On Thermonuclear War, New Statesman* (1 May 1961): 754.

19. Frank Meyer, review of *On Thermonuclear War, National Review* (March 1961): 189.

20. Norman Thomas, "Roads that Bypass Peace," *Saturday Review* (4 February 1961): 18, 33, quoted in Ghamari-Tabrizi, 303.

21. Paul D. Aligica, "Herman Kahn, founder," *Hudson Institute*, 2007, Hudson Institute, Inc., accessed 21 June 2007 <http://www.hudson.org/learn/index.cfm?fuseaction=staff_bio&eid=HermanKahn>.

CHAPTER 7: IN RAND'S ORBIT

1. Roger D. Launius, "*Sputnik* and the Origins of the Space Age," *NASA History Division*, January 2007, NASA, accessed 21 June 2007 <http://history.nasa.gov/sputnik/sputorig.html>.

2. Ibid.

3. Fred Kaplan, *The Wizards of Armageddon* (New York: Simon and Schuster, 1983), 135.

4. James Killian, *Sputnik, Scientists, and Eisenhower* (Cambridge: The MIT Press, 1977), 8.

5. Launius, op. cit.

6. Ibid.

7. Andrew David May, *The RAND Corporation and the Dynamics of American Strategic Thought,* doctoral dissertation (Dickinson College, October 1998), 365.

8. Killian, op. cit., 8.

9. Gregg Herken, *Counsels of War* (New York: Oxford University Press, 1987), 106–7.

10. "Preliminary Design of an Experimental World-Circling Spaceship," Santa Monica Plant, Engineering Division, report number SM-11827, Contract W33-038 (Santa Monica, CA: Douglas Aircraft Company, Inc., 2 May 1946).

11. David R. Jardini, *Out of the Blue Yonder: The RAND Corporation's Diversification into Social Welfare Research, 1946–1968,* doctoral dissertation (Carnegie Mellon University, May 1996), 115.

12. Herken, 112.

13. Ibid.

14. United States, Office of Defense Mobilization, Security Resources Panel of the Science Advisory Committee, *Deterrence and Survival in the Nuclear Age* (Washington, DC: GPO, 1957), 31–34.

15. Sprague Electric Company, accessed 9 November 2006 at <http//www.massmoca.org/about.html> and <http://www.comsprague.com/about.htm>.

16. Kaplan, op. cit., 145.

17. Ibid., 141.

18. *Deterrence and Survival in the Nuclear Age,* op. cit., 5.

19. Gwynne Dyer, *War: The Lethal Custom* (New York: Carroll & Graf, 2005), 303–4; and Stephen Daggett, *Military Operations: Precedents for Funding Contingency Operations in Regular or in Supplemental Appropriations Bills* (CRS Report for Congress) (Washington, DC: GPO, 2006), Federation of American Scientists Online, accessed 26 June 2007 <http://www.fas.org/sgp/crs/natsec/RS22455.pdf>.

20. Kaplan, 146.

21. Ibid., 147.

22. "Group Discusses Threat to Nation," *New York Times* (11 December 1957): 8; Chalmers M. Roberts, "Enormous Arms Outlay Is Held Vital to Survival," the *Washington Post* (20 December 1957).

23. Richard Reeves, *President Kennedy: Profile of Power* (New York: Simon and Schuster, 1993), 37.

24. Kaplan, 159–61.

25. Stuart Symington entry in Biographical Directory of the U.S. Congress, accessed 9 November 2006 at <http://bioguide.congress.gov/scripts/biodisplay.pl?index=S001136>.

26. Herken, 128–32.

27. X, "The Sources of Soviet Conduct," *Foreign Affairs* (July 1947) accessed 7 September 2005 at <http://www.foreignaffairs.org/19470701faessay25403/x/the-sources-of-soviet-conduct.html>

28. Albert Wohlstetter, "The Delicate Balance of Terror," *Foreign Affairs* (January 1959): 211–34.

29. Ibid.

30. Ibid.

31. John Lewis Gaddis, *We Now Know: Rethinking Cold War History* (Oxford: Oxford University Press, 1997), 264.

32. Wohlstetter, "The Delicate Balance of Terror," op. cit.

33. Ibid.

34. Gordon W. Prange, Donald M. Goldstein, Katherine V. Dillon, *Pearl Harbor: The Verdict of History* (New York: Penguin, 1991), 479–83.

35. John Lewis Gaddis, *Strategies of Containment* (New York: Oxford University Press, 2005), 283–88.

CHAPTER 8: A DELICATE DANCE

1. Personal papers of Deirdre Henderson, Box 1, John F. Kennedy Library, Boston, MA.

2. Joseph W. Alsop recorded interview by Elspeth Rostow, 18 June 1964, 12–18. John F. Kennedy Library Oral History Program accessed 12 September 2006 at <http://www.jfklibrary.org>

3. See note 1, chapter 4.

CHAPTER 9: WHIZ KIDS RULE

1. President Dwight D. Eisenhower, Farewell Address, 17 January 1961, accessed 10 December 2006 at <http://www.eisenhower.archives.gov/speeches/farewell_address.html>.

2. See Alain Enthoven interview, in David R. Jardini, *Out of the Blue Yonder: The RAND Corporation's Diversification into Social Welfare Research, 1946–1968,* doctoral dissertation (Carnegie Mellon University, May 1996), 165.

3. Robert McNamara, *In Retrospect* (New York: Vintage Books, 1996), 16–17.

4. Ibid.

5. Charles Hitch and Roland N. McKean, *Economics of Defense in the Nuclear Age* (New York: Holiday House, 1965).

6. Jardini, 165.

7. "Faculty Profiles: Alain C. Enthoven," Stanford School of Business, 2007, Stanford University, accessed 26 June 2007 <https://gsbapps.stanford.edu/facultybios/biomain.asp?id=00464891>.

8. Kaplan, 253.

9. Jardini, 166.

10. Paul H. Nitze, *From Hiroshima to Glasnost: At the Center of Decision* (New York: Grove Weidenfeld, 1989), 218.

11. Richard Bellman, *I Am the Hurricane,* manuscript, Brownlee Haydon Box, RAND Archives, 287.

12. Daniel Ellsberg, *Secrets: A Memoir of Vietnam and the Pentagon Papers* (New York: Penguin Books, 2002), 25; and Ellsberg, personal interview, October 2004, and January and June 2005.

13. Kaplan, 124.

14. Ibid., 256.

15. Ibid., 254.

16. Jardini, 288–89.

17. Ibid., 169.

18. Kaplan, 256.

19. General Thomas D. White, "Strategy and the Defense Intellectuals," *Saturday Evening Post* (4 May 1963), 10. Also cited in Jardini, 221.

20. Jardini, 183.

21. Ibid., 256.

CHAPTER 10: THE ART OF SCIENCE

1. George Gilder, "Inventing the Internet," *Forbes* (2 June 1997).

2. Stewart Brand, interview with Paul Baran, "Founding Father," *Wired Magazine,* March 2001, accessed 12 October 2005 at <http://www.wired.com/wired/archive/9.03/baran.html>

3. Warren McCulloch, *Embodiments of Mind* (Cambridge, MA: MIT Press, 1965).

4. "What is the difference between analog and digital signals?" *NTT East Website,* 2007, Nippon Telegraph and Telephone East Corporation, accessed 10 July 2007 <http://www.ntt-east.co.jp/isdn_e/e_page/e_faq02/faq003.html>.

5. Virginia Campbell, "How RAND Invented the Postwar World," *Invention and Technology* (Summer 2004): 50–59.

6. Stewart Brand, interview with Paul Baran.

7. Jardini, 87.

8. Campbell, op. cit.

9. The RAND Corporation, *A Million Random Digits with 100,000 Normal Deviates* (Glencoe, IL: Free Press, 1955).

10. Bruno W. Augenstein, "Evolution of the U.S. Military Space Program, 1949–1960: Some Key Events in Study, Planning, and Program Development," *The RAND Paper Series,* P-6814 (Santa Monica, CA: RAND, September 1982), 6.

11. Bruno W. Augenstein and Bruce Murray, *Mert Davies: A RAND Pioneer in Earth Reconnaissance and Planetary Mapping from Spacecraft* (Santa Monica, CA: RAND Corporation, 2004), 84.

12. Dwayne A. Day, John M. Logsdon, and Brian Latell, editors, *Eye in the Sky: The Story of the Corona Spy Satellites* (Washington, DC: Smithsonian Institution Press, 1998), 187.

13. Ibid., 30.

14. Ibid., 121.

15. Augenstein and Murray, 7.

16. Day et al., 102.

17. Interview with Oleg Troyanovski, "Episode 8: Sputnik," *CNN Perspectives Cold War Series,* Turner Original Productions, 1998.

18. Day et al., 31.

19. Ibid., 1.

20. William Burrows, *Deep Black* (New York: Random House, 1986), viii.

21. Joseph W. Hamaker, "But What Will It Cost? The History of NASA Cost Estimating," NASA Cost Estimating, at <http://www.NASA.htm>.

22. Robert Buchheim et al., *Space Handbook: Astronautics and Its Applications,* Staff Report of the Select Committee of Astronautics and Space Exploration, 85th Congress (Santa Monica, CA: RAND, 1958).

CHAPTER 11: A FINAL SOLUTION TO THE SOVIET PROBLEM

1. Secretary of Defense Thomas Gates, "Notes by the Secretaries to the Joint Chiefs of Staff on Strategic Target Planning," 27 January 1991, copy 33, limited distribution "I," declassified 1995, National Archives.

2. Robert S. McNamara, *In Retrospect* (New York: Vintage Books, 1996), 21–25; and Kaplan, 269.

3. R. P. Turco, O. B. Toon, T. P. Acherman, J. B. Pollack, Carl Sagan, "Global Atmospheric Consequences of Nuclear War," 25 July 1983, NASA-TM-101281, 20–22.

4. Herken, 138.

5. Kaplan, 272.

6. Herken, 139.

7. Kaplan, 260.

8. Ibid., 273.

9. Ibid., 279.

10. John Lewis Gaddis, *We Now Know: Rethinking Cold War History* (Oxford: Oxford University Press, 1997), 256–57.

11. Gaddis, *The Cold War,* 114–15.

12. Dean Rusk, *As I Saw It* (New York: The Penguin Press, 1991), 207–17.

13. Ibid., 221.

14. McNamara, 21.

15. Gaddis, *The Cold War,* 112–14.

16. Bart Barnes, "Dean Rusk, 60's Foreign Policy Leader, Dies," the *Washington Post* (22 December 1994): 1.

17. Kaplan, 293–94.

18. Tom Wicker, "No New Tax Now; 207 Million Is Sought for Civil Defense in Speech on Berlin; Kennedy Asks Increase in Defenses," *New York Times* (26 July 1961): 1.

19. Herken, 159.

20. Carl Kaysen, "Memorandum for General Maxwell Taylor, Military Representative to the President, September 5, 1961," record group 218 of the Joint Chiefs of Staff (records of Maxwell Taylor), National Archives.

21. Kaplan, 299.

22. Paul H. Nitze, *From Hiroshima to Glasnost: At the Center of Decision* (New York: Grove Weidenfeld, 1989), 199–208.

23. Gaddis, *The Cold War,* 115.

24. Robert F. Kennedy and Arthur Schlesinger Jr., *Thirteen Days: A Memoir of the Cuban Missile Crisis* (New York: W. W. Norton, 1999), 83–84.

CHAPTER 12: AN IRRESISTIBLE FORCE

1. *Time* magazine, 23 April 1973, accessed 4 July 2007 at <http://www.time.com/time/magazine/article/0,9171,945221-1,00.html>; Anthony Russo, "Inside the RAND Corporation and Out: My Story," *Ramparts* (April 1972), 45–55; Anthony Joseph (Tony) Russo biography accessed 23 September 2005 at <http://pentagonpaperstrusso.com>.

2. David R. Jardini, *Out of the Blue Yonder: The RAND Corporation's Diversification into Social Welfare Research, 1946–1968*, doctoral dissertation (Carnegie Mellon University, May 1996), 263.

3. Gabriel Kolko, *Confronting the Third World: United States Foreign Policy 1945–1980* (New York: Pantheon Press, 1980), 132.

4. Maxwell Taylor, *The Uncertain Trumpet* (New York: Harper and Row, 1960), 29.

5. Fred Kaplan, *The Wizards of Armageddon* (New York: Simon and Schuster, 1983), 292.

6. For Kennedy's inaugural address, see <http://www.jfklibrary.org/Historical+Resources/Archives/Reference+Desk/Speeches/JFK/Inaugural+Address+January+20+1961.htm>.

7. Jardini, 173.

8. Albert and Roberta Wohlstetter, "Notes on the Cuban Crisis" (Santa Monica, CA: RAND Corporation, 1962); and "Studies for a Post-Communist Cuba" (Santa Monica, CA: RAND Corporation, 1963).

9. Joan Wohlstetter, personal interview, March 2004.

10. W. Phillips Davison, "User's Guide to the RAND Interviews in Vietnam" (Santa Monica, CA: RAND Corporation, 1972); Anthony Russo, "Looking Backward: RAND Vietnam in Retrospect," *Ramparts* (November 1972).

11. Paul Dickson, *Think Tanks* (New York: Atheneum, 1971), 67.

12. Jardini, 279.

13. *Counterinsurgency: A Symposium, April 16–20, 1962* (Santa Monica, CA: RAND Corporation, 2006, reprint), 5–7.

14. Stanley Karnow, *Vietnam: A History* (New York: The Viking Press, 1983), 254.

15. Ibid., 396.

16. Charles Wolf, *Insurgency and Counterinsurgency: New Myths and Old Realities* (Santa Monica, CA: RAND Corporation, 1965).

17. Konrad Kellen, personal interview, May 2004.

18. Austin Long, *On "Other War": Lessons from Five Decades of RAND Counterinsurgency Research* (Santa Monica, CA: RAND Corporation, 2006), 9.

19. Leon Gouré, *Civil Defense in the Soviet Union* (Westport, CT: Greenwood Press, 1986); Leon Gouré, "Soviet Civil Defense," P-1887 (Santa Monica, CA: RAND, 1960).

20. Stanley Karnow, *Vietnam: A History* (New York: The Viking Press, 1983), 20.

21. Jardini, 282.

22. Jardini, 284.

23. Thomas Schelling, *The Strategy of Conflict* (Cambridge, MA: Harvard University Press, 1963), 123–25.

24. Fred Kaplan, "All Pain, No Gain: Nobel Laureate Thomas Schelling's Little-Known Role in the Vietnam War," *Slate* (11 October 2005), accessed 4 July 2007 at <http://www.slate.com/id/2127862>.

25. Karnow, op. cit., 500–1.

26. William Kaufmann, *Military Policy and National Security* (Princeton, NJ: Princeton University Press, 1956), 128.

27. Robert S. McNamara, *In Retrospect* (New York: Vintage Books, 1996), 33.

28. Robert Komer, "The Other War in Vietnam: A Progress Report" (Washington, DC: Agency for International Development, 1966), 29.

29. Neil Sheehan, *A Bright Shining Lie: John Paul Vann and America in Vietnam* (New York: Vintage Books, 1989), 380.

30. Lyndon B. Johnson, address, Cam Ranh Bay, December 1967.

31. See Daniel Hallin, "Vietnam on Television," Museum of Broadcast Communications at <http://www.museum.tv/archives/etv/V/htmlV/vietnamonte/vietnamonte.htm>.

32. Tim Weiner, "Robert Komer, 78, Figure in Vietnam, Dies," the *New York Times* (12 April 2000).

33. National Security Action Memorandum 343, 28 March 1966, papers of Lyndon B. Johnson, Papers as President, National Security File, Komer-Leonhart File. LBJ Library, Austin, TX.

34. Weiner.

35. Sheehan, 732.

36. Ibid., 733.

37. Nomination of William E. Colby. Hearing, 93rd Congress, 1st Session, on Nomination of William E. Colby to be Director of Central Intelligence, U.S. Senate, Committee on Armed Services, U.S. Government, Printing Office, Washington DC, 1970, 315–21.

38. Ibid.

39. Robert Komer, "Military and Political Policy: Maritime Strategy vs. Coalition Defense," *Foreign Affairs* (Summer 1982).

40. *Project Air Force 50th Anniversary (1946–1996)* (Santa Monica, CA: RAND Corporation, 1996), 31–32.

41. Irving Lewis Horowitz, *The Rise and Fall of Project Camelot: Studies in the Relationship Between Social Science and Practical Politics* (Cambridge: The MIT Press, 1967).

42. Jardini, 299.

43. Thomas Schelling, "Thomas C. Schelling: Autobiography," *Les Prix Nobel 2005,* Karl Grandin, ed. (Stockholm: Nobel Foundation, 2006).

44. Sheehan, 740.

45. Jardini, 274.

46. Interview with Albert Wohlstetter, 27 January 1989, RAND Collection (RU 9536), Smithsonian Video History Collection (Washington, DC), noted in Jardini, 267.

47.   Eugene M. Zuckert biography at <www.af.mil/bios/bio.asp?bioID=7326>.
48.   Jardini, 292.
49.   Ibid., 295.
50.   Ibid., 300.
51.   Smith, 136.
52.   Jardini, 301.
53.   Franklin R. Collbohm biography, RAND document (Santa Monica, CA:
      RAND Corporation, 28 August 1986), 1–2.

CHAPTER 13: A NIGHT IN RACH KIEN

1.   Daniel Ellsberg, personal interview, October 2004, and January and June
      2005; and Ellsberg, *Secrets: A Memoir of Vietnam and the Pentagon
      Papers* (New York: Penguin Books, 2002), 143–50.

CHAPTER 14: THE PRICE OF SUCCESS

1.   Martin Collins and Gus Shubert, interview with Albert Wohlstetter,
      Smithsonian Video History Collection, Smithsonian Institution Archives,
      RAND, Santa Monica, 27 January 1989.
2.   Sam Tanenhaus, interview with Paul Wolfowitz, *Vanity Fair* (9 May 2003)
      at <http://www.DoD%20Deputy%20Secretary%20Wolfowitz%
      20Interview%20with%20Sam%20Tanenhaus,%20Vanity%20Fair.htm>.
3.   Earl Shorris, "Ignoble Liars: Leo Strauss, George Bush and the Politics of
      Deception," *Harper's* (June 2004); and Anne Norton, *Leo Strauss and the
      Politics of American Empire* (New Haven, CT: Yale University Press,
      2004).
4.   Henry Jackson biography, Henry M. Jackson Foundation at <http://www
      .hmjackson.org/bio.html>.
5.   Richard Perle, personal interview, November 2005.
6.   Robert Gordon Kaufman, *Henry M. Jackson: A Life in Politics* (Seattle:
      University of Washington Press, 2000), 322.
7.   "PBS: Think Tank: Richard Perle: The Making of a Neoconservative," at
      <www.pbs.org/thinktank/show_1017.html>.
8.   Perle interview.
9.   Jardini, 357.
10.   Henry Rowen, personal interview, 27 April 2004.
11.   Ibid.
12.   Memorandum from William L. Hooper, Office of Science and Technology,
      to Donald F. Honig, Special Assistant to the President for Science and
      Technology, quoted in Jardini, 393.
13.   Jardini, 379–83.
14.   Joseph Califano, *The Triumph and Tragedy of Lyndon Johnson: The
      White House Years* (New York: Simon and Schuster, 1991), 24.

15. Jardini, 399.
16. Lyndon Johnson, "Great Society Speech," University of Michigan
     Commencement, Ann Arbor, MI, 22 May 1964, *Public Papers of the
     Presidents of the United States: Lyndon B. Johnson,* Vol. I, 1963–64
     (Washington, DC: Government Printing Office, 1967), 704–7.
17. Jardini, 405.
18. Nat Hentoff, *A Political Life: The Education of John V. Lindsay* (New
     York: Knopf, 1969), 78.
19. Rudolph Giuliani, eulogy, Memorial Service for Mayor John V. Lindsay,
     26 January 2001 at <http://clanlindsay.com/john_vliet_lindsay.htm>.
20. Nat Hentoff, "The Man Who Stood Up to Bobby Kennedy," *The Village
     Voice* (24 January 2001).
21. Thomas P. Ronan, "Lindsay Says City Needs Arbitration in Labor
     Disputes; Lindsay in Call for Arbitration," *New York Times* (17
     November 1965).
22. Vincent Cannato, *The Ungovernable City: John Lindsay and His Struggle
     to Save New York* (New York: Basic Books, 2001), 82.
23. Jardini, 416.
24. "John Lindsay's Ten Plagues," *Time* (1 November 1968).
25. Jardini, 412.
26. Richard Reeves, "City Hires RAND Corporation to Study Four Agencies,"
     the *New York Times* (9 January 1968): 31.
27. *Annual Report 1972* (Santa Monica, CA: RAND, 1972).
28. Rae Archibald, personal interview, September 2004.
29. Ibid.
30. Bernard Cohen, "The Police Internal Administration of Justice in New
     York City," R-621 (New York: RAND Corporation, November 1970); and
     Cohen and Jan M. Chaiken, "New York City Police: The Background and
     Performance of the Class of 1957" (New York: RAND Corporation,
     February 1973).
31. David Burnham, "Study Questions Handling of Police Misconduct," *New
     York Times* (20 November 1970): 1, 46.
32. Jardini, 432.
33. David K. Shipler, "Rent Control End and City Subsidies Linked in a
     Study," *New York Times* (13 February 1970): 1, 43.
34. Jardini, 433.
35. Archibald interview.
36. Cannato, 557.
37. Jardini, 436.
38. The Council for Aid to Education—a subsidiary of RAND. CAE became
     an independent nonprofit in October 2005. See <http://www.cae.org/
     content/about/htm>.

CHAPTER 15: STEALING AWAY

1. Henry Rowen, personal interview, 27 April 2004.
2. Daniel Ellsberg interview, October 2004; *Secrets,* 299–301.

CHAPTER 16: *PLUS ÇA CHANGE*

1. Joan Wohlstetter, personal interview, February 2006.
2. Frances Fitzgerald, *Fire in the Lake: The Vietnamese and the Americans in Vietnam* (New York: Little, Brown and Company, Back Bay Books, 2002), 403–20.
3. Stanley Karnow, *Vietnam: A History* (New York: The Viking Press, 1983), 632.
4. Charles Wolf, personal interview, November 2003.
5. Donald Rice, personal interview, January 2006.
6. "Is the Think Tank Thought Out?" *Los Angeles* (January 1982): 254.
7. Konrad Kellen, personal interview, May 2004.
8. Daniel Ellsberg, personal interview, October 2004, and January and June 2005.
9. Karnow, 634.
10. Ellsberg interview, January 2005.
11. Rice interview.
12. "Is the Think Tank Thought Out?"
13. Herken, 260.
14. "Watching Birds and Budgets," *Time* (11 February 1974): 16–17.
15. Herken, 258.
16. Emmett B. Keeler, "Effects of Cost Sharing on Use of Medical Services and Health," *Medical Practice Management* (Summer 1992): 317.
17. Ibid., 318.
18. RAND Research, 1997, 43.
19. Louis W. Miller et al., *Operations Research and Policy Analysis at RAND, 1968–1988,* N-2937-RC (Santa Monica, CA: RAND Corporation, April 1989).
20. Rice interview.
21. "RAND Europe Research," RAND Europe, 25 April 2007, RAND Corporation, accessed 11 July 2007 <http://www.rand.org/randeurope/research/>.
22. Donald B. Rice biography, Wells Fargo Board of Directors, accessed 26 October 2006 at <http://www.wellsfargo.com/about/corporate/boardofdirectors/rice>.
23. Rice interview.
24. Pardee RAND Graduate School yearbook, 1980.

25.   Confidential interview, 2003.

26.   See <http://www.whitehouse.gov/government/rumsfeld-bio.html> accessed on 12/21/07.

27.   See <<http://www.rand.org/about/annual_report/1996/admin/trustees .htm>> accessed on 1/10/08.

28.   Dave Goldberg, "In Rand's Defense: It's Not All Military," *Chicago Tribune* (20 June 1982): Section 3: 6.

CHAPTER 17: TEAM B STRIKES

1.   "U.S. Negotiator on Arms Quits, Citing the Effects of Watergate," the *New York Times* (15 June 1974).

2.   *Cong. Rec.* (4 August 1969): 22016–19.

3.   Albert Wohlstetter, "Is There a Strategic Arms Race?" *Foreign Policy* 15 (Summer 1974): 3–20.

4.   Anne Hessing Cahn, *Killing Détente: The Right Attacks the CIA* (University Park, PA: The Pennsylvania State University Press, 1998), 15.

5.   Ibid.

6.   Ibid., 7.

7.   Ibid.

8.   Ibid., 9.

9.   Henry Kissinger, *The White House Years* (Boston: Little, Brown, 1979), 119.

10.   Robert Scheer, *With Enough Shovels* (New York: Vintage Books, 1983), 37–38.

11.   Kissinger, 208.

12.   Ibid., 210.

13.   Peter J. Ognibene, *Scoop: The Life and Politics of Henry M. Jackson* (New York: Stein and Day, 1975), 182–95.

14.   Tad Szulc, "Pentagon Cool," *Washingtonian Magazine,* 10.1 (1974): 16.

15.   Gerald R. Ford, *A Time to Heal: The Autobiography of Gerald R. Ford* (New York: Harper and Row, 1979), 132.

16.   Donald Rumsfeld biography at <http://www.defenselink.mil/bios/ rumsfeld.html>.

17.   Richard D. Lyons, "Senate Confirms Bush as C.I.A. Director," the *New York Times* (28 January 1976).

18.   Ford, 346.

19.   Martin Weil, "Eugene Rostow Dies," the *Washington Post* (26 November 2002): B6.

20.   Eugene V. Rostow, "Defining Détente in Terms of the United Nations Charter," the *New York Times* (27 April 1974): 31.

21.   Cahn, 27.

22. Ibid.
23. Albert Wohlstetter, "Optimal Ways to Confuse Ourselves," *Foreign Policy* 20 (Fall 1975): 170–98; and "The Uncontrolled Upward Spiral," *Strategic Review* 3 (Winter 1975): 71–86.
24. Max Boot, "Think Again: Neocons," *Foreign Policy* (January/February 2004).
25. Thomas Powers, *The Man Who Kept the Secrets: Richard Helms and the CIA* (New York: Knopf, 1979), 145.
26. William Colby, *Honorable Men: My Life in the CIA* (New York: Simon and Schuster, 1978), 338–46.
27. *Report by the Presidential Commission on CIA Activities Within the United States (Rockefeller Commission)* (Washington, DC: GPO, 1975).
28. Powers, 129–31.
29. Wohlstetter, "Is There a Strategic Arms Race?" 3–20.
30. John Prados, *The Soviet Estimate: U.S. Intelligence Analysis and Soviet Strategic Forces* (Princeton, NJ: Princeton University Press, 1986), 186, cited in Cahn, 102.
31. Cahn, 104.
32. "Intelligence Community Experiment in Competitive Analysis—Soviet Strategic Objectives—An Alternative View—Report of Team B," Washington DC, December 1976, 2–6, National Archives.
33. William Colby, letter to President Gerald Ford, 21 November 1975, cited in Cahn, 119.
34. Jerry Wayne Sanders, *Peddlers of Crisis: The Committee on the Present Danger and the Politics of Containment* (Boston: South End Press, 1983), 199.
35. Leo Cherne, letter to George H. W. Bush, 8 June 1976, cited in Cahn, 139.
36. Cahn, 147.
37. Richard Pipes, interview with Sam Tanenhaus, "The Hard-liner," *Boston Globe* (2 November 2003).
38. Richard Pipes, *The Formation of the Soviet Union: Communism and Nationalism, 1917–23* (Cambridge, MA: Harvard University Press, 1954).
39. Cahn, 158.
40. Richard Pipes interview.
41. Cahn, 160.
42. David Binder, "New CIA Estimate Finds Soviet Seeks Superiority," the *New York Times* (26 December 1976): 1.
43. Tim Weiner, "Jeane Kirkpatrick, Reagan's Forceful Envoy, Dies," the *New York Times* (9 December 2006): 1.
44. "U.S. Military Spending 1949–2009," Infoplease, 2007, accessed 11 July 2007 <http://www.infoplease.com/ipa/A0904490.html>.

45.   Max Kampelman, *Entering New Worlds: The Memoirs of a Private Man in Public Life* (New York: HarperCollins, 1991), 234, quoted in Cahn, op. cit., 30.

CHAPTER 18: WITNESSING END TIMES

1.   Ronald Reagan, "Remarks at the Presentation Ceremony for the Presidential Medal of Freedom," 7 November 1985, at <http://www.reagan.utexas.edu/archives/speeches/1985/110785a.htm>.

2.   Charles Wolf Jr., *Extended Containment: Countering Soviet Imperialism and Applying Economic Realism* (Santa Monica, CA: A RAND Note, 1983).

3.   For Reagan's inaugural address, see <http://www.reagan.utexas.edu/archives/speeches/1981/12081a.htm>.

4.   Ronald Reagan, "Address to Member of the British Parliament," 8 June 1982, at <http://www.reagan.utexas.edu/archives/speeches/1982/60882a.htm>.

5.   Zalmay Khalilzad, personal interview, January 2006.

6.   Khalilzad interview.

7.   Jacques Steinberg, "Robert L. Bartley, 66, Dies," the *New York Times* (11 December 2003).

8.   Kaplan, 387–89.

9.   John H. Cushman, "Applying Military Brain to Military Brawn, Again," *The New York Times* (17 December 1986): B10; Ballistic Missile Defense History, Missile Defense Agency history link, accessed 20 November 2006 at <http://www.mda.mil/mdalink/html/mdalink.html>.

10.   "Thursday, August 16, 1984 International," *New York Times* (16 August 1984).

11.   Benjamin B. Fischer, "A Cold War Conundrum: The 1983 Soviet War Scare" (Washington, DC: Center for the Study of Intelligence, 1997).

12.   Konrad Kellen, *The Germans and the Pershing II* (RAND Report P-6950) (Santa Monica, CA: RAND, 1983).

13.   Albert Wohlstetter, "Between an Unfree World and None: Increasing Our Choices," *Foreign Affairs* 63 (Summer 1985): 962–94.

14.   Lawrence S. Wittner, "Reagan and Nuclear Disarmament," *Boston Review* (April/May 2002), accessed 4 September 2005 at <http://bostonreview.net/BR25.2/wittner.html>.

15.   Alexander Yakovlev, "Memorandum to Mikhail Gorbachev: The Imperative of Political Development," 25 December 1985, National Security Archives, accessed 20 November 2006 at <http://www.gwu.edu/~nsarchiv/>.

16.   President Ronald Reagan, "Letter to General Secretary Mikhail Gorbachev," 11 March 1985, National Security Archives, accessed 20 November 2006 at <http://www.gwu.edu/~nsarchiv/NSAEBB/NSAEBB172/Doc2.pdf>.

17. Thomas Schelling, *The Strategy of Conflict* (Cambridge, MA: Harvard University Press, 2006, 1963).
18. See <http://nobelprize.org/nobel_prizes/economics/laureates/2005/index.html>.
19. For Nobel Prize recipients who had been employed by RAND, see <http://www.rand.org/about/history/nobel/>, accessed 20 November 2006.
20. Alan Greenspan, "Remarks on the Reagan Legacy," 9 April 2003, accessed 7 July 2007 at <http://federalreserve.gov/BOARDDOCS/SPEECHES/2003/200304092/default.htm>.
21. Jude Wanniski, "Sketching the Laffer Curve," 14 June 2005, accessed 7 July 2007 at <www.wanniski.com>.
22. William A. Niskanen, *Reaganomics: An Insider's Account of the Policies and the People* (New York: Oxford University Press, 1988), 273.

CHAPTER 19: THE TERROR NETWORK

1. Ben R. Rich and Leo Janos, *Skunk Works* (New York: Back Bay Books, 1996).
2. Michael Rich, personal interview, June 2003.
3. Natalie Crawford e-mail of 13 September 2001 to Michael Rich, RAND.
4. Chronology of Terror, 12 September 2001, at CNN.com.
5. Ibid.
6. Ibid.
7. Richard A. Clarke, *Against All Enemies: Inside America's War on Terror* (New York: The Free Press, 2004), 7.
8. Natalie Crawford, e-mail message to RAND staffers, 14 September 2001.
9. Rich interview.
10. Bruce Hoffman, "Terrorism and Beyond: The 21st Century," conference dinner address, Oklahoma City, OK (17 April 2000), accessed 5 May 2005 at <http://www.terrorisminfo.mipt.org/hoffman-ctb.asp>.
11. Bruce Hoffman, personal interview, April 2004.
12. Brian Jenkins, "International Terrorism: The Other World War," R-3302AF (Santa Monica, CA: RAND Project Air Force, 1985), 1.
13. Paul Wolfowitz, "Paul Nitze's Legacy: For a New World," remarks delivered to the Aspen Institute at the U.S. Chamber of Commerce, Washington, DC, 25 April 2004. See <file:///C:/Documents%20and%20Settings/alex/My%20Documents/DefenseLINK%20News%20Paul%20Nitze's%20Legacy%20For%20a%20New%20World.htm>.
14. Bruce Hoffman, "Rethinking Terrorism in Light of a War on Terrorism. Testimony before the Subcommittee on Terrorism and Homeland Security, House Permanent Select Committee on Intelligence," U.S. House of Representatives, 26 September 2001. Accessed 13 September 2005 at <http://www.rand.org./pubs/testimonies/CT182/>.

15. Brian Jenkins and Janera Johnson, *International Terrorism: A Chronology 1968–1974* (Santa Monica, CA: RAND, 1975), 1–4.

16. Donald Rice, personal interview, January 2006.

17. Caleb Carr, *The Lessons of Terror: A History of Warfare Against Civilians* (New York: Random House, 2003), 32.

18. Konrad Kellen, "Terrorists: What Are They Like? How Some Terrorists Describe Their World and Actions," in *Terrorism and Beyond: An International Conference on Terrorism and Low-Level Conflict*, R-2714-DOE/DOJ/DOS/RC (Santa Monica, CA: RAND Corporation, December 1982), 130.

19. Jenkins, v.

20. Bruce Hoffman, *Countering the New Terrorism* (Santa Monica, CA: RAND Corporation, 2003), vi.

21. Bruce Hoffman and Karen Gardela, "RAND Chronologies of International Terrorism," in Ian Lesser, *Countering the New Terrorism: Implications for Strategy* (Santa Monica, CA: RAND Corporation, 1999), 85.

22. Brian Jenkins, "Defense Against Terrorism," *Political Science Quarterly* 101. 5 (1986): 773–86.

23. Brian Jenkins, "Where I Draw the Line," *Perspectives on Terrorism*, 2002, *Christian Science Monitor* (11 July 2007) at <http://www.csmonitor.com/specials/terrorism/lite/expert.html>.

24. Franz Fanon, *The Wretched of the Earth* (New York: Grove Press, 1961), 40.

25. Daniel Ellsberg, "Judo Politics" (Santa Monica, CA: RAND Corporation, 1959).

26. "Frequently Asked Questions: What's asymmetric warfare?" Center for Asymmetric Warfare, 2000, Center for Asymmetric Warfare at the Naval Air Warfare Center Weapons Division, 11 July 2007, at <http://www.ctrasymwarfare.org/faq.htm >.

27. Brian Jenkins, "*The Lessons of Beirut: Testimony before the Long Commission*" (Santa Monica, CA: RAND, 1984), 12.

28. "Monday, October 24, 1983 Bombings in Beirut," *New York Times* (24 October 1983): B1.

29. "May 29 1972: Japanese kill 26 at Tel Aviv airport," BBC On This Day, 2007, British Broadcasting Company, 11 July 2007, <http://news.bbc.co.uk/onthisday/hi/dates/stories/may/29/newsid_2542000/2542263.stm>.

30. *Terrorism and Beyond*, op. cit., 145.

31. Bruce Hoffman, *Inside Terrorism* (New York: Columbia University Press, 1999); Nicholas Lemann, "What Terrorists Want," the *New Yorker* (29 October 2001), accessed 3 April 2005 at <http://newyorker.com/fact/content/?011029fa_FACT1>.

32. Kellen, 132.

33. John Arquilla, David Ronfeldt, and Michele Zanini, "Networks, Netwar, and Information-Age Terrorism," in Ian O. Lesser et al., *Countering the*

New Terrorism (Santa Monica, CA: RAND Corporation, MR-989-AF, 1999), 47.

34. Brian Michael Jenkins, *Unconquerable Nation: Knowing Our Enemy, Strengthening Ourselves* (Santa Monica, CA: RAND Corporation, 2006), 15.

35. Ibid., 19.

CHAPTER 20: YODA AND THE KNIGHTS OF COUNTERFORCE

1. Sally B. Donnelly, "Long-Distance Warriors," *Time* (12 December 2005).

2. Michael R. Gordon, "The Strategy to Secure Iraq Did Not Foresee a 2nd War," the *New York Times* (19 October 2004): A1; L. Paul Bremer III, *My Year in Iraq: The Struggle to Build a Future of Hope* (New York: Simon and Schuster, 2006), 24; and James T. Quinlivan, "Force Requirements in Stability Questions," *Parameters* (Winter 1995): 59–69.

3. Jason Vest, "The Dubious Genius of Andrew Marshall," American Prospect Online, accessed 17 December 2004 at http://www.prospect .org/cs/articles?article=the_dubious_genius_of_andrew_marshall; Khurram Husain, "Neocons: The men behind the curtain," *Bulletin of the Atomic Scientists,* vol. 59, no. 06 (November/December 2003): 62–71.

4. James G. Roche, "Serving the Patriots of America's Air Force," Order of the Sword Induction Ceremony, Andrews Air Force Base, Maryland, 13 September 2003. Accessed 23 April 2005 at <http://www .accessmylibrary.com/coms2/summary_0286-2303653_ITM>.

5. Nicholas Lemann, "Dreaming About War," *New Yorker* (16 July 2001), accessed 28 December 2004 at <<http://newyorker.com>>.

6. Andrew Marshall, in Andrew Krepinevich Jr., *The Military-Technical Revolution: A Preliminary Assessment* (Washington, DC: Center for Strategic and Budgetary Assessments, 2002), i.

7. "Discriminate Deterrence: Report of the Commission on Integrated Long-Term Strategy," Fred C. Iklé and Albert Wohlstetter, cochairmen (Washington, DC: Government Printing Office, 1988).

8. Krepinevich, ii.

9. Neil Swidey, "The Mind of the Administration, Part Two: The Analyst," the *Boston Globe* (18 May 2003).

10. Sam Tanenhaus, interview with Paul Wolfowitz, *Vanity Fair* (9 May 2003) at <http://www.DoD%20Deputy%20Secretary%20Wolfowitz%20Interview %20with%20Sam%20Tanenhaus,%20Vanity%20Fair.htm>.

11. Albert Wohlstetter, "On Vietnam and Bureaucracy," accessed 24 December 2004 at <http://www.rand.org/publications/classics/wohlstetter/ D17276.1/D17276.1.html>.

12. Ibid.

13. This assumption is applicable to all RAND work. As just one example, see

Todd C. Helmus, Christopher Paul, Russell W. Glenn, *Enlisting Madison Avenue: The Marketing Approach to Earning Popular Support in Theaters of Operation* (Santa Monica, CA: RAND, 2007).

14. Anne Norton, *Leo Strauss and the Politics of American Empire* (New Haven, CT: Yale University Press, 2004), 185.
15. Zalmay Khalilzad, personal interview, January 2006.
16. Norton, 186.
17. Khalilzad interview; Robert F. Worth, "The Juggler," the *New York Times* (12 March 2006): 4:1.
18. Donald Kagan, Gary Schmitt, Thomas Donnelly, "Rebuilding America's Defenses: Strategy, Forces and for a New Century." A Report of the Project for a New American Century (Washington, DC: Project for the New American Century, 2000), 11.
19. Max Boot, "The Case for American Empire," the *Weekly Standard* (15 October 2001); and Charles Krauthammer, "Bless Our Pax Americana," the *Washington Post* (22 March 1991).
20. Lemann, op. cit.
21. Ken Silverstein, "Buck Rogers Rides Again," the *Nation* (25 October 1999); Hundley, *Past Revolutions,* op. cit., 7–20; Douglas McGray, "The Marshall Plan," *Wired* (February 2003).
22. Zalmay Khalilzad et al., *Deterrence Theory and Chinese Behavior* (Santa Monica, CA: RAND Corporation, 1998).
23. Khalilzad interview. China is still in Marshall's sight. His office considers Beijing a very real military rival. See Neil King Jr., "Secret Weapon: Inside Pentagon, A Scholar Shapes Views of China," the *Wall Street Journal* (8 September 2005): A1.
24. Jason Vest, "The New Marshall Plan," *In These Times.com.* Accessed 17 December 2004 at <http://www.inthesetimes.com/issue/25/09/vest2509.html>.
25. Brad Roberts, "1995 and the End of the Post–Cold War Era," *Washington Quarterly* 18, 1 (Winter 1995).
26. Jude Wanniski, "An American Empire," Supply-side University, accessed 24 August 1995, 12 July 2007 <http://wanniski.com/searchbase/amemp1.htm>; Charles Krauthammer, "Bless Our Pax Americana," *Washington Post* (22 March 1991).
27. Joan Wohlstetter, personal interview, March 2004.
28. Albert Wohlstetter and Fred Hoffman, "Confronting Saddam: A Model Danger," *The Wall Street Journal* (9 August 1990): 24.

CHAPTER 21: BACK TO IRAQ

1. Ahmed Chalabi, e-mail interview, January 2006.
2. Bernard Lewis, "Put the Iraqis in Charge," the *Wall Street Journal* (29

August 2003); Frederick Kempe, "Mideast Doctrine's Domestic Hurdle," the *Wall Street Journal* (13 December 2005): A11.

3. Dexter Filkins, "Baghdad Boys," the *New York Times* (12 December 2005): A1.

4. Chalabi, e-mail interview.

5. David L. Phillips, *Losing Iraq: Inside the Postwar Reconstruction Fiasco* (New York: Westview Press, 2005), 69–76.

6. Hugh Pope, "Ahmed Chalabi: Profile," *Los Angeles Times* (19 July 1994): 3.

7. Patrick E. Tyler, "U.S. and Iraqis Tell of a Coup Attempt Against Baghdad," *The New York Times* (3 July 1992): A1.

8. Rob Zone, "Chalabi's Hour, Controversial Exile Leader Back in Iraq," *The Seattle Times* (9 April 2003): A5.

9. Phillips, 62.

10. Zalmay Khalilzad, personal interview, January 2006.

11. Zone, op. cit.

12. Project for the New American Century, letter to President Clinton (Washington, DC: Project for the New Century, 26 January 1998).

13. Iraq Liberation Act, Public Law 105-338, 31 October 1998. 105th Congress, Congressional Record, Volume 144.

14. Phillips, 72.

15. Jane Mayer, "The Manipulator," *New Yorker* (7 June 2004): 58.

16. Ron Suskind, *The Price of Loyalty: George W. Bush, the White House and the Education of Paul O'Neill* (New York: Simon & Schuster, 2004), 75; and Richard A. Clarke, *Against All Enemies: Inside America's War on Terror* (New York: The Free Press, 2004), 30–33.

17. Eric Alterman, "When Presidents Lie," *The Nation* (25 October 2004).

18. Ken Adelman, "Cakewalk in Iraq," *Washington Post* (13 February 2002): A27.

19. Norman Brownstein, "War Now Drives the Presidency," *Los Angeles Times* (29 January 2003): A1.

20. Dexter Filkins, "Where Plan A Left Ahmed Chalabi," *The New York Times Magazine* (5 November 2006): 46.

21. Ibid.

22. James Dobbins et al., *America's Role in Nation Building: From Germany to Iraq* (Santa Monica, CA: RAND Corporation, 2003), xxvi.

23. Nina J. Easton, "The Briefing," *The Boston Globe* (20 November 2005): A8.

24. Ahmed Chalabi, "An Insider's View: Democratic Politics at Work in Iraq: A Foreign Policy Briefing from Iraqi Deputy Prime Minister Ahmed Chalabi," transcript prepared from a tape recording (Washington, DC: American Enterprise Institute, 9 November 2005).

25. Filkins, "Plan A," 48.

26. Ahmed Chalabi, interview with National Interest online, "Questions for Ahmed Chalabi," *National Interest Online,* 28 February 2007, The Nixon Center, accessed 12 July 2007 <http://www.nationalinterest.org/Article .aspx?id=13758>.

27. Interview with Baha al-Araji, "Why America Will Fail in Iraq," *Foreign Policy* (November/December 2006): 20.

28. Supplied by BB Monitoring Service, from Al Arabiya TV, Dubai, in Arabic, 29 September 2006, at 16:00 GMT, found in Voice of Iraq, Iraqi National Congress, accessed 5 November 2006 at <http://inciraq.com/ English/Press/Sep/060929_DR%20Chalabi%20intervie_Arabiya %20TV.htm>.

CHAPTER 22: DEATH OF A STRATEGIST

1. Joan Wohlstetter, personal interview, April 2004.

2. Program notes, RAND Corporation memorial service for Albert Wohlstetter, 2 March 1997.

3. Richard Perle, personal interview, November 2005.

4. John Lewis Gaddis, *The Cold War: A New History* (New York: The Penguin Press, 2005), 195–203.

5. Neil Swidey, "The Mind of the Administration, Part Two: The Analyst." *The Boston Globe,* 18 May 2003, accessed at <<http://www.boston.com/ news/globe/ideas/articles/2003/05/18/the_analyst/>> on 2/21/05.

CHAPTER 23: WHITHER RAND?

1. "Projects: RAND Education's work in Qatar," *RAND Education,* 13 April 2007, RAND Corporation, accessed 12 July 2007 at <http://www .rand.org/education/qatar/index.html>.

2. Andrew Rathmell et al., *Developing Iraq's Security Sector: The Coalition Provisional Authority's Experience* (Santa Monica, CA: RAND, 2005).

3. Doug Suisman et al., *The Arc: Formal Structure for a Palestinian State* (Santa Monica, CA: RAND Corporation, 2005).

4. David Galula, *Pacification in Algeria, 1956–1958,* foreword by Bruce Hoffman (Santa Monica, CA: RAND Corporation, 2006, reprint of 1963 edition).

5. Richard Perle, personal interview, November 2005.

6. Larry Diamond, personal interview, October 2005.

7. James Thomson, personal interview, February 2006.

8. James A. Thomson, Colorado ACLU Speech, 1 October 2005 at <http//www.rand.org/pubs/corporate/_pubs/2005/RAND_CP507.pdf>.

9. Thomson interview.

10. Sydney E. Ahlstrom, *A Religious History of the American People* (New York: Doubleday and Company, 1975), 346–62.

11. George Washington, "Farewell Address," *American Daily Advertiser* (19 September 1796): A1.

12. Interview with Baha al-Araji, "Why America Will Fail in Iraq," *Foreign Policy* (November/December 2006): 20.

13. Arthur Kennickell, "A Rolling Tide: Changes in the Distribution of Wealth in the U.S., 1989–2001," *Survey of Consumer Finances* (Washington, DC: Federal Reserve Board, September 2003), 10, at <http://www.federalreserve.gov/pubs/oss/oss2/scfindex.html>.

14. Aaron J. Klein, *Striking Back: The 1972 Munich Olympics Massacre and Israel's Deadly Response* (New York: Random House, 2005), 96.

Bibliography

BOOKS

Aaron, Raymond. *The Imperial Republic: The United States and the World.* Englewood Cliffs, NJ: Prentice Hall, 1974.

Acheson, Dean. *Present at the Creation: My Years in the State Department.* New York: Norton, 1969.

Amadae, S. M. *Rationalizing Capitalist Democracy: The Cold War Origins of Rational Choice Liberalism.* Chicago: The University of Chicago Press, 2003.

Andre, David J. "Competitive Strategies: An Approach Against Proliferation." In Henry D. Sokolski, editor, *Prevailing in a Well-Armed World: Devising Competitive Strategies Against Weapons Proliferation.* Washington, DC: Storming Media, 2000, 3–25.

Arquilla, John, and David Ronfeldt. *In Athena's Camp: Preparing for Conflict in the Information Age.* Santa Monica, CA: RAND Corporation, 1997.

Arquilla, John, David Ronfeldt, and Michele Zanini. "Networks, Netwar, and Information-Age Terrorism." In Ian O. Lesser et al., *Countering the New Terrorism.* MR-989-AF. Santa Monica, CA: RAND Corporation, 1999.

Arrow, Kenneth. *Social Choice and Individual Values.* New York: Wiley, 1952. (Originally published as "Social Choice and Individual Values." RM-291. Santa Monica, CA: RAND Corporation, 1949.)

Bacevich, Andrew J. *The New American Militarism: How Americans Are Seduced by War.* Oxford: Oxford University Press, 2005.

Berkowitz, Bruce. *The New Face of War: How War Will Be Fought in the 21st Century.* New York: The Free Press, 2003.

Beschloss, Michael R. *The Crisis Years.* New York: HarperCollins, 1991.

Boot, Max. *The Savage Wars of Peace: Small Wars and the Rise of American Power.* New York: Basic Books, 2002.

Bracken, Paul. "Instabilities in the Control of Nuclear Forces." In Martin Hellman, editor, *Breakthrough: Emerging New Thinking.* New York: Walker and Company, 1988.

Bremer III, L. Paul. *My Year in Iraq: The Struggle to Build a Future of Hope.* New York: Simon and Schuster, 2006.

Brodie, Bernard. *A Layman's Guide to Naval Strategy.* Princeton, NJ: Princeton University Press, 1942.

———. *Sea Power in the Machine Age.* Princeton, NJ: Princeton University Press, 1941.

———. *Strategy in the Missile Age.* Princeton, NJ: Princeton University Press, 1959.

———. "War in the Atomic Age" and "Implications for Military Policy." Editor, *The Absolute Weapon: Atomic Power and World Order.* New York: Harcourt Brace, 1946.

Buchanan, Patrick J. *Where the Right Went Wrong.* New York: St. Martin's Press, 2004.

Cahn, Anne Hessing. *Killing Détente: The Right Attacks the CIA.* University Park, PA: The Pennsylvania State University Press, 1998.

Califano, Joseph. *The Triumph and Tragedy of Lyndon Johnson: The White House Years.* New York: Simon and Schuster, 1991.

Cannato, Vincent. *The Ungovernable City: John Lindsay and His Struggle to Save New York.* New York: Basic Books, 2001.

Carr, Caleb. *The Lessons of Terror: A History of Warfare Against Civilians.* New York: Random House, 2003.

Chomsky, Noam. *Year 501: The Conquest Continues.* Boston: South End Press, 2003.

Clarke, Richard A. *Against All Enemies: Inside America's War on Terror.* New York: The Free Press, 2004.

Coffey, Thomas M. *Iron Eagle: The Turbulent Life of General Curtis LeMay.* New York: Avon Books, 1988.

Colby, William. *Honorable Men: My Life in the CIA.* New York: Simon and Schuster, 1978.

Coll, Steve. *Ghost Wars: The Secret History of the CIA, Afghanistan, and Bin Laden, from the Soviet Invasion to September 10, 2001.* New York: The Penguin Press, 2004.

Collins, Martin J. *Cold War Laboratory: RAND, the Air Force and the American State, 1945–1950.* Washington, DC: Smithsonian Institution Press, 2002.

Crile, George. *Charlie Wilson's War: The Extraordinary Story of the Largest Covert Operation in History*. New York: Atlantic Monthly Press, 2003.

Delong, Lt. General Michael, USMC, Ret. *Inside CentCom: The Unvarnished Truth About the Wars in Afghanistan and Iraq*. Washington, DC: Regnery, 2004.

Diamond, Larry. *Squandered Victory: The American Occupation and Bungled Effort to Bring Democracy to Iraq*. New York: Times Books, 2005.

Dickson, Paul. *Think Tanks*. New York: Atheneum, 1971.

Dobbins, James, et al. *America's Role in Nation-Building: From Germany to Iraq*. Santa Monica, CA: RAND Corporation, 2003.

Drew, Elizabeth. *Fear and Loathing in George W. Bush's Washington*. New York: New York Review of Books, 2004.

Ellsberg, Daniel. *Papers on the War*. New York: Touchstone Books, 1972.

———. *Secrets: A Memoir of Vietnam and the Pentagon Papers*. New York: Penguin Books, 2002.

Fanon, Franz. *The Wretched of the Earth*. New York: Grove Press, 1961.

Feldman, Noah. *What We Owe Iraq: War and the Ethics of Nation Building*. Princeton, NJ: Princeton University Press, 2004.

Ferguson, Niall. *Colossus: The Price of America's Empire*. New York: The Penguin Press, 2004.

———. *Empire: The Rise and Demise of the British World Order and the Lessons for Global Power*. New York: Basic Books, 2002.

Fitzgerald, Frances. *Fire in the Lake: The Vietnamese and the Americans in Vietnam*. New York: Little, Brown and Company, Back Bay Books, 2002.

Franks, Tommy. *American Soldier*. New York: Regan, 2004.

Fukuyama, Francis. *The End of History and the Last Man*. New York: The Free Press, 1992.

———. *State Building: Governance and World Order in the 21st Century*. New York: Cornell University Press, 2003.

Gaddis, John Lewis. *The Cold War: A New History*. New York: The Penguin Press, 2005.

———. *Strategies of Containment: A Critical Appraisal of American National Security Policy During the Cold War*. Oxford: Oxford University Press, 2005.

———. *Surprise, Security and the American Experience*. Cambridge: Harvard University Press, 2004.

———. *The United States and the Origins of the Cold War, 1941–1947*. New York: Columbia University Press, 2000.

———. *We Now Know: Rethinking Cold War History*. Oxford: Oxford University Press, 1997.

Ghamari-Tabrizi, Sharon. *The Worlds of Herman Kahn: The Intuitive Science of Thermonuclear War*. Cambridge: Harvard University Press, 2005.

Gouré, Leon. *Civil Defense in the Soviet Union*. Westport, CT: Greenwood Press, 1986.

Gray, Colin S. *Modern Strategy*. Oxford: Oxford University Press, 1999.

Grayling, A. C. *Among the Dead Cities: The History and Moral Legacy of the WWII Bombing of Civilians in Germany and Japan*. New York: Walker and Company, 2006.

Greider, William. *Fortress America: The American Military and the Consequences of Peace*. New York: Public Affairs, 1998.

Halberstam, David. *The Fifties*. New York: Fawcett Columbine, 1993.

Halper, Stefan, and Jonathan Clarke. *America Alone: The Neo-Conservatives and the Global Order*. Cambridge: Cambridge University Press, 2004.

Hammes, Colonel Thomas X. *The Sling and the Stone: On War in the 21st Century*. St. Paul, MN: Zenith Press, 2004.

Hardt, Michael, and Antonio Negri. *Empire*. Cambridge: Harvard University Press, 2001.

Hentoff, Nat. *A Political Life: The Education of John V. Lindsay*. New York: Knopf, 1969.

Herken, Gregg. *Counsels of War*. New York: Oxford University Press, 1987.

Hersh, Seymour M. *Chain of Command: The Road from 9/11 to Abu Ghraib*. New York: HarperCollins, 2004.

Hershberg, James G. *James B. Conant: Harvard to Hiroshima and the Making of the Nuclear Age*. New York: Knopf, 1993.

Hiro, Dilip. *Secrets and Lies: Operation "Iraqi Freedom" and After*. New York: Nation Books, 2004.

Hitch, Charles, and Roland N. McKean. *Economics of Defense in the Nuclear Age*. New York: Holiday House, 1965.

Hoffman, Bruce. *Inside Terrorism*. New York: Columbia University Press, 1999.

———. Foreword. In David Galula, *Pacification in Algeria, 1956–1958*. Santa Monica, CA: RAND Corporation, 2006 (original edition, 1963).

Hoffman, Bruce, and Karen Gardela. "RAND Chronologies of International Terrorism." In Ian Lesser, *Countering the New Terrorism: Implications for Strategy*. Santa Monica, CA: RAND Corporation, 1999.

Hoffman, Fred S., Albert Wohlstetter, and David S. Yost, editors. *Swords and Shields: NATO, the USSR, and New Choices for Long-Range Offense and Defense*. Lexington, MA: Lexington Books, 1987.

Horowitz, Irving Louis. *The Rise and Fall of Project Camelot: Studies in the Relationship Between Social Science and Practical Politics*. Cambridge: The MIT Press, 1967.

Howe, Irving. *Leon Trotsky*. New York: Viking Press, 1979.

Hundley, Richard O. *Past Revolutions, Future Transformations*. Santa Monica, CA: RAND Corporation, 1999.

Iklé, Fred Charles. *Every War Must End*. New York: Columbia University Press, 1991.

Imperial Hubris—Why the West Is Losing the War on Terror. Washington, DC: Brassey's Inc., 2004.

Isaacson, Walter. *Kissinger: A Biography*. New York: Touchstone, 1992.

Isserman, Maurice. *The Other American: The Life of Michael Harrington.* New York: Public Affairs, 2000.

Johnson, Chalmers. *Blowback: The Costs and Consequences of American Empire.* New York: Metropolitan Books, 2000.

———. *The Sorrows of Empire: Militarism, Secrecy, and the End of the Republic.* New York: Metropolitan Books, 2004.

Johnson, Haynes. *Sleepwalking Through History.* New York: Doubleday/Anchor Books, 1992.

Kagan, Robert. *Of Paradise and Power: America and Europe in the New World Order.* New York: Knopf, 2003.

Kagan, Robert, and William Kristol, editors. *Present Dangers: Crisis and Opportunity in American Foreign and Defense Policy.* San Francisco: Encounter Books, 2000.

Kahn, Herman. *On Thermonuclear War.* Princeton, NJ: Princeton University Press, 1960.

———. *Thinking About the Unthinkable in the 1980s.* New York: Simon and Schuster, 1984.

Kahn, Herman, and Andrew Marshall. *Methods of Reducing Sample Size in Monte Carlo Computations.* Santa Monica, CA: RAND Corporation, 18 August 1953.

Kaplan, Fred. *The Wizards of Armageddon.* New York: Simon and Schuster, 1983.

Karnow, Stanley. *Vietnam: A History.* New York: The Viking Press, 1983.

Kellen, Konrad. "Terrorists: What Are They Like? How Some Terrorists Describe Their World and Actions." In *Terrorism and Beyond: An International Conference on Terrorism and Low-Level Conflict.* R-2714-DOE/DOJ/DOS/RC. Santa Monica, CA: RAND Corporation, December 1982.

Khalilzad, Zalmay, et al. *Deterrence Theory and Chinese Behavior.* Santa Monica, CA: RAND Corporation, 1998.

Killian, James. *Sputnik, Scientists, and Eisenhower.* Cambridge: The MIT Press, 1977.

Kissinger, Henry. *Ending the Vietnam War.* New York: Simon and Schuster, 2003.

———. *Nuclear Weapons and Foreign Policy.* New York: W. W. Norton, 1969.

———. *The White House Years.* Boston: Little, Brown, 1979.

Kolko, Gabriel. *Confronting the Third World: United States Foreign Policy 1945–1980.* New York: Pantheon Press, 1980.

Leites, Nathan. *The Operational Code of the Politburo.* New York: McGraw-Hill, 1951.

LeMay, Curtis. *Mission with LeMay: My Story.* New York: MacMillan, 1965.

Lewis, Bernard. *The Emergence of Modern Turkey.* Second edition. Cambridge: Oxford University Press, 1968.

Light, Paul. *The Four Pillars of High Performance.* New York: McGraw-Hill, 2005.

Mann, James. *Rise of the Vulcans: The History of Bush's War Cabinet.* New York: The Viking Press, 2004.

Marshall, Andrew. *Bureaucratic Behavior and the Strategic Arms Competition.* Santa Monica, CA: Southern California Arms Control and Foreign Policy Seminar, 1971.

———. Foreword. In Andrew Krepinevich Jr., *The Military-Technical Revolution: A Preliminary Assessment.* Washington, DC: Center for Strategic and Budgetary Assessments, 2002.

———. Preface. In Henry D. Sokolski, editor, *Prevailing in a Well-Armed World: Devising Competitive Strategies Against Weapons Proliferation.* Washington, DC: Storming Media, 2000.

———. Foreword. In Zalmay Khalilzad, editor, *Strategic Appraisal: The Changing Role of Information in Warfare.* Santa Monica, CA: RAND Corporation, 1999.

Marshall, Andrew W., J. J. Martin, and Henry S. Rowen, editors. *On Not Confusing Ourselves: Essays on National Security Strategy in Honor of Albert and Roberta Wohlstetter.* Boulder, CO: Westview Press, 1991.

McCullough, David. *Truman.* New York: Simon and Schuster, 1992.

McNamara, Robert S. *Argument Without End: In Search of Answers to the Vietnam Tragedy.* New York: Public Affairs, 1999.

———. *In Retrospect.* New York: Vintage Books, 1996.

McNamara, Robert, and James G. Blight. *Wilson's Ghost.* New York: Public Affairs, 2003.

Mitchell, Elizabeth. *W: Revenge of the Bush Dynasty.* New York: Hyperion, 2000.

Nasar, Sylvia. *A Beautiful Mind.* New York: Touchstone, 1998.

Neumann, John von, and Oskar Morgenstern. *Theory of Games and Economic Behavior.* 60th anniversary edition. Princeton, NJ: Princeton University Press, 2004.

Newhouse, J. P. *Free for All.* Cambridge: Harvard University Press, 1993.

Niskanen, William A. *Reaganomics: An Insider's Account of the Policies and the People* (New York: Oxford University Press, 1988).

Nitze, Paul H. *From Hiroshima to Glasnost: At the Center of Decision.* New York: Grove Weidenfeld, 1989.

Norton, Anne. *Leo Strauss and the Politics of American Empire.* New Haven, CT: Yale University Press, 2004.

Ognibene, Peter J. *Scoop: The Life and Politics of Henry M. Jackson.* New York: Stein and Day, 1975.

Packer, George. *The Assassins' Gate: America in Iraq.* New York: Farrar, Straus and Giroux, 2005.

The Pentagon Papers. Senator Gravel edition. Boston: Beacon Press, 1971.

Perle, Richard, and David Frum. *An End to Evil: How to Win the War on Terror.* New York: Random House, 2003.

Phillips, David L. *Losing Iraq: Inside the Postwar Reconstruction Fiasco*. New York: Westview Press, 2005.

Pillsbury, Michael. *China Debates the Future Security Environment*. Washington, DC: National Defense University Press, 2000.

Poundstone, William. *Prisoner's Dilemma*. New York: Doubleday, 1992.

Powers, Thomas. *The Man Who Kept the Secrets: Richard Helms and the CIA*. New York: Knopf, 1979.

Prange, Gordon W., Donald M. Goldstein, Katherine V. Dillon. *Pearl Harbor: The Verdict of History*. New York: Penguin, 1991.

Reeves, Richard. *President Kennedy: Profile of Power*. New York: Simon and Schuster, 1993.

Rice, Donald B. *The Battle of the Budget Deficit*. Santa Monica, CA: RAND Corporation, 1985.

———. *Commencement Remarks: RAND Graduate Institute's Fourth Commencement Exercises, April 29, 1983*. Santa Monica, CA: RAND Corporation, 1983.

———. *Commencement Remarks: RAND Graduate Institute's Third Commencement Exercises, September 4, 1980*. Santa Monica, CA: RAND Corporation, 1980.

———. *Defense Resource Management Study: Case Studies of Logistics Support Alternatives*. Washington, DC: U.S. Government Printing Office, 1979.

———. *Defense Resource Management Study: Final Report*. Washington, DC: U.S. Government Printing Office, 1979.

———. *Regulatory Policy: Some Advice for Government and Business*. Santa Monica, CA: RAND Corporation, 1979.

Risen, James. *State of War: The Secret History of the CIA and the Bush Administration*. New York: The Free Press, 2006.

Rosten, Leo. *Captain Newman, M.D.* New York: Harper, 1962.

———. *The Education of H*Y*M*A*N K*A*P*L*A*N*. New York: Harvest, 1965.

Sanders, Jerry Wayne. *Peddlers of Crisis: The Committee on the Present Danger and the Politics of Containment*. Boston: South End Press, 1983.

Scarborough, Rowan. *Rumsfeld's War*. Washington, DC: Regnery, 2004.

Scheer, Robert. *With Enough Shovels*. New York: Vintage Books, 1983.

Schelling, Thomas. *The Strategy of Conflict*. Cambridge, MA: Harvard University Press, 1963.

Schumpeter, Joseph. *Capitalism, Socialism and Democracy*. London: Allen and Unwin, 1943.

Shachtman, Max. *Dog Days: James P. Cannon vs. Max Shachtman in the Communist League of America*. New York: Prometheus Research Library, 2002.

———. *Race and Revolution*. London: Verso, 2003.

Sheehan, Neil. *A Bright Shining Lie: John Paul Vann and America in Vietnam*. New York: Vintage Books, 1989.

Smith, Bruce. *The RAND Corporation: CSE Study of a Nonprofit Advisory Corporation.* Cambridge: Harvard University Press, 1966.

Sorensen, Ted. *Kennedy.* New York: Harper and Row, 1965.

Sperry, Paul. *Crude Politics.* Nashville, TN: WND Books, 2003.

Suskind, Ron. *The Price of Loyalty.* New York: Simon and Schuster, 2004.

Taylor, Maxwell. *The Uncertain Trumpet.* New York: Harper and Row, 1960.

Trachtenberg, Marc, editor. *Development of American Strategic Thought.* New York: Garland, 1987.

Tripp, Charles. *A History of Iraq.* Cambridge: Cambridge University Press, 2000.

Trotsky, Leon. *Revolution Betrayed.* New York: Dover Publications, 2004.

Ullman, Harlan, and James P. Wade Jr. *Rapid Dominance, a Force for All Seasons: Technologies and Systems for Achieving Shock and Awe: A Real Revolution in Military Affairs.* London: Royal United Services Institute for Defence Studies, 1998.

Wald, Alan. *The New York Intellectuals.* Chapel Hill, NC: University of North Carolina Press, 1987.

Wells, Tom. *Wild Man: The Life and Times of Daniel Ellsberg.* New York: Palgrave, 2001.

White, Morton G. *A Philosopher's Story.* University Park, PA: Pennsylvania State University Press, 1999.

Williams, John D. *The Compleat Strategyst.* New York: McGraw-Hill, 1954.

Wohlstetter, Albert. Foreword. In K. Scott McMahan and Dennis M. Gormley, *Controlling the Spread of Land-Attack Cruise Missiles.* Marina del Rey, CA: American Institute for Strategic Cooperation, January 1995.

―――. *Legends of the Strategic Arms Race.* Washington, DC: United States Strategic Institute, 1975.

Wohlstetter, Albert, Roberta Wohlstetter, Victor Gilinsky, and Robert Gillete. *Nuclear Policies: Fuel without the Bomb.* Cambridge, MA: Ballinger Publishing Company, 1978.

Wohlstetter, Charles. *The Right Place.* New York: Applause Books, 1997.

Wohlstetter, Roberta. *Pearl Harbor: Warning and Decision.* Stanford, CA: Stanford University Press, 1962.

Woodward, Bob. *Plan of Attack.* New York: Simon and Schuster Paperbacks, 2004.

Zubok, Vladislav, and Constantine Pleshakov. *Inside the Kremlin's Cold War: From Stalin to Khrushchev.* Cambridge: Harvard University Press, 1996.

ARCHIVES, JOURNALS, MAGAZINES, NEWSPAPERS, WEB SITES

"Agensys Names Donald B. Rice as Chairman." Press release. Agensys.com (11 March 2002). Agensys, Inc. Accessed 7 November 2005 at <http://www.agensys.com/pressrelease_031102.html>.

Air & Space Power Chronicles, Curtis LeMay biography at <http://www
.airpower.maxwell.af.mil>.

Air Force Magazine (January 2004), at <http://www.afa.org/magazine/jan2004/
0104vonkarman.asp>.

Allardice, James. "RAND Breaks Ground for New Complex." *Santa Monica
Mirror* (21 August 2002).

"Arming to Disarm in the Age of Détente." *Time* (11 February 1974): 15–24.

Augenstein, Bruno W. "Evolution of the U.S. Military Space Program, 1949–
1960: Some Key Events in Study, Planning, and Program Development." *The
RAND Paper Series,* P-6814 (Santa Monica, CA: RAND, September 1982).

Augenstein, Bruno W., and Bruce Murray. *Mert Davies: A RAND Pioneer in
Earth Reconnaissance and Planetary Mapping from Spacecraft* (Santa Monica,
CA: RAND Corporation, 2004).

Barry, John, and Evan Thomas. "The Pentagon's Guru." *Newsweek* (21 May
2001).

Bartley, Robert L. "A Wohlstetter Life." The *Wall Street Journal* (13 January 1997).

Bellman, Richard. *I Am the Hurricane.* Manuscript. Brownlee Haydon Box.
RAND Archives.

Berkowitz, Bruce. "War in the Information Age." *Hoover Digest* 2 (2002).

Boot, Max. "Think Again: Neocons." *Foreign Policy* (January/February 2004).

Bourgin, Si. Memorandum (Santa Monica, CA: RAND Corporation, 4 April
1962).

Bowles, Edward L. RAND History Project. 14 and 15 July 1987, 20 August
1987.

Brodie, Bernard, et al. "Implications of Large Yield Weapons." Project RAND
(Santa Monica, CA: RAND Corporation, 10 July 1952).

Brownstein, Norman, "War Now Drives the Presidency." *Los Angeles Times* (29
January 2003): A1.

Burnham, David. "Study Questions Handling of Police Misconduct." The *New
York Times* (20 October 1970): 1, 46.

Byman, Daniel, Kenneth Pollack, and Gideon Rose. "The Rollback Fantasy."
Foreign Affairs (January/February 1999).

Catanzaro, Michael. "The 'Revolution in Military Affairs' Has an Enemy:
Politics." *The American Enterprise* (October/November 2001): 24–27.

Chalabi, Ahmed. "An Insider's View: Democratic Politics at Work in Iraq: A
Foreign Policy Briefing from Iraqi Deputy Prime Minister Ahmed Chalabi."
Transcript prepared from a tape recording. American Enterprise Institute:
Washington, DC, 9 November 2005.

———. Interview by Ariana Huffington. 10 November 2005. At <www
.HuffingtonPost.com>.

"Charles Hitch: In Memoriam." Obituary. University of California, 1995.
Accessed 7 July 2006 at <http://sunsite.berkeley.edu/~ucalhist/general_history/
overview/presidents/index2.html#hitch>.

"Chevron Names Donald Rice to Board." AP Online, 28 September 2005. Accessed 7 November 2005 at <http://www.forbes.com/associatedpress/feeds/ap/2005/09/28/ap224998.html>.

Clifford, Peggy. "RAND and the City: Part I." *Santa Monica Mirror* (27 October 1999).

————. "RAND and the City: Part II." *Santa Monica Mirror* (3 November 1999).

Cohen, Bernard. "The Police Internal Administration of Justice in New York City." R-621 (New York: RAND Corporation, November 1970).

Cohen, Bernard, and Jan M. Chaiken. "New York City Police: The Background and Performance of the Class of 1957" (New York: RAND Corporation, February 1973).

Collbohm, Franklin. RAND History Project. Martin Collins and Joseph Tatarewicz, interview. (Santa Monica, CA: RAND, 28 July 1987).

————. Collbohm biography, RAND document (Santa Monica, CA: RAND Corporation, 28 August 1986).

Congressional Record. 1 May 1969: 10955–57.

————. 18 July 1969: 20122.

————. 4 August 1969: 22016–19.

————. 7 August 1969: 22936–38.

Cushman, John H. "Applying Military Brain to Military Brawn, Again." The *New York Times* (17 December 1986).

Davis, Carmel. Review of *The Military Use of Space: A Diagnostic Assessment* by Barry Watts. *Naval War College Review* (Autumn 2001): 168–70.

Derain, James Der. "The Illusion of a Grand Strategy." The *New York Times* (25 May 2001).

"The Development of Strategic Thinking at RAND, 1948–1966: A Mathematical Logician's View." An interview with Albert Wohlstetter (5 July 1985). Interviewers: Jim Digby, Joan Goldhamer. Transcribed by Dana Bursk. (Santa Monica, CA: RAND, 1997).

"Donald B. Rice." Biography. *Wells Fargo* (2005). Accessed 7 November 2005 at <http://www.wellsfargo.com/about/corporate/boardofdirectors/rice>.

"Donald B. Rice Elected to Chevron Board of Directors." Press release. Chevron.com (2005). Chevron Corporation. Accessed 7 November 2005 at <http://www.chevron.com/news/press/2005/2005-09-28_1.asp>.

Donnelly, Sally. "Long-Distance Warriors," *Time* (12 December 2005).

Dreyfuss, Robert. "Tinker, Banker, NeoCon, Spy." The *American Prospect* 13, 21 (18 November 2002).

Dreyfuss, Robert, and Jason Vest. "The Lie Factory." *Mother Jones* (January/February 2004).

Dwyer, Jim. "Defectors' Reports on Iraq Arms Were Embellished, Exile Asserts." The *New York Times* (9 July 2004): 1.

Easton, Nina J. "The Briefing." The *Boston Globe* (20 November 2005): A8.

Ellsberg, Daniel. "Judo Politics" (Santa Monica, CA: RAND Corporation, 1959).

———. "Revolutionary Judo" (Santa Monica, CA: RAND Corporation, January 1970).

Enthoven, Alain. "Tribute to Charles J. Hitch." OR/MS Today at <http://www.lionhrtpub.com/orms/orms-12-95/hitch-tribute.html>.

Fallows, James. "Blind into Baghdad." The *Atlantic Monthly* (January/February 2004).

Filkins, Dexter. "Baghdad Boys." The *New York Times* (12 December 2005): A1.

———. "Where Plan A Left Ahmed Chalabi." The *New York Times Magazine* (5 November 2006): 46.

Filler, Martin. "Landscape Visionary for a New American Dream." The *New York Times* (2 February 1997): Section H 32–33.

Gaither, H. Rowan. "Memorandum to Frank R. Collbohm. Subject: Formation of Non-Profit Corporation for RAND Project." 18 December 1947. Santa Monica, CA.

Gertz, Bill, and Rowan Scarborough. "Inside the Ring." The *Gertz File* (6 April 2001). Accessed 13 October 2005 at <http://www.gertzfile.com/gertzfile/ring040601.html>.

Glazer, Nathan. "Neoconservative from the Start." The *Public Interest* 159 (Spring 2005).

Goldberg, Dave. "In RAND's Defense: It's Not All Military." *Chicago Tribune* (20 June 1982): section 3: 6.

Goldstein, J. R. *RAND: The History.* Paper P-2336-1 (Santa Monica, CA: RAND Corporation, 1960).

Gordon, Michael R. "The Strategy to Secure Iraq Did Not Foresee a 2nd War." The *New York Times* (19 October 2004).

Gouré, Leon. "Soviet Civil Defense," P-1887 (Santa Monica, CA: RAND, 1960).

Greenspan, Alan. "Remarks on the Reagan Legacy," 9 April 2003, accessed 7 July 2007 at <http://federalreserve.gov/BOARDDOCS/SPEECHES/2003/200304092/default.htm>.

Helmus, Todd C., Christopher Paul, Russell W. Glenn. *Enlisting Madison Avenue: The Marketing Approach to Earning Popular Support in Theaters of Operation* (Santa Monica, CA: RAND, 2007).

Hinkle, Bart. "New Weapons for New Wars?" The *American Enterprise* (October/November 2001): 18–23.

Hitch, Charles. "An Appreciation of Systems Analysis," P-699 (Santa Monica, CA: RAND, 18 August 1955).

Hoffman, Bruce. "Terrorism and Beyond: The 21st Century." Conference dinner address. Oklahoma City, OK (17 April 2000).

———. "Rethinking Terrorism in Light of a War on Terrorism. Testimony before the Subcommittee on Terrorism and Homeland Security, House Permanent Select Committee on Intelligence," U.S. House of Representatives, 26 September 2001. Accessed 13 September 2005 at <http://www.rand.org./pubs/testimonies/CT182/>.

Hounshell, David. *The Cold War, RAND, and the Generation of Knowledge, 1946–1962* (Santa Monica, CA: RAND Reprints, 1998).

Husain, Khurram. "Neocons: The men behind the curtain." *Bulletin of the Atomic Scientists,* Vol. 59, no. 06 (November/December 2003).

Iraq Liberation Act. Public Law 105-338, 31 October 1998. 105th Congress, Congressional Record, Volume 144.

Jardini, David R. *Out of the Blue Yonder: The RAND Corporation's Diversification into Social Welfare Research, 1946–1968.* Doctoral dissertation. Carnegie Mellon University, May 1996.

Jenkins, Brian. "International Terrorism: The Other World War." R-3302AF (Santa Monica, CA: RAND Project Air Force, 1985).

———. "Defense Against Terrorism." *Political Science Quarterly* 101. 5 (1986): 773–86.

———. "Where I Draw the Line." *Perspectives on Terrorism,* 2002, *Christian Science Monitor* (11 July 2007). <http://www.csmonitor.com/specials/terrorism/lite/expert.html>.

———. "The Lessons of Beirut: Testimony before the Long Commission" (Santa Monica, CA: RAND, 1984).

———. *Unconquerable Nation: Knowing Our Enemy, Strengthening Ourselves* (Santa Monica, CA: RAND Corporation, 2006).

Kagan, Donald, Gary Schmitt, Thomas Donnelly. "Rebuilding America's Defenses: Strategy, Forces and for a New Century." A Report of the Project for a New American Century (Washington, DC: Project for the New American Century, 2000).

Kaplan, Fred. "*Force Majeure:* What Lies Behind the Military's Victory in Iraq." Slate.com (10 April 2003) at <http://www.slate.com/id/2081388>.

Kellen, Konrad. "Adenauer at 90." *Foreign Affairs* (January 1966).

———. *The Germans and the Pershing II* (RAND Report P-6950) (Santa Monica, CA: RAND, 1983).

———. "Terrorists: What Are They Like? How Some Terrorists Describe Their World and Actions," in *Terrorism and Beyond: An International Conference on Terrorism and Low-Level Conflict,* R-2714-DOE/DOJ/DOS/RC (Santa Monica, CA: RAND Corporation, December 1982): 130.

Keller, Bill. "The Fighting Next Time." The *New York Times* (10 March 2002, late edition): section 6: 32+.

Kempe, Frederick. "Mideast Doctrine's Domestic Hurdle." The *Wall Street Journal* (13 December 2005): A11.

Khalilzad, Zalmay, and George W. Casey Jr. "A Path to Success in Iraq." *Los Angeles Times* (11 April 2004).

King, Neil Jr. "Secret Weapon: Inside Pentagon, a Scholar Shapes Views of China." The *Wall Street Journal* (8 September 2005): 1.

Kirchick, James. "Cold Warriors Return for War on Terrorism." The *Hill* (30 June 2004).

Kraft, Joseph. "Rand: Arsenal for Ideas." *Harper's Magazine* (July 1960): 69–76.

Krauthammer, Charles. "Bless Our Pax Americana." The *Washington Post* (22 March 1991).

Kurth, James. "Iraq: Losing the American Way." *American Conservative* (15 March 2004).

Lafferty, Elaine. "Missile Defense Is About Money and It's Here to Stay." The *Irish Times* (25 July 2001).

Launius, Roger D. "*Sputnik* and the Origins of the Space Age." NASA *History Division,* January 2007, NASA, <http://history.nasa.gov/sputnik/sputorig .html>.

Leavitt, William. "RAND: The Air Force's Original 'Think-Tank.'" *Air Force/ Space Digest* (May 1967): 100–9.

Lemann, Nicholas. "Dangers Present." The Talk of the Town. The *New Yorker* (23 July 2004).

———. "What Terrorists Want." The *New Yorker* (29 October 2001).

Lewis, Bernard. "Put the Iraqis in Charge." The *Wall Street Journal* (29 August 2003).

———. "The West and the Middle East." *Foreign Affairs* (January 1997).

Lewis, George. "Pentagon Defense Strategist Previews Future Warfare." *Campus News* (July 2002). University of Kentucky Public Relations. Accessed 14 October 2005 at <http://www.uky.edu/PR/News/Archives/2002/July2002/ AndyMarshall.html>.

Life Magazine. "Valuable Batch of Brains." Photographed by Leonard McCombe (11 May 1959).

Lind, William. "Understanding Fourth Generation War." Accessed 15 January 2004 at <http://antiwar.com/lind/index.php?articleid=1702>.

"The Lindsay Legacy." Editorial. The *New York Times* (21 December 2000).

"The Marshall Plan." Center for Security Policy. Publications of the Center for Security Policy. 12 February 2001. Accessed 3 November 2005 at <http://www .security-policy.org/papers/2001/01-D13.html>.

May, Andrew David. *The RAND Corporation and the Dynamics of American Strategic Thought.* Doctoral dissertation. Dickinson College (October 1998).

Mayer, Jane. "The Manipulator." The *New Yorker* (7 June 2004).

McGray, Douglas. "The Marshall Plan." *Wired* (February 2003).

McNamara, Robert S. Biography. Secretary of Defense Histories at <http://www .defenselink.mil/specials/secdef_histories/bios/mcnamara.htm>.

Morris, Stephen J. "The War We Could Have Won." The *New York Times* (1 May 2005): 15.

Novick, David. Interview by Martin Collins. RAND History Project. Martin Collins interview, 24 February, 20 June 1988 (Santa Monica, CA: RAND, 1989).

Nye, Mary Jo. "The Most Versatile Physicist of His Generation." *Science Magazine* (April 2002): 49–50. At <http://www.sciencemag.org/cgi/content/ full/296/5565/49>.

Oliver, Myrna. "Franklin Collbohm Dies; Founder of RAND Corp." The *Los Angeles Times* (14 February 1990): A3, A13.

Pace, Eric. "Albert Wohlstetter, 83, Expert on U.S. Nuclear Strategy, Dies." The *New York Times* (13 January 1997).

Parker, Thomas. "High-Tech to the Rescue in the Persian Gulf." The *Middle East Quarterly* 6, 2 (1999). Accessed 14 October 2005 at <http://www.meforum.org/article/458>.

Podhoretz, Norman. "How to Win World War IV." *Commentary* 113 (February 2002): 19–29.

Pope, Hugh. "Ahmed Chalabi: Profile." *Los Angeles Times* (19 July 1994).

Project for the New American Century. Declaration of Principles. Washington, DC: Project for the New Century, 1997.

———. Letter to President Clinton. Washington, DC: Project for the New Century, 26 January 1998.

———. "Rebuilding America's Defenses." Washington, DC: Project for the New Century, 2000.

Quinn, Sally. "A Lightning Rod's Striking Return." The *Washington Post* (17 November 2005): C1.

RAND Corporation, Articles of Incorporation and By-Laws (Santa Monica, CA: RAND Corporation, 14 May 1948).

"RAND Corporation: Its Origin, Evolution and Plans for the Future" (Santa Monica, CA: RAND Corporation, February 1971).

"RAND Elects Donald B. Rice to Board of Trustees." News release. RAND Corporation. RAND.org, 19 March 2001. Accessed 7 November 2005 at <http://rand.org/news/Press/rice.html>.

Rathmell, Andrew. "Planning Post-Conflict Reconstruction in Iraq: What Can We Learn?" (Santa Monica, CA: RAND Corporation, 2006).

Rathmell, Andrew, et al. *Developing Iraq's Security Sector: The Coalition Provisional Authority's Experience* (Santa Monica, CA: RAND, 2005).

Reagan, Ronald. The Presidential Papers of Ronald W. Reagan. At <http://www.reagan.utexas.edu/archives/speeches/publicpapers.html>.

Ricks, Thomas E. "Pentagon Study May Bring Big Shake-up: Unconventional Defense Thinker Conducting Review." The *Washington Post* (9 February 2001, final edition): A1+.

———. "Warning Shot: How Wars Are Fought Will Change Radically." The *Wall Street Journal* (15 July 1994): 1.

Roche, James G. "Serving the Patriots of America's Air Force." Order of the Sword Induction Ceremony. Andrews Air Force Base, Maryland. 13 September 2003. Accessed 23 April 2005 at http://www.accessmylibrary.com/coms2/summary_0286-2303653_ITM.

Rosten, Leo. Interview by Brownlee Haydon. August 1969. (Santa Monica, CA: RAND, 1971): 4.

Rostow, Eugene V. "Defining Détente in Terms of the United Nations Charter." The *New York Times* (27 April 1974): 31.

Ryn, Claes G. "The Ideology of American Empire." *Orbis* (Summer 2003).

Schelling, Thomas C. "What Went Wrong with Arms Control?" *Foreign Affairs* 64 (Winter 1985–86): 219–33.

Schwartz, Stephen. "Trotskycons? Past and Present." *National Review Online* (11 June 2003).

Schelling, Thomas C. "A Tribute to Bernard Brodie and (Incidentally) to RAND." *International Security,* Vol. 3, No. 3 (1978/79 Winter).

Shipler, David K. "Rent Control End and City Subsidies Linked in a Study." The *New York Times* (13 February 1970): 1:43.

Shorris, Earl. "Ignoble Liars: Leo Strauss, George Bush and the Politics of Deception." *Harper's* (June 2004).

Silverstein, Ken. "Buck Rogers Rides Again." The *Nation* (25 October 1999).

———. "The Man from ONA." The *Nation* (25 October 1999).

Specht, R. D. "RAND: A Personal View of Its History" (Santa Monica, CA: RAND Corporation, 1958).

Stipp, David. "Climate Collapse: The Pentagon's Worst Nightmare." *Fortune* (26 January 2004).

Swidey, Neil. "The Mind of the Administration, Part Two: The Analyst." The *Boston Globe* (18 May 2003).

Szulc, Tad. "Pentagon Cool." *Washingtonian Magazine* 10, 1 (1974): 115–34.

Tanenhaus, Sam. Interview with Paul Wolfowitz. *Vanity Fair* (9 May 2003). At <http://www.DoD%20News%20Deputy%20Secretary%20Wolfowitz%20Interview%20with%20Sam%20Tanenhaus,%20Vanity%20Fair.htm>.

Thomson, James A. Colorado ACLU Speech. 1 October 2005. At <http//www.rand.org/pubs/corporate/_pubs/2005/RAND_CP507.PDF>.

Turco, R. P., O. B. Toon, T. P. Acherman, J. B. Pollack, Carl Sagan. "Global Atmospheric Consequences of Nuclear War." 25 July 1983, NASA-TM-101281.

Tyler, Patrick E. "U.S. and Iraqis Tell of Coup Attempt against Baghdad." The *New York Times* (3 July 1992): 1.

United States Air Force. Biography. Dr. Donald B. Rice. Accessed 7 November 2005 at <http://www.af.mil/bios/bio.asp?bioID=6895>.

United States Air Force. Biography. Dr. James G. Roche. February 2004. Accessed 14 October 2005 at <http://www.af.mil/bios/bio.asp?bioID=6942>.

United States Commission to Assess the Ballistic Missile Threat to the United States. Executive Summary of the Report. Washington, DC: Government Printing Office, 1998.

"Unocal Appoints James Crownover, Donald Rice to Company Board of Directors." *UCLnews,* 7 December 1998. Accessed 7 November 2005 at <http://www.unocal.com/uclnews/98news/120798a.html>.

"Vance R. Wanner Memorial Award 1999 Recipient." Mors.org, 15 July 2004.
    Military Operations Research Society. Accessed 7 November 2005 at <http://
    www.mors.org/awards/wanner/rice.html>.
Van Orman Quine, Willard. "Obituary." The *Guardian* (30 December 2000).
Vest, Jason. "The Dubious Genius of Andrew Marshall." The *American Prospect
    Online,* 15 February 2001. Accessed 13 October 2005 at <http://www
    .prospect.org/webfeatures/2001/02/vest-j-02-15.html>.
Vogel, Jack. "Project RAND: Some Payoffs from Non-Directive Research."
    D-14147-PR (Santa Monica, CA: RAND Corporation, 8 October 1965).
Wanniski, Jude. "Albert Wohlstetter, R.I.P." 16 January 1997. At <http://www
    .polyeconomics.com/searchbase/fyi01-16-97.html>.
———. "An American Empire." Supply-side University, 24 August 1995,
    accessed 12 July 2007 at <http://wanniski.com/searchbase/amemp1.htm>.
———. "Sketching the Laffer Curve." 14 June 2005, accessed 7 July 2007 at
    <www.wanniski.com>.
Wattenberg, Ben. "Peddling 'Son of Manifest Destiny.'" The *Washington Times*
    (21 March 1990).
Weiner, Tim, and Barbara Crosette. "George F. Kennan, Leading U.S. Strategist
    of the Cold War, Dies at 101." The *New York Times* (19 March 2005): B11.
White, Annahrae. "The House That Hangs in the Sky." *Los Angeles Examiner,
    Pictorial Living* (7 August 1955).
Winik, Jay. "Secret Weapon." *Washingtonian* (April 1999): 45–55.
Wittner, Lawrence S. "Reagan and Nuclear Disarmament." *Boston Review*
    (April/May 2002).
Wohlstetter, Albert. "A Purpose Hammered Out of Reflection and Choice." *Life
    Magazine* (20 June 1960): 124–34.
———. "Between an Unfree World and None: Increasing Our Choices." *Foreign
    Affairs* 63 (Summer 1985): 962–94.
———. "California Seminar on Arms Control and Foreign Policy. Proof of
    Evidence of Albert Wohlstetter on behalf of Friends of the Earth Ltd." 5–6
    September 1977. File brief.
———. "Clocking the Strategic Arms Race." The *Wall Street Journal* (24
    September 1974): 24.
———. "Critique of a Brookings Agenda for the Nation on Military Strategy,
    Military Forces, and Arms Control." Document DE(L)-1790-ISA (Santa
    Monica, CA: RAND Corporation, October 1968).
———. "The Delicate Balance of Terror." *Foreign Affairs* (January 1959).
———. "Economic and Strategic Considerations in Air Base Location: A
    Preliminary Review." Document D-1114 (Santa Monica, CA: RAND
    Corporation, 29 December 1951).
———. "Is There a Strategic Arms Race?" *Foreign Policy* 15 (Summer 1974):
    3–20.

————. "Objectives of the United States Military Posture" (Santa Monica, CA: RAND Corporation, May 1959).

————. "On Vietnam and Bureaucracy." Accessed 24 December 2004 at <http://www.rand.org/publications/classics/wohlstetter/D17276.1/D17276.1.html>.

————. "Optimal Ways to Confuse Ourselves." *Foreign Policy* 20 (Fall 1975): 170–98.

————. "Rivals, But No 'Race.'" *Foreign Policy* 16 (Fall 1974): 48–92.

————. "Safeguard Critics Contradict Selves." *Los Angeles Times* (4 August 1969).

————. "Scientists, Seers, and Strategy." *Foreign Affairs* 41 (Spring 1963): 466–78.

————. "The Uncontrolled Upward Spiral." *Strategic Review* 3 (Winter 1975).

————. "The Uses of Irrelevance." The *New York Times* (25 February 1979).

————. "Who Are 'Good' and 'Bad' Guys?" *Los Angeles Times* (3 August 1969).

Wohlstetter, Albert, and Brian Chow. "Recommended Changes in U.S. Military Space Policies and Programs." *Commission on Integrated Long-Term Strategy.* Washington DC, October 1988.

Wohlstetter, Albert, and Fred Hoffman. "Confronting Saddam: A Model Danger." The *Wall Street Journal* (9 August 1990).

Wohlstetter, Albert and Roberta. "Metaphors and Models: Inequalities and Disorder at Home and Abroad." Document D-17664-RC/ISA (Santa Monica, CA: RAND Corporation, 27 August, 1968).

————. "Notes on the Cuban Crisis" (Santa Monica, CA: RAND Corporation, 1962).

————. "On Dealing with Castro's Cuba: Part I." Document D(L)-17906-ISA (Santa Monica, CA: RAND Corporation, 16 January 1965).

————. "Studies for a Post-Communist Cuba" (Santa Monica, CA: RAND Corporation, 1963).

"Wohlstetters' Downtown Apartment." *Chicago Tribune* (22 May 1967): section 2.

Wolf, Charles. "Extended Containment: Countering Soviet Imperialism and Applying Economic Realism" (Santa Monica, CA: A RAND Note, 1983).

————. "Insurgency and Counterinsurgency: New Myths and Old Realities" (Santa Monica, CA: RAND Corporation, 1965).

Wolfowitz, Paul. "Paul Nitze's Legacy: For a New World." Remarks delivered to the Aspen Institute at the U.S. Chamber of Commerce, Washington, DC (25 April 2004).

Woo, Elaine. "Roberta Wohlstetter, 94; wrote Pearl Harbor Study." *Los Angeles Times* (11 January 2007).

Worth, Robert F. "The Juggler." The *New York Times* (12 March 2006).

Yakovlev, Alexander. "Memorandum to Mikhail Gorbachev: The Imperative of Political Development," 25 December 1985, National Security Archives.

Zone, Rob. "Chalabi's Hour, Controversial Exile Leader Back in Iraq." The *Seattle Times* (9 April 2003): A5.

PERSONAL INTERVIEWS

Aaron, Chester. Personal interview. August 2003.

Archibald, Rae. Personal interview. September 2004.

Benjamin, Roger. Personal interview. May 2004.

Chalabi, Ahmed. E-mail interview. January 2006.

Diamond, Larry. Personal interview. October 2005.

Ellsberg, Daniel. Personal interview. October 2004, January 2005, and June 2005.

Hoffman, Bruce. Personal interview. April 2004.

Glazer, Nathan. Personal interview. October 2005.

Kellen, Konrad. Personal interview. May 2004.

Khalilzad, Zalmay. Personal interview. January 2006.

Perle, Richard. Personal interview. November 2005.

Rice, Donald. Personal interview. January 2006.

Rich, Michael. Personal interview. June 2003.

Rowen, Henry. Personal interview. 27 April 2004.

Schulman, Julius. Personal interview. June 2004.

Sokolski, Henry. Personal interview. March 2004.

Thomson, James. Personal interview. February 2006.

Van der Car, Peter. Personal interview. March 2004.

Wohlstetter, Joan. Personal interview. April 2004 and February 2006.

Wolf, Charles. Personal interview. November 2003.

Index